D1628055

100 Masterpieces from the Vitra Design Museum Collection

**100 Masterpieces
from the
Vitra Design Museum
Collection**

Exhibition
Vitra Design Museum, Weil am Rhein
July 10, 1995 - January 21, 1996
Tour of Europe, Israel, Japan, and the
United States
1996 through 2000

Concept
Peter Dunas in collaboration
with Mathias Schwartz-Clauss, Serge Mauduit,
and Petra Rhode

Organization
Mathias Schwartz-Clauss, Peter Dunas,
Matthias Kries

Design
Dieter Thiel in collaboration
with Thorsten Romanus

Public relations
Gabriella Gianoli

Catalogue
Editors
Alexander von Vegesack,
Peter Dunas, Mathias Schwartz-Clauss

Texts by
Peter Dunas, Mathias Schwartz-Clauss,
Matthias Kries, Petra Rohde, Alexander von
Vegesack, Christopher Wilk

Biographies and bibliography
Serge Mauduit, Andreas Nutz, Matthias Kries

Editing
Marianne Dunas, Anne-Marie Katins,

Translations
Jeremy Gaines, Rebecca Wallach

Production management
Elke Henecka

Photos
Thomas Dix, Andreas Jung, Roland Engerisser,
Miron Landreau

Illustrations
Bernard Monestier, Miron Landreau,
Jourii Movtchan

Repros
Miron Landreau

Layout
Heinz Hiltbrunner, Gabriela Eichmüller, Basel

Lithos
Fotolitho Stampfer, Bolzano

Printers
Druckhaus Uhl, Radolfzell

The Vitra Design Museum wishes to thank the following persons and institutions for their willingness to support the exhibition and the catalogue by providing documentation and information, or by donating individual objects:

Alias s.r.l., I-Grumello del Monte, Renato Stauffacher and Chiara Finazzi
Alvar Aalto Foundation, SF-Helsinki, Mia Hipeli
Alvar Aalto-Museo, SF-Jyväskylä, Kaarina Mikonranta and Katariina Pakoma
Amat-3 Internacional s.a., E-Martorell-Barcelona, Lidia Amat
Ron Arad & Associates Ltd., GB-London, Ron Arad and Caroline Thorman
Aram Designs Ltd., GB-London, Zeev Aram
Archives Modernes de l'Architecture Lorraine, F-Nancy, Catherine Coley
Artek oy ab, SF-Helsinki, Ben af Shultén
Helmut Bätzner, D-Karlsruhe
Albrecht Bangert, D-Schopfheim
Andreas Baresel-Bofinger, D-Munich
B&B Italia s.p.a., I-Novedrate/Como, Federico Busnelli and Fiorella Villa
B.D. ediciones de diseño, E-Barcelona, Maite Serra
Brigitta Bertoia, USA-Bally/Pennsylvania
Galerie Maria de Beyrie, F-Paris, Maria de Beyrie
Blattmann Metallwarenfabrik AG, CH-Wädenswil, W. Wegmann
Andrea Branzi, I-Milan
Cassina s.p.a., I-Meda/Milan, Franco Cassina, Anna Spadoni and Mariangela Viterbo
Castelli GmbH, D-Ahlen, Roland Schieffer
Castelli s.p.a., I-Orrano dell'Emilia, Livia Cassai
Achille Castiglioni, I-Milan
Centre Georges Pompidou, MNAM/CCI Design, F-Paris, Raymond Guidot and Marie-Laure Jousset
ClassiCon, D-Munich, Stefan von Fischer-Poturzyn
Coop Himmelblau, A-Vienna, Wolf D. Prix and Helmut Swiczinsky
DDL Studio, I-Milan, Donato D'Urbino and Paolo Lomazzi
Paolo Deganello, I-Milan
Studio De Lucchi, I-Milan, Michele De Lucchi and Gabriella Furlan
Design Institut Cologne, D-Cologne, Julia Lang
Galerie Down Town, F-Paris, François Laffanour and Sonja Ganne
Eames Office, USA-Petaluma/California, Lucia Eames-Demetrios
Ecart International, D-Munich, Wolf Bruns
Ecart s.a., F-Paris, Isabelle Fraysse
Eternit AG, CH-Niederurnen, Linus B. Fetz
Jean-Paul Felley, CH-Geneva
Fulvio Ferrari, I-Turin
Galerie Ulrich Fiedler, D-Cologne, Ulrich Fiedler
Galerie Yves Gastou, F-Paris, Yves Gastou
Objekt-Koordination Gillesen GmbH, D-Langenfeld, Renate and Klaus Gillesen
Gufram s.r.l., I-Balangero, Eliana Enrietti
Willy Guhl, CH-Hemmishofen
Ai und Yoshinobu Hagita, D-Düsseldorf
David Hanks, USA-New York
Fritz Hansen A/S, DK-Allerød, Anne Margrethe Hauge
IMD AG, CH-Hausen, Frans Baars
Galerie Jousse Seguin, F-Paris, Philippe Jousse

The Knoll Group, USA-New York/New York, Carl Magnusson
Knoll International Deutschland GmbH, D-Murr, Hartmut Dörrie
Kunstmuseum Düsseldorf, D-Düsseldorf, Wolfgang Schepers und Marianne Dunas
Kuramata Design Office, J-Tokyo, Mieko Kuramata
Wolfgang Laubersheimer, D-Cologne
Fondation Le Corbusier, F-Paris, Evelyne Trehin
Markku Lehtinen, SF-Kaarina
Library of Congress, USA-Washington DC, Ford Peatross
Alberto Meda, I-Milan
Memphis s.r.l., I-Milan, A. Bianchi Albrici
Studio Mendini, I-Milan, Alessandro Mendini and Beatrice Felis
Herman Miller Inc., USA-Zeeland/Michigan, John Berry and Linda Folland
Bernard Monestier, F-Paris
Moormann Möbel GmbH, D-Aschau/Chiemgau., Nils Holger Moormann
Jasper Morrison, GB-London
Musée des arts décoratifs, F-Paris, Guillemette Delaporte
Museum of Modern Art, USA-New York/New York, Pierre Adler
Jaqueline Nelson, USA-New York/New York
Marc Newson, F-Paris
Jeffrey J. Osborne, USA-New York/New York
Panton Design, CH-Basel, Verner Panton and R. Troxler
Jorge Pensi Diseño, E-Barcelona, Jorge Pensi
Charlotte Perriand, F-Paris
Pesce Ltd., USA-New York/New York, Gaetano Pesce and Helena Gambo
Poltronova, I-Agliana/Pistoia
Lisa Licitra Ponti, I-Milan
Andrée Putman, F-Paris
Galerie Sentou, F-Paris, Pierre J. Romanet
Brüder Siegel GmbH + Co KG, D-Leipheim/Donau
Studio Starck, F-Paris, Philippe Starck and Laurence Shukor
Stedelijk Museum, NL-Amsterdam, Reyer Kras
Stiletto, D-Berlin
Erika and Peter Sulzer, D-Geisweiler
Roger Tallon, F-Paris
Tecno s.p.a., I-Varedo, Paolo Borsani and Carla Corbella
Tecta, D-Lauenförde, Axel Bruchhäuser
Gebrüder Thonet GmbH, D-Frankenberg, Georg Thonet and Jutta Sachsenröder
Top System Burkhard Lübke, D-Gütersloh, Burkhard Lübke
Victoria & Albert Museum, GB-London, Christopher Wilk
Vitra GmbH, D-Weil am Rhein, Judith Brauner, Egon Bräuning, Ricardo Lopez, Susanne Papke, Gudrun Rüb, Bernadette Weinkötz
Peter Vöge, NL-Leiden
Hans J. and Marianne Wegner, DK-Gentofte
Frank Lloyd Wright Foundation, USA-Scottsdale/Arizona, Bruce Brooks Pfeiffer and Penny Fowler
Zanotta s.p.a., I-Nova Milanese, Duilio Gregorini
Federica Zanuso, I-Milan

Table of Contents

Foreword
Alexander von Vegesack
Director, Vitra Design Museum

All the Vitra Design Museum's activities focus on documenting and interpreting the history of industrial furniture design. Drawing on the Museum's own collection and extensive archives, we assemble changing exhibitions which, after being held here, go on tour internationally. At the same time, we publish catalogues to accompany these exhibitions and, independently, present discussions of various aspects of furniture design.

In the past six years, we have succeeded in setting up a museum that generates the lion's share of its finances. Aside from a basic sum contributed by our sponsors, the Vitra companies, the Vitra Design Museum receives no funding from the private or public sectors, but by means of its own activities meets its annual budget for program and staff. The fact that this experiment has worked has to do, on the one hand, with our international team of young and highly motivated staff members and, on the other, with growing interest in the domain of everyday life. Besides clothes and automobiles, no objects accompany us so closely through life as do pieces of furniture on which we sit or sleep, or work, or in which we keep our possessions. Many facets of our culture's development, even the most short-lived fashions, have an impact on the construction, the materials, and the design of furniture. In this context the chair, as an impression of our body with legs, seat, backs, and arms, occupies a special place. No item of furniture has been subject to so many different influences, and architects and furniture designers have constantly been challenged to design chairs optimally to meet the consequent demands.

The Museum's public are also the users of furniture. Each of them is an expert, as each of them uses chairs every day. So people do not shy away from entering our Museum; and our exhibitions as well as our workshops, organized almost every summer together with select designers on diverse subjects, repeatedly encounter great interest.

Naturally, the attractiveness of our theme must be seen in connection with the architecture surrounding us. Alongside our own building designed by Frank O. Gehry, the pavilion by Tadao Ando, the factories by Nicholas Grimshaw, Frank O. Gehry, and Alvaro Siza, above all the fire station by Zaha Hadid is impressive – it will soon be used by the Vitra Design Museum as additional exhibition premises.

Looking back on our museum work to date, it seemed obvious to present key items from our collection in the light of insights gained over the years. Therefore the museum curators responsible endeavored to go beyond merely exhibiting twenty to thirty undisputed masterpieces, and additionally to forge thematic links to show the hundred most representative model types in due context. The allocation of the objects to groups underlines their essential significance and thus makes it easier for viewers to approach them. But primarily the presentation is intended to encourage viewers to create their own links between the objects, as many pieces of furniture can clearly be allocated to several groups.

Research work for the exhibition and catalogue was part of our publication project of compiling an *Atlas of Modern Furniture Design*. This reference book will appear in sections over the next few years and is meant to provide comprehensive and reliable statements about each piece of furniture that has had significant influence on industrial furniture production. A CD-ROM, being made in cooperation with the Karlsruhe Center for Art and Media Technology, will hold information that goes beyond the bounds of a book, such as interviews and film documentation.

The work on the *Atlas of Modern Furniture Design* began five years ago when I met the expert Bernard Monestier in Paris, and we agreed to cooperate on such a project. I wish to offer him my heartfelt thanks for his unflagging support. In addition, I am deeply grateful to Christopher Wilk, Curator of the Furniture and Woodwork Collection in London's Victoria and Albert Museum, who found the time to enrich our project with his continued advice and also with his Introduction to this volume. Within the Vitra Design Museum, I would like especially to thank Peter Dunas, who was in charge of the furniture atlas project, and Mathias Schwartz-Clauss, who has been strongly involved in many exhibitions since the opening of the Museum. Without the persevering research of Serge Mauduit, with whom I have now worked for fifteen years, we would not have been able to realize the project. An extremely important part was played by our staff members Matthias Kries and Andreas Nutz as well as Petra Rohde and Miron Landreau. As with all Museum projects, at some point, for a shorter or longer period of time, everyone was involved in the current exhibition – our

secretarial staff, the Department for Loans and Traveling Exhibitions, the Marketing Department and in particular our management team as well as the Head of our Visitors Department, Katja Takvorian, who plays a major role in conveying our ideas to the public. Finally, I would like most cordially to thank Rolf Fehlbaum, who as the chairman and managing partner of the Vitra companies has always been a source of critical and reliable counsel on all questions related to our work.

⌐ Zaha M. Hadid, Vitra Fire Station, 1993
∧ "African Seats" exhibition, 1994
< "African Seats" summer workshop, 1994
> "Czech Cubism" exhibition, 1991

Introduction
Christopher Wilk
Curator Furniture and Woodwork Collection,
Victoria and Albert Museum, London

What is Vitra?

Within the European design community, no manufacturer of office furniture is better known and more respected than Vitra. While such a statement might be regarded as the sort of unctuous hyperbole that fills honorific book prefaces or uncritical, advertiser-driven design magazines, the fact is that the firm is synonymous with the highest quality design and manufacture. Its roster of designers is a "who's who" of contemporary European design – Mario Bellini, Antonio Citterio, Philippe Starck, Jasper Morrison – and its manufacture of classic furniture by Charles and Ray Eames gives it an association with the most distinguished furniture of the postwar period. Design is part of the company's ethos, not only in terms of the furniture it sells but in every aspect of Vitra's operation. This includes not merely a corporate collection of modern furniture, unusual in itself, but a museum with an active exhibition program, open to the public. How the Vitra Design Museum came into being and the nature of its collection deserve brief explanation.

Collection and Museum

Vitra is a Swiss firm, founded by Willi Fehlbaum in 1934 as a manufacturer of shop fittings. In 1957 they expanded into the production of office furniture and began manufacturing, under license from the Herman Miller Company in America, furniture designed by Charles and Ray Eames, and George Nelson. In 1977 Willi Fehlbaum's son Rolf took over the running of the company. Rolf Fehlbaum began collecting early examples of furniture designed by the Eameses and Nelson, as well as the work of other classic Modern designers including Jean Prouvé and Alvar Aalto. In 1987 he met Alexander von Vegesack, an equally passionate collector, from whom he acquired a large group of classic furniture design from 1880-1945, which considerably enlarged the size of the collection. Originally, Fehlbaum intended to house the collection in a building adjacent to a new factory commissioned from the North American architect Frank Gehry. The Gehry factory was part of Vitra's ambitious building program which involved commissioning, some would say collect-ing, major international architects including Nicholas Grimshaw, Tadao Ando, Eva Jiricna, Zaha Hadid, and Alvaro Siza to design new structures at Vitra's main manufacturing site in Weil am Rhein, Germany. Gehry's collection building was intended to be open to business customers. However, as the collection grew and von Vegesack was hired as a free-lance director, it evolved into a museum, open to the public. It attracted considerable attention not only because of the objects it displayed but primarily because it was Gehry's first European building, a dynamic and complex structure which drew, in part, on German Expressionist and Czech Cubist architecture for inspiration.

What is in the Collection?

The Vitra collection consists of more than 1800 pieces of furniture of which the vast majority are chairs. Although the furniture ranges in date from 1820 to the present day, most dates from 1925 and after, and virtually all of the pieces made before the 1970s can be characterized as in the Modernist tradition or part of what is seen as that style's prehistory. Although it is said that only furniture intended for mass production is collected, that policy is not strictly adhered to. In addition, a small collection of lighting supplements the furniture holdings.

The Vitra Design Museum owns a particularly large collection of Eames furniture, including models and prototypes, which was acquired en masse in 1988 during the closure of the Eames office, following the death of Ray Eames. This acquisition was an especially dramatic one by virtue of its size and importance, but it also signaled the unique nature of the Vitra Design Museum's activities. Not only does it stand as testimony to Vitra's passion for Eames furniture but also for the Museum's interest in documenting the furniture it owns by means of the acquisition of documentary material, including entire archives (the Eames collection includes approximately 250 pieces of furniture as well as photographs, trade catalogues, and other advertising material). Besides the Eames collection, Vitra owns archives relating to the German tubular steel industry during the 1920s and 1930s (in particular the papers of Anton Lorenz), a collection of furniture designs by Eero Saarinen, and archives of the work of Harry Bertoia and Verner Panton. Both the Director and the Museum itself own large and important holdings of twentieth-century trade catalogues, photographs, patents, and contemporary literature.

The Museum points to its collection of prototypes and archives as proof that its interests go beyond the precious museum object to the process of design. Displays of its collection within the setting of its beautiful, abstract museum building and exhibition titles including the word "masterpieces" may subvert this view but, over time, a more analytical didacticism is emerging. While other design and decorative arts museums around the world wrestle with the complex meaning and hierarchies of objects, this Museum takes a pragmatic, object-based view, partly inspired by its beginnings in the activity of collecting but also by its close contact with working designers.

The specialist nature of the collection, concentrating mainly on one category of object, means that within its field the Vitra Design Museum is more active than any other museum in the world. It is driven by a fierce desire to acquire and is unencumbered by the need to share resources among different departments. As a small, private institution, it is notably free of the bureaucracy that afflicts most museums which, in Europe, are almost all state-sponsored. Finally, although some individual pieces of furniture may cost a great deal of money, the types of objects Vitra collects are not extraordinarily expensive compared to the sums expended by museums which also collect so-called fine art.

The Philosophy behind the Collection

The Museum's collection cannot be called a comprehensive collection of modern furniture as it has consciously chosen to espouse what might be called a Pevsnerian approach to the history of furniture (derived from Nikolaus Pevsner's influential book, *Pioneers of the Modern Movement*, London, 1936). In this view, the ahistorical, utopian, functional, and geometrically pure Modernist style codified in the 1920s, is seen as the true style of this century (although contemporaries viewed it as anti-style,

believing that it was styleless and timeless, nothing less than the only appropriate form for the time). Within the Museum collection, the nineteenth century is represented by those pieces thought somewhat fancifully to have provided the twentieth century with pure, unornamented form and/or forward-looking technology – Schinkel, the Shakers and Thonet thus find their way in. The collection is dominated by leading edge, mainly architect, designs from Vienna at the turn of the century, from Germany and France during the 1920s and 1930s, and from Scandinavia, Italy, and America after 1945. Furniture other than that in the Modernist tradition is largely ignored, as is everyday or vernacular furniture, and, particularly, the decorative (including Art Nouveau and Art Deco, despite the former's acceptance as part of the history of Modernism). The craft revival since the 1960s is equally unrepresented.

The demise of Modernism itself, from the 1970s especially, means that objects from that decade and after recognize a plurality of styles, although the framework remains high-style, avant-garde design. So, while a Postmodern Queen Anne chair by Robert Venturi is in the Museum's collection, there is none by a true classical revival architect of the 1930s or, for that matter, the 1990s. Objects designed by leading architects who challenged the purity and simplicity of modern design by insisting on decoration, color, irony, and the validity of popular taste and irrationality, such as Alessandro Mendini and Ettore Sottsass, are well represented in the collection. The work of traditional decorative designers who followed the same path but without ironical or irrational intent are not included.

Corporate Collections and Design Museums

The Vitra Design Museum and its collection are different from other corporate collections or design museums or centers in numerous ways. Many manufacturers have collections of their own products, although these tend to be relatively small. Few companies place value on original objects and are likely to consider the keeping of products or papers to be unrelated to their core business. Resources are rarely available to preserve and make them accessible, and unless a senior company official takes a personal interest, they tend to be treated badly. Companies that own such collections rarely place them on public view; instead, they are seen as an adjunct to the showroom and perhaps occasionally lent to exhibitions or trade shows. At the heart of these corporate collections lies the promotion of the firm's own products and no further purpose. Although it is true that the Vitra Design Museum collection includes some examples of Vitra furniture, that the museum is located on the factory site, and that it frequently lends its holdings to exhibitions and trade shows, it cannot in any way be described as a collection of the company's products; indeed, it is difficult to believe that any corporate collection in the world includes such a small percentage of its own firm's productions.

It is no coincidence that the Vitra Design Museum was founded during the 1980s, a period of economic expansion when design or, in some instances, the perceived marketing value of design, found expression in all manner of consumer products, artwork, and new private institutions. Among the latter were the Design Museum in London, the Wolfsonian [sic] Foundation in Florida, and the Domino's Pizza Collection of Frank Lloyd Wright material in Michigan. Behind these and others, as with Vitra, was an individual committed to the enduring value of design and to the activity of collecting. It is worth noting, however, that by the time the full effects of the recession were felt in the early 1990s, one of these institutions had closed, and the future of others rests on shaky ground. Like most cultural organizations, the future of the Vitra Design Museum relies on its ability to expand its audience and fund its own operating budget by earning income – hence its publications program and production of lines of miniature furniture – and the commitment of the Vitra company itself.

Unlike most design museums or centers, the Vitra Design Museum focuses almost entirely on furniture, and it has more than once been referred to as a chair museum. It does not address the entire world of design, even if such a thing were possible. But equally unlike other such institutions, it has attempted to bridge the gap between museum and practice, by bringing leading designers into the Museum to teach residential courses to young desi-gners, by making its participation in trade shows a key element of its policy, and through active contact with designers whose work it collects.

This link with practising designers is one of the unique features of the Museum. However, it again suggests that the museum cannot be separated entirely from the Vitra furniture company. The products and the image of the company attract designers. Indeed, it is rare to meet an architect or designer who is not an admirer of Vitra; most long to work for a firm they perceive as committed to excellence in design and willing to support activities beyond the core ones of manufacturing and selling. Much as the Museum stresses its independence from the company, the two are intimately connected in the eyes of the design community.

Museum and Marketing

It would be naive to think that Vitra's collecting has nothing to do with the company's overall marketing strategy. Although the collection did not begin as part of a conscious effort to contribute to the firm's identity, and it retains its independence, the Museum has undeniably grown into a valuable affirmation of the passion for design felt by Vitra's owner. When the Museum appears at major trade shows, either on its own (with a complete exhibition or merely an information booth) or within the Vitra company display, the message is clear: Vitra is a company committed to design, even when this is not directly profitable. It also, not incidentally, aligns current production with what is perceived to be the most significant work of previous decades. This does not in any way detract from the Museum enterprise, but awareness of this is essential.

In an age when the values of Modernism have been turned upside-down and the notion of a canon of good design has been rejected by many, the ideological position of the Vitra Design Museum may be seen as anachronistic; but it may equally be seen as an attempt to uphold an important and viable set of design values which still inspire contemporary work, in particular that manufactured by Vitra and other leading furniture manufacturers. The Museum thus becomes a celebration and reinforcement of the firm's activities, even if it does not use the company's products to do so. Although its acquisition of more recent objects has moved beyond Modernism, its outlook still adheres to a Modernist belief in the moral, even redemptive, power of design and in the validity of furniture as an autonomous and deeply important area of work.

While practising designers and academics may argue the validity of such a position, it is clear that the Vitra Design Museum has found a large audience which fervently believes in those values. That public is part of cosmopolitan European society where, with the notable exception of Britain, design matters. Vitra speaks to that public more successfully than most institutions and, rather than detracting from the Museum's credibility, the relationship between company and museum is seen by them as an asset.

Note on the Use of the Catalogue

Technical specifications:
The technical specifications above the texts refer only to the object shown. The names in parentheses do not originate from the manufacturer or designer and serve solely for identification.
To the extent that this is not noted otherwise, the objects are made by the first manufacturer/s. Possible later manufacturers as well as later changes in name, size, or material are not given in the technical specifications. The technical specifications on the manufacturing refer only to the manufacturer stated, although changes to the object and changes of name by this manufacturer are not taken into account.

Production dates are indicated in the following ways. "Production: 1910" would mean production in that year only. "Production: 1910–1915" would mean production from 1910 to 1915. "Production 1910 to the present" would mean production began in 1910 and continued to today. "Production: since 1910" would mean production began in 1910 but the date it stopped is unknown. "Production: from around 1910" would mean production began in approximately 1910 and the date it stopped is unknown.

The size of the objects is given in height x width x depth.

Illustrations:
The illustrations alongside the technical specifications point to other objects in the catalogue which are comparable in historical, formal or technical terms

Technology

Technological achievements have always comprised the powerhouse behind industrial society. At the beginning of industrialization, new production methods relied on a formal canon of objects and equipment produced by individual craftsmen. They increasingly influenced design and emancipated themselves by means of designs of their own from the dictates of prevalent styles and ideals of beauty, gradually shaping styles themselves.

Many innovative items from a technological point of view were mass-produced by the million and yet became well-received design classics – such as the bentwood "Chair No.14" manufactured by Gebrüder Thonet, or Marcel Breuer's steel-tube cantilever chair, and often a public awareness of these designs first resulted from cheap copies. Other examples demonstrate what was technologically feasible, but rarely got past the preproduction stage, such as Alberto Meda's "LightLight" chair, of which only fifty were made.

Ideally, technology combines the wish for an economic use of materials with automated production methods, such as became possible with the advent of plastics – the "Bofinger Chair" is the first consistent result of widely conducted research and efforts in this regard. Mass-produced goods designed for manufacture by machine and low-priced as well were the sociocultural goal of several generations of designers and soon led in rich industrialized countries to a mentality of not buying things that lasted. A changed environmental awareness and the search for greater individuality caused the uniformity of the large series to be disrupted in many areas and prompted a stronger degree of product differentiation. The use of valuable, in part natural materials, labor-intensive production methods, and considerable logistic outlays, leading to low unit output, tend to push prices up and to negate the original aims of rationalized, technological production processes. *PD*

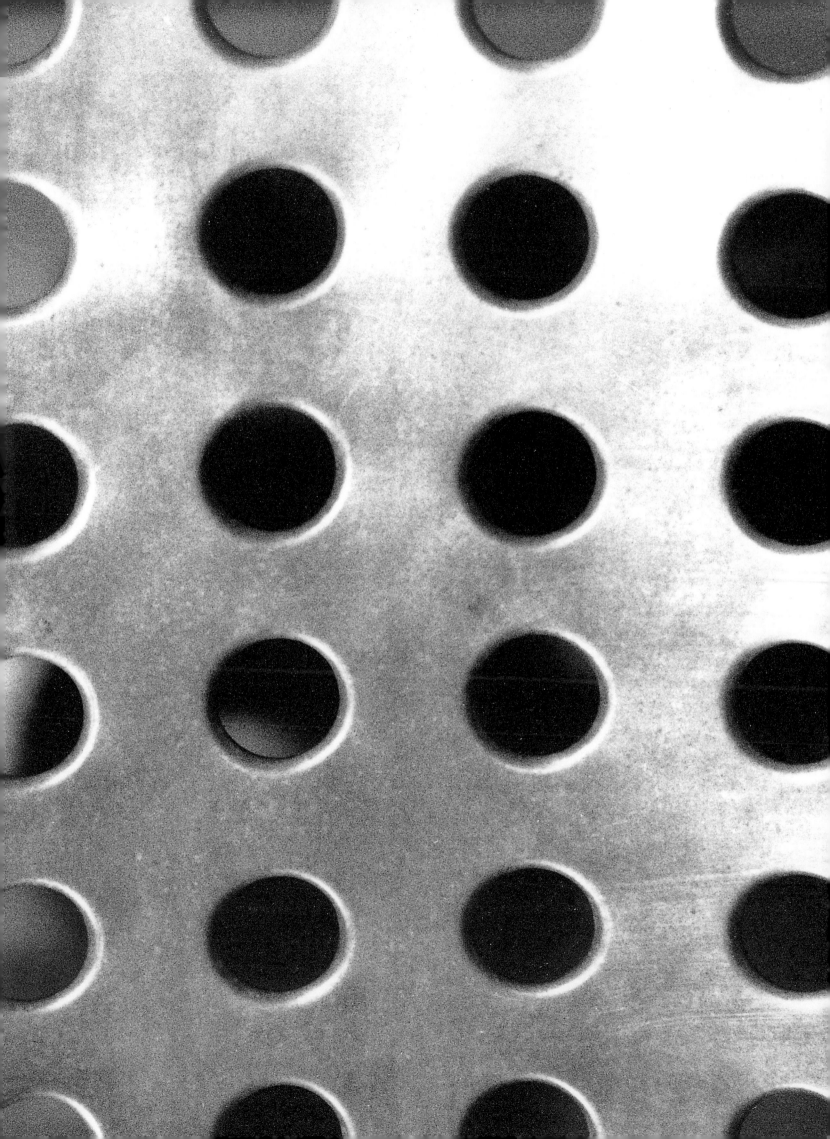

1

Name: (Garden Chair)
Designer: Karl Friedrich Schinkel
Design: 1820-5
Production: unknown

Manufacturer: presumably the
Königliche Eisengießerei Saynerhütte
Size: 86 x 46 x 54; seat height 43.5 cms
Material: cast iron, wrought-iron rods

With its new manufacturing processes and materials, industrialization squeezed the traditional trades of turners and carvers out of furniture construction. One of the most important innovations in this area was the use of iron. Long before Michael Thonet's first bentwood experiments, which enabled the first real mass production of furniture, a large weapons factory, founded by Czar Peter the Great and later converted to civilian use, was already producing considerable quantities of cast-iron furniture in 1736.

Karl Friedrich Schinkel, the Prussian architect, also utilized the cast-iron process to produce furniture efficiently. It is primarily for his architectural work that Schinkel is considered the most important representative of German Classicism, but as a furniture maker he achieved great recognition as well. As a founding member of the Technische Deputation (technical buildings inspectorate), he regularly presented his models in the publication *Vorbilder für Fabrikanten*

und Handwerker (examples for manufacturers and craftsmen) which was supported by the inspectorate and thus able to exert considerable influence on the taste of the day. His elegant interpretations of the Classical period resulted in formally stringent designs for various purposes. In addition to wooden furniture, he also designed numerous iron table bases, garden chairs, and other furniture.

Schinkel's iron garden chair consists essentially of two identical side pieces, each cast as an entire unit. Since these side pieces are not rods but flat rolled beams in cross section, they offer great stability with the use of minimum materials. Ornamental rosettes adorn the intersection points of the legs as well as the outer and inner sides. This allows the same casting mold to be used for both sections. The wrought-iron rods of the seat and the strecher between the legs are set into drilling holes and riveted from the outside, thus enabling manufacture of the side

sections for a bench with the same mold, the latter simply being assembled using longer rods. The back is also riveted by two transverse braces to the side sections. Their decorative filling, which was made using so-called open hearth casting and was molded while still hot to fit the curve of the seatback, shows typical Classicist motives. A lyre is situated in the center and flanked by lion heads on both sides, surrounded by identical acanthus foliage on the left and right. The symmetry that dominates all parts of the design is repeated here, dictated by the technique and style.

The chair is being manufactured as a reproduction today by the Tecta company in Lauenförde, Germany. *MSC*

< K. F. Schinkel: Altes Museum Berlin, 1822-30, rebuilt 1958-66
∨ K. F. Schinkel: Garden bench, 1820-5

Name: Chair No. 14
Designer: Michael Thonet and sons
Design: 1859-60
Production: 1865 to the present

Manufacturer: Gebrüder Thonet, Vienna
Size: 92.5 x 42 x 50; seat height 46.5 cms
Material: bent beechwood

Worldwide, "No.14" is one of the most successful products in the history of industrial mass production. It also established the international reputation of the Thonet Company. By 1930 over 50 million chairs had already been sold. In 1930 the price was DM 8.50 and this was the most reasonably priced model within the Thonet line. Even today it is being produced in modified form.

Starting in 1830, Michael Thonet began to experiment with shaping laminated wood. He boiled wood strips in glue and bent them into prepared iron molds. He is recognized as the founder of industrial bentwood processing and in 1836 introduced the first chair made of laminated wood. Efficient methods of manufacturing, a reduction in the individual parts of a chair, and finally the development of its own distribution network via sales offices in all major cities around the globe enabled Thonet to develop into an international company. Laminated and molded wooden furniture sold in subtropical countries with high humidity led to a flood of complaints since the glue tended to dissolve. Because of this pressure, Michael Thonet developed a procedure of bending solid wood with steam, replacing the glued peg jointing with screws. Model "No.14" was the first product utilizing this new bentwood technique and, after about 1865, the entire fabrication was switched over. Thanks to the screwed connections, it was now possible to ship the chairs in their individual parts for final assembly at their destination. Thirty-six dismantled "No.14" chairs could be packed into a crate with a volume of only one cubic meter. Since the connections could be retightened as necessary, the lifespan of the chair was also enhanced as an added benefit. *PD*

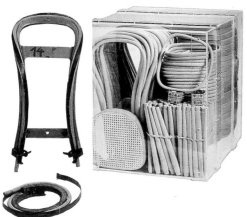

⌐ Today's bending shop at Thonet's successor company, Ton, in Bystrice, Czech Republic
« Thonet bending molds for "No.14"
‹ Thirty-six dismantled "No.14s" in one cubic meter
∧ Banquet hall in Grundtvig Haus, Copenhagen, c.1920
› German post office in Africa, 1900

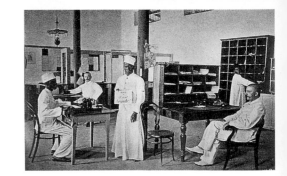

3
Name: (French Terrace Chair)
Designer: Anonymous
Design: around 1926
Production: from around 1926

Manufacturer: Société industrielle des meubles multiples, Lyon
Size: 83 x 43.5 x 47.5; seat height 45.5 cms
Material: varnished steel, wood veneer

Not much is known about the origins of this stackable metal chair. It is included as one of the exemplary "types of chairs" which Adolf Gustav Schneck, professor at the Württemberg State College of Applied Art in Stuttgart presented in the exhibition "Der Stuhl" (the chair) in Stuttgart in 1928.
The underside of the seat is stamped with a crowned, two-headed heraldic eagle and the year, 1896. Below that: "Grands Prix-Paris-1900-Luterma-Made in Esthonia-Fabriqué en Esthonie." The plywood seat was decorated on the top with a historicizing claw motif in embossed relief. The thin veneer layer is connected to the frame by eight split-pin rivets, thus allowing easy changing. There is evidence that different models of this chair were produced. In Stuttgart the chair was shown with both a perforated plywood seat and a perforated metal one. The interchangeability also implies that only the embossed seat stemmed from Estonia

and that only this part was identified from the year 1900. The reverse side of the back is stamped "Société Industrielle des Meubles Multiples, Lyon."
The catalogue of the Stuttgart exhibition includes the following interesting remarks by Schneck: "In addition to these simple chairs of today, and there are a large number in this category, we are presenting simple chairs of the past; not museum objects, but such as are still on the market and have proven their value as standard models. The metal chairs which were deleted from German catalogues 30 years ago because of their lack of taste have continued to be sold in France and have now been reintroduced in Germany at the major exhibition "Pressa" in Cologne. It was discovered that this chair offers great sitting comfort and that this is perhaps an important advantage."[1]
This chair can be considered an early example of a space-saving, low-cost chair produced in large

numbers. The economical use of materials is illustrated in the molding of the legs, which are thin but still sturdy. Furthermore, the shape allows the chairs to be stacked. The perfect fit of the individual parts points to the high degree of craftsmanship involved.
In 1934 the Frenchman Xavier Pauchard modified the metal chair by extending the side sections of the back to armrests and by changing the molding of the legs. This chair was produced under the model name "A 56" by Fenêtre sur cour and is still being marketed today by various firms.
Today's terrace furniture, produced in large numbers due to improved production methods, mostly in a plastic injection-molding process, can probably trace its origins to this French terrace chair. *PD*

∧ From a German mail-order catalogue, 1976
> Xavier Pauchard: "A 56," 1943

Name: B 64, Cesca
Designer: Marcel Breuer
Design: 1928
Production: 1929 to the present

Manufacturer: Gebrüder Thonet AG,
Frankenberg on Eder, Germany
Size: 81 x 57 x 62.5; seat height 45 cms
Material: chrome-plated tubular steel,
varnished wood, bentwood, wicker

■

Marcel Breuer's cantilever chair is one of the best-known chairs in the world, but it often first came to the attention of consumers through cheap imitations. Breuer's fondness for tubular steel and his knowledge of how to use it in chair construction was already illustrated in the Club chair "B 3" (Wassily) introduced in 1925. Breuer was revolutionary in abandoning the traditional construction of a chair based on four legs, but he was not the originator of this idea. The Dutch architect Mart Stam had already introduced the notion of a cantilevered chair to Heinz Rasch and Ludwig Mies van der Rohe in 1926 during the preparation of the Werkbund exhibition "Die Wohnung" (the apartment) for the Weissenhof Settlement in Stuttgart. The design was a far cry from a free-swinger for it was rigid. Ludwig Mies van der Rohe was the first to pick up on the idea of a chair without traditional leg support with his model "MR 10" and continued the straight barrel shape in a single curve to the seat. Both chairs were presented in the exhibition "Die Wohnung" (the apartement) in 1927 where Marcel Breuer saw them. Although Breuer allowed many of his tubular steel designs to be produced as standard furniture, he gave the production rights for the "B 32" (without armrests) and the "B 64" to Thonet. Stam's complaint about the use of his designs was rejected by Breuer with the argument that he had already designed a U-shaped stool in 1925-6 for the canteen of the Bauhaus which – if it were laid on its side – anticipated the principle of the cantilevered chair. The main difference from Stam's model lay in the combination of tubular steel construction with wooden frames for the seat and back, with a bentwood technique referring to the origins of the bending of tubular steel. Even if Breuer was not the originator of the cantilevered chair, his springy free-swinger became his greatest commercial success. When the Italian company Gavina s.p.a. took over production of the Breuer designs in 1962, the "B 64" received the nickname "Cesca" after Breuer's adopted daughter, Francesca. *PD*

< Tubular steel bending works at Carl Beck & Alfred Schulze Co., 1930-1
^ Interior designed by Le Corbusier with "B 32"

Name: Chaise Longue No. 313
Designer: Marcel Breuer
Design: 1932
Production: since 1934

Manufacturer: Embru AG
(Eisen- und Metallbettenfabrik AG, Rüti)
for Wohnbedarf AG, Zurich
Size: 75.5 x 58 x 137 cms
Material: aluminum "Anticorodal"
alloy, varnished wood

The "Chaise Longue No. 313," part of a collection of different springy aluminum chairs and recliners, is the product of two different developments. Marcel Breuer, who emigrated from Dessau to Zurich, had already applied to the National Patent Office for the German patent for a "frame for springy chairs or recliners" on November 22, 1932. A lawsuit ensued which continued for a year between the companies of Mauser (Cologne) and Arnold (Schorndorf) and Mies van der Rohe, until finally on September 10, 1936, the patent application was turned down. The point at issue was the copyright for the rigid connection of the (rear) so-called "auxiliary spring supports" which, by relieving the burden, enabled a reduction in the tube diameter. At the end of 1932, Marcel Breuer directed the modernization of a new shop in Talstrasse 11 for Wohnbedarf AG in Zurich, which had been founded in 1931 by, among others, the architectural critic, Sigfried Giedeon. The goal of Wohnbedarf AG was to develop, more or less as a distributer, contemporary furniture with a light appearance for

apartments made in the New Building style in cooperation with designers and the industry. When the Alliance Aluminium Cie. announced the competition "Concours international du meilleur siège en aluminium" in Paris in 1933, Giedeon succeeded in establishing a second jury, parallel to that of industry representatives, with artistically oriented members, such as representatives of CIAM (Les Congrès Internationaux d'Architecture Moderne). As CIAM secretary, Giedeon invited his colleagues Le Corbusier and Walter Gropius to be members of the jury. Marcel Breuer participated in the competition, submitting prototypes of springy chairs and recliners made of aluminum which he had had produced by Embru. He was awarded first prize on November 23 and 24 by two juries that had reached their decisions independently of each other. The intelligent construction principle was quite striking, with a symmetrical aluminum section sawed lengthwise and then bent to form both the front and the back auxiliary spring supports.

Earlier, on October 21, 1933, Breuer had signed a license agreement with Embru for the exclusive production and sales rights, initially for Switzerland and Liechtenstein, and had applied for a Swiss patent on October 31, 1933. This application was more or less equivalent to the previously rejected Berlin patent but was expanded to include solid materials, such as wood and metal. A patent was granted on November 1, 1934, by the Swiss Office for Intellectual Property after Embru had already begun mass production, also in lacquered strip steel. Other license partners for the springy "Anticorodal" or "Duralumin" series included Arnold in Germany, A.L. Colombo in Italy, and Stylclair in France.
The designs in the aluminum series met with great popular acclaim and formed the link between the tubular steel furniture of Breuer's days at the Bauhaus in Germany and the plywood furniture which he developed after his emigration to England between 1935 and 1937. *PD*

∧ Wohnbedarf advertising photograph with aluminum furniture by M. Breuer, 1930s
> Cover of a Wohnbedarf brochure, 1934
⌐ M. Breuer: "Isokon Chaise Longue," 1936

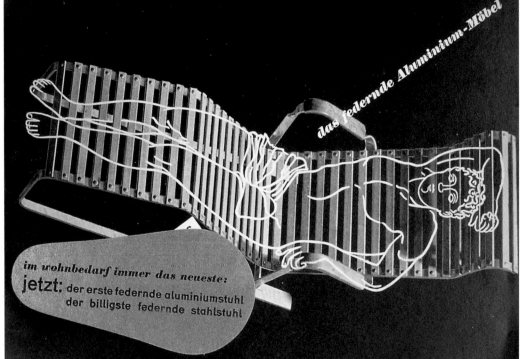

6
Name: (Garden Chair)
Designer: Jacques André
Design: 1936
Production: 1937

Manufacturer: Ateliers Jean Prouvé, Nancy
Size: 70 x 74.5 x 97.5; seat height 31,5 cms
Material: varnished sheet metal,
acrylic glass

■

Like Jean Prouvé, Jacques André came from a family of architects and craftsmen in Nancy. Their fathers were actively involved in the Ecole de Nancy which played an important role in Art Nouveau. Jean Prouvé was a founding member in 1929 of the avant-garde Union des Artistes Modernes (UAM) and in 1934 recruited Jacques André as well, who had just received his architecture degree and had been working with him since the 1920s.
In 1936 the two of them suggested to UAM on the occasion of the 1937 world's fair in Paris that the union present a comprehensive collection of furniture. The intention was to create a combination of steel with acrylic glass and thus create an equivalent in furniture to high-tech architecture which, through its skeletal steel construction and generous use of glass, created an increasingly light appearance.
Prouvé had produced a prototype for a plexiglass object that same year and had presented it at the Paris autumn salon. In February of 1937, Jacques André began production of the series which was only intended to comprise six parts. The chair was made of folded and perforated sheet metal and was constructed in Jean Prouvé's workshop. Folding the sheet metal increased its resilience, while perforation reduced the weight and supported the visual sense of dematerialization. The material acrylic glass only appears to be light and was at that time very difficult to produce and to process. At the presentation of the series in 1937, André also encountered problems with the weatherproofing of the material which tended to develop cracks in direct sunlight. The anticipated positive response was not forthcoming and no producer was found for the production of the series as hoped. *MK*

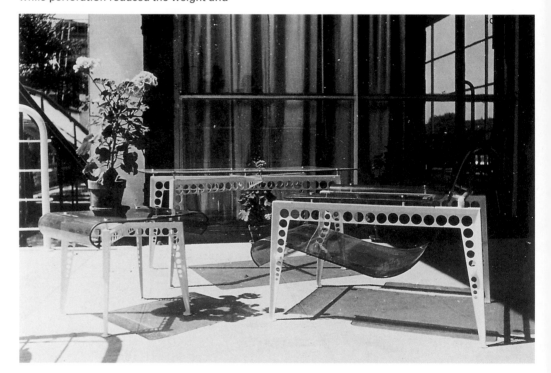

Pavilion of the Union des Artistes Modernes, 1937, Paris world's fair, with plexiglass furniture by J. André

Name: Landi
Designer: Hans Coray
Design: 1938
Production: 1939 to the present

Manufacturer: P. & W. Blattmann
Metallwarenfabrik, Wädenswil, Switzerland
Size: 77 x 54 x 58; seat height 43 cms
Material: molded, heat-treated, and stained
aluminum alloy; rubber

"Landi" is the official outdoor chair of the Schweizerische Landesausstellung (Swiss National Exhibition), nicknamed the "Landi," which was held in Zurich in 1939.

The "Landi" architect, Hans Fischli, invited submissions to a competition for over 1,500 new chairs for gardens, squares and parks in 1938. Since these were meant to have a link to Switzerland, it was decided that the material of choice be the "Swiss metal," aluminum. Aluminum was one of the most important export articles, stood for modernity, and could only be produced using great quantities of electricity, these being readily available through hydroelectric power plants. As early as November 1933, the parent company of the Schweizerische Aluminiumwerke in Paris had initiated a competition to identify the best aluminum chair. Walter Gropius and Le Corbusier were members of the jury, and Marcel Breuer won first prize (see "Chaise Longue No. 313").

1938, Hans Coray, student of Romance languages and self-taught designer, won the first prize of SF 500 with a miniature model consisting of a perforated steel seat with a wire base. The cooperation between Fischli-Coray-Blattmann (the metal-working company) and the Rorschach aluminum works finally resulted in a sensational chair that weighed a mere three kilos. One innovative feature was the development of a shell from a hard material – even prior to the Eameses' attempts at bending metal (see "DAX") – which was molded using a 300-ton drawing press. The perforation of the metal, an idea borrowed from the aviation industry, reduced the weight while the three-dimensional shape of the perforation edges improved the stability. The development was supported by concurrent experiments by the Swiss Federal Railway. The base of the feet was also made of molded metal strips, the innovative Argon metal-arc welding joined the identical pairs of legs by the cross beams beneath the seat. All individual parts underwent special heat treatment, rendering the aluminum as hard as steel, and afterward all that remained was to mount the seat on the lower base with screwed connections.

Since the "Landi" was intended for outdoor use, no caps were placed under the feet. In various stages these were first made of plastic wood, later of plastic, and at the end of the fifties in the present form of black or white rubber since the chair was increasingly used indoors. In 1962 the manufacturers changed the number and arrangement of the perforations, reducing the rows from 7 to 6 and the original 91 holes to 60; after 1971 also marketed under the name "2070 Spartana" by Zanotta s.p.a. This enabled mass production rather than individual processing and gave the springy seat greater stability, since in the first models cracks sometimes appeared in the curved area between the seat and the back.

At the end of the "Landi," the chairs were sold to visitors for SF 5. *PD*

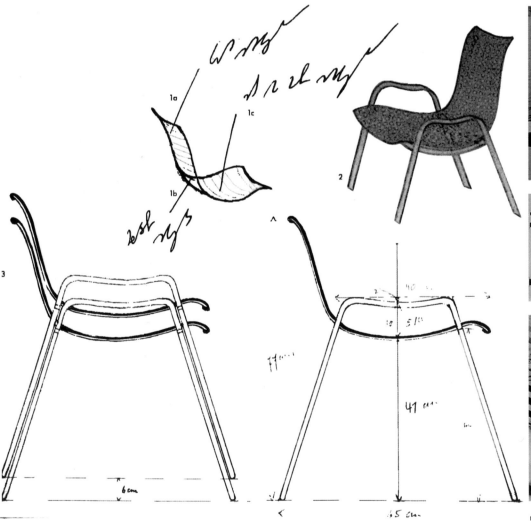

⌐ H. Coray: Sketch for "Landi," 1938
≪ The "Landi" National Exhibition, 1939
≪ From a 1959-60 P. & W. Blattmann-prospectus
∧ Production process of the "Landi"

8
Name: (Children's Chair)
Designer: Charles and Ray Eames
Design: 1945
Production: 1945

Manufacturer: Molded Plywood Division of Evans Products Company, Venice, California
Size: 36.5 x 35 x 28; seat height 23 cms
Material: molded plywood

■

The stackable children's chair is part of a small group of stools, chairs, and tables made of untreated or colored stained birch plywood and was the first mass-produced non-war application of the technical experience Charles and Ray Eames had gained during World War II in molding three-dimensional plywood.
In a trial run, 5,000 stools and chairs were produced and introduced to the public at great marketing expense. Despite overall recognition, the children's chair was a disaster financially speaking. Since the Evans Products Company did

not have a distribution network at its disposal, the sales figures lagged far below expectations. Once the trial run in 1946 and 1947 sold out completely, no further production followed. The patented children's chair was basically forgotten after that.
The chair consists of only two parts: the seat and legs are made of one continuous piece of plywood, and the back is attached. In contrast to the prototypes from 1940 made of molded plywood for competitions (see "Organic Armchair") or the leg splints developed for the

navy, the three-dimensional design of the chair appears very reduced. The skillful arrangement and sequence of the angles guarantees rigidity, while avoiding the difficult and extreme three-dimensional dilatation and compression of the individual layers of veneer.
Due to the heavy burden placed on children's furniture, only a few examples exist today. *PD*

⌐ Individual parts in the producer's warehouse
∧ Photograph from the Eameses' office
« C. and R. Eames: Leg splints, 1942
‹ C. and R. Eames: Elephant made of molded plywood, 1945

9
Name: Knoll #70, Womb Chair
Designer: Eero Saarinen
Design: 1947
Production: 1948-93

Manufacturer: Knoll Associates, Inc.,
New York
Size: 89 x 100 x 90; seat height 43 cms
Material: fabric-covered and fiberglass
reinforced latex padding, tubular steel base

Eero Saarinen's "Womb Chair" was the result of collaboration with Charles Eames and their joint attempt to mold laminated wood three-dimensionally. These experiments led to the two winning the "Organic Design in Home Furnishings" competition held by the New York Museum of Modern Art in 1940. Eero Saarinen's contact with Florence (Schuster) Knoll, who had studied together with him, Charles and Ray Eames, Harry Bertoia, and Don Albinson under Eero's father, Eliel Saarinen at the Cranbrook Academy of Art, helped him develop the first chair with a plastic shell produced in large quantities.

According to Florence Knoll, Saarinen sought to design a comfortable chair, which would allow several sitting positions rather than one rigid one, and incorporated a number of loose cushions. During the search for an appropriate carpenter for building the model, they discovered a shipbuilder in New Jersey named Winter who worked with fiberglass. Since this material has no structure of its own, it was more suitable than laminated wood for shaping even complicated curves and molds. Winter, however, did not believe this technology could be applied to furniture. But developing the plastic shell itself was less difficult than connecting it to the base.

Numerous attempts were necessary to ensure permanent connection while retaining the flexibility of the shell. The latex-foam padding and loose seat and back cushions provided the desired comfort.

Because of its overall popularity – the consumer liked feeling safe and sound as if in their mother's womb – the chair was a commercial success. Saarinen set new standards from both a technological and a formal standpoint with this model and was granted a patent for the "Womb Chair."
PD

Contemporary interior with "Womb Chair"

Cover of *The Saturday Evening Post* of May 16, 1959

10

Name: DKR (Dining Height, K-Wire Shell,
R-Wire Base/Rod Iron Base)
Designer: Charles and Ray Eames
Design: 1951
Production: 1951-67

Manufacturer: Banner Metals, Compton,
California, for Herman Miller Furniture
Company, Zeeland, Michigan
Size: 82 x 48 x 52.5; seat height 45.5 cms
Material: varnished wire

Charles and Ray Eames demonstrated their fondness for industrial production methods and materials with a technological thrust in their designs for the New York MoMA's 1948 "Low-Cost Furniture Design" competition (see "La Chaise" and "DAX").

After rejecting the idea of an organic, i.e. human-body-shaped, shell designed of pressed sheet steel or aluminum, and modifying the use of fiberglass technology, Charles and Ray Eames duplicated the shape of the S-Shell (Side-Chair) using welded wire. The choice of wire was certainly influenced by Harry Bertoia who, as a sculptor, employed metal wire and pipes and had worked in the Eameses' office from 1943 to 1946. In 1952, just one year following the marketing introduction of the "DKR," Bertoia introduced his "Diamond Chair" to the public which was produced by Knoll. In a lawsuit between Herman

Miller and Knoll, Charles and Ray Eames were awarded intellectual ownership of the copyright. Wire had already proven itself as a material in various bases for fiberglass shells and for the bases of tables. Its delicate transparency and visual lightness combined with high resiliency could now also be applied to the shell construction. After experiments with triangular mesh, a rectangular structure and spot-welding were eventually chosen. The loose ends of wire were bound at the edge by two thicker wires. Thus the tips of the wires were less sharp and the shell shape was stabilized. This technological innovation was awarded a patent, the first for a mechanical solution for furniture. With its use of a single material for the base and seat the design of the "Wire Chair," as the "DKR" is also known, offered a holistic appearance, but, like the plastic shell, it was also available in different base

options; the most well known is the "Eiffel-Tower Base."

It proved possible to enhance seating comfort on the rigid wire chair additionally by a single – or, after 1955, a two-piece (bikini version) – removable, thin cushion. This allowed a variety of possibilities for combining individual parts and different colors. In 1952, the "Wire Chair" was awarded the Trail Blazer Award by the Home Fashions League of America. The "Wire Chair" has also been manufactured and marketed by Vitra AG, Basel since 1958. *PD*

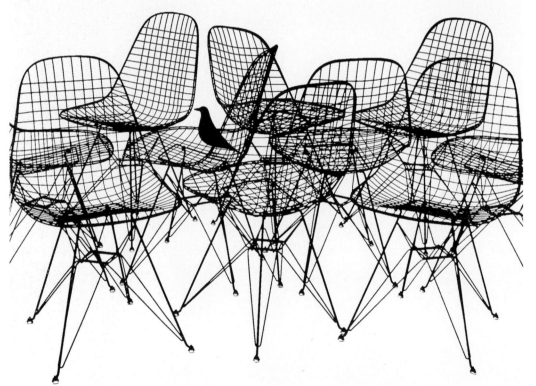

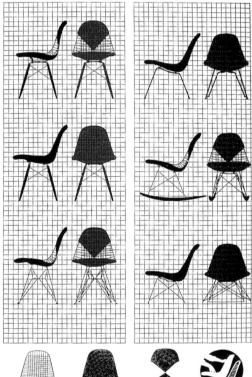

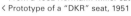

wire shell   *one piece pad*   *two piece pad*   *pad removed*

^From a 1952 Hermann Miller catalogue
⌐ From a 1952 Hermann Miller catalogue
< Prototype of a "DKR" seat, 1951

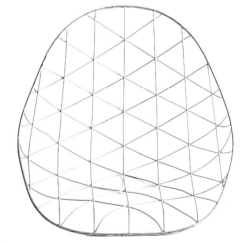

40

11
Name: Indoor-Outdoor "Reclining Armchair" No. 684 (swiveling and tilting)
Designer: Charles and Ray Eames
Design: 1958
Production: 1958 to the present

Manufacturer: Herman Miller Furniture Company, Zeeland, Michigan
Size: 100 x 65 x 77; seat height 40 cms
Material: polished and clear-coated cast aluminum, synthetic fiber

The "Indoor-Outdoor" or "Leisure Group" stems from a suggestion by Alexander Girard and Eero Saarinen who were looking for suitable furniture for a house they had just completed for Irvin Miller. Girard, who as an architect was also interested in horticulture and was the director for textile production at Herman Miller, complained that although contemporary furnishings existed for inside, there was no good-looking terrace or garden furniture. Charles Eames could not get this idea out of his head, and he tried to help his friend. During an airplane flight, he thought of the idea of material stretched across an aluminum frame construction.

Even prior to that Eames had intended to produce metal furniture (in 1948 using embossed aluminum for the New York Museum of Modern Art competition "Low-Cost Furniture Design" or in 1951 using welded wire for the "Wire Chairs"). Again he wanted to develop a body-shaped form, not as a hard shell but as an elastic length of material between the side pieces which followed the body contours. He sketched the profile of the

sides on the back of an envelope. The material was reinforced on the side by means of a narrow strip of plastic and was fixed in a groove turned to the outside. After returning from his trip, his former student at the Cranbrook Academy of Art and then colleague, Don Albinson, began immediately with the construction of wood models of the profile and the crossbeams or stretcher. It was soon decided that a symmetrical arrangement of the grooves in a double T-beam configuration would be more stable. The inner groove could then serve as an opening for the crossbeams and thus the right and left profile would be identical (except for the drilling); thereafter, all that remained was to develop the side sections. The synthetic fiber Saran, developed by Alexander Girard and the Eames Office in four colors, seemed to be appropriate for use outdoors, and triple layers of the fiber were stretched between the sides, overlapping in the spots where the seat, back, and headrest would be subject to the greatest wear and tear. Unfortunately their expectations with regard to

the material were sadly dashed, for it soon rotted when left outside. Saran had to be replaced by a heat-sealed artificial leather, called Koroseal or Naugahide.
Further experiments led to a padded sandwich construction featuring two layers of Naugahide with a thin padding of vinyl foam and vinyl padding which was "quilted" every $1\frac{7}{8}$ inches by high-frequency welding, which lent the "Aluminum Group" chairs and armchairs the look they have today. Originally developed for outdoors, the first mass-produced aluminum chairs and armchairs are now only used indoors and as classics have not lost any of their modernity. *PD*

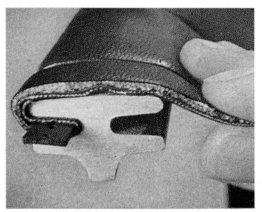

Ⱶ The fabric is fixed in the double T-beam of the frame
⩓ Production of the "Reclining Armchair," c. 1958
⅂ Production of the "Reclining Armchair," c. 1958
Γ C. and R. Eames: Study for developing the frame crosssection of the "Reclining Armchair," c. 1958
⋏ From a Hermann Miller catalogue, 1958

12
Name: Lambda
Designer: Marco Zanuso, Richard Sapper
Design: 1959-64
Production: 1964

Manufacturer: Gavina s.p.a., Bologna
Size: 77.5 x 39.5 x 46; seat height 44 cms
Material: stamped steel, varnished; rubber

Marco Zanuso is considered the great rationalist of postwar Italian design. In 1939 he took a degree in architecture at the Milan Polytechnic and opened his own office in 1945. Between 1958 and 1977 he collaborated closely with Richard Sapper.
Zanuso dedicated himself intensively to material analysis and technology research.
In 1959 he received a contract for the development of a low-cost kitchen chair whose seat and back should be made out of plastic; his client gave him complete design freedom in creating the connections of the parts and the shape of the base. After producing numerous prototypes, Zanuso disregarded the original specifications and developed an all-metal chair. One of these trial models was awarded the silver medal of the XII Milan Triennial.

He envisioned mass-production as in the automobile industry and was involved with preliminary technological studies over the course of five years.
The "Lambda" consists of a total of ten stamped, thin sheets of metal, which could also be shaped and assembled by small metalworking shops. The seat shell has a double-walled construction. In the space inbetween the seat and back sections, the inner and outer form differ from each other to the greatest degree, thus creating the greatest hollow space. This increases the stability. The four U-shaped folded legs blend with the inner shell and are securely connected with the outer shell by curved gussets. All connections are electrically spot-welded together. At the end of the process, the chair is sprayed in high-gloss paint.

This particular construction affords a great degree of stability despite the use of a thin material and its minimal weight.
The fold of the legs predates the later style of low-cost plastic garden chairs. Unlike these, the "Lambda" cannot be stacked.
A later version was planned with a leather pad which was to be glued into the shell.
Despite the already mentioned advantages, it still was not possible for Zanuso to succeed in automating production. Since the individual parts had to be assembled by hand, the expected high unit output was not achieved. The design was discontinued after the trial series. *PD*

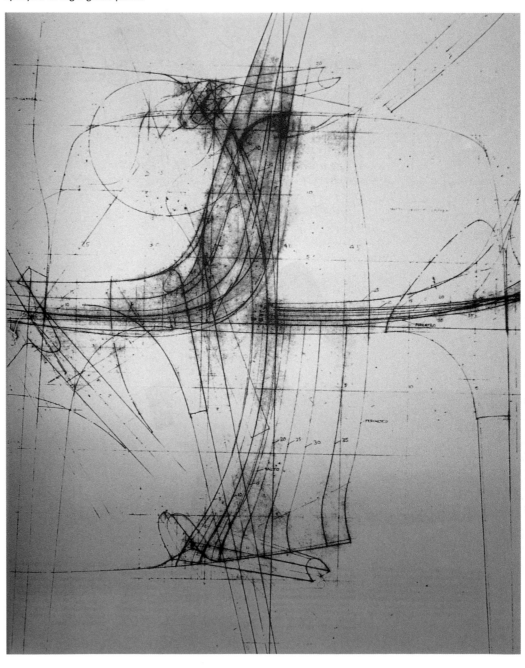

^M. Zanuso: Drawing for "Lambda," 1958-9
Γ Structure of "Lamda"

13
Name: BA 1171, Bofinger Chair
Designer: Bätzner Architectural Office
(Helmut Bätzner with Alfred Bätzner and
Friedhelm Bös)
Design: 1964-5
Production: 1966/8-1984

Manufacturer: Menzolit-Werke, Albert
Schmidt, Kraichtal-Menzingen, Germany,
for Wilhelm Bofinger KG, Ilsfeld, Germany
Size: 75 x 52.5 x 53.5; seat height 44 cms
Material: solid color, fiberglass-reinforced
polyester resin

Plastic reinforced with fiberglass has been commonly used in furniture ever since the late 1940s with the work of Eero Saarinen and Charles Eames. When he developed his "Tulip Chair" in 1956, Eero Saarinen had hoped one day to be able to produce this model completely in plastic. His desire for an all-plastic chair was shared by many designers, and throughout Europe research was initiated to accomplish this end.

But only in 1966 did architect Helmut Bätzner succeed in presenting the first mass-producable one-piece plastic chair at the furniture fair in Cologne.

This chair was developed in 1964 and 1965 in connection with construction work for the State Theater in Karlsruhe for which Bätzner's architecture office was handling the planning. The chair was intended as additional seating for the experimental stages, foyer, café, canteen, and terrace area. Versatile use both indoors and out, as single or as row seating, called for special qualities: the chair had to be light, movable, stackable, compact, linkable, and weatherproof. The material chosen was fiberglass-reinforced polyester. It was possible to guarantee stability of

the legs, seats and back, with minimal material inputs by opting for molding. The special shape of the legs follows a double curve. After creating the optimal design in model form, Helmut Bätzner presented the idea to Bofinger, the well-known furniture manufacturer. Together they investigated possibilities for mass production and discovered a suitable partner in the Menzolit-Werke, Albert Schmidt. Since the mid-fifties, this company had specialized in development, production, and processing of preimpregnated polyester resin mats, which among other things were used for molds in car body construction. Rudolf Baresel-Bofinger, the general manager of Bofinger KG, convinced the chair would be a success, signed a license agreement on January 14, 1966 with Helmut Bätzner and commissioned production of the double-shell heated ten-ton press. During the so-called "prepreg-process," in a single operating cycle lasting only five minutes, a near-finished chair was produced. The polyester resin was stained throughout in eight colors and, because of the smooth surface of the press molds, chairs were created which required no further finishing (only the edges of the press seams had to be smoothed). In the same year as

its introduction, the "Bofinger Chair" received the Rosenthal-Studio-Preis in the presence of Federal Chancellor Ludwig Erhard and the founding director of the Bauhaus, Walter Gropius. Designed as a relatively low-cost piece of furniture, the "Bofinger Chair" became an ideal seating for public places due to its minimal weight of only four kilos, its enormous stability, its weatherproofing and easy care. Its stackability was also remarkable – eighty chairs took up merely one square meter. Altogether more than 120,000 chairs were produced. Millions of units of cheap plastic garden chairs with similarly shaped legs have duplicated this model in numerous variations.

At the end of 1994, there were attempts by the successors Baresel-Bofinger and the Habit Company factories in Kürten-Engeldorf, Germany, to manufacture the "Bofinger Chair" using recycled material. The first examples were shown at the Cologne furniture fair in 1995. *PD*

^ Developmental series of the "Bofinger Chair"
< From a Menzolit-Werke brochure, c. 1975

14
Name: Blow
Designer: Jonathan De Pas, Donato
D'Urbino, Paolo Lomazzi, Carla Scolari
Design: 1967
Production: 1968-9, 1988-92

Manufacturer: Zanotta s.p.a., Nova
Milanese, near Milan
Size: 83 x 110 x 95; seat height 42 cms
Material: transparent PVC foil, mangled
and electronically high-frequency welded

"Blow" is the first piece of inflatable living room furniture to be mass-produced and to score high unit sales. "Blow" also helped the manufacturer Zanotta to first gain an international reputation. "Blow" reflects the changing attitudes toward interior design objects at the end of the sixties. Traditional bourgeois values, such as permanence, material assets, and solidity, were questioned and rejected. Inspired by pop culture and leisure-time activities, the four architects designed their first piece of furniture, adopting

the construction principle behind an inflatable raft: light, transparent, mobile, compact to store, and inexpensive! Just as with the "Throw-Away" sofa designed by Willie Landels for the same manufacturer in 1965, the temporary nature of a formless polystyrene foam body with a synthetic covering is an expression of the desire for change as soon as one has grown tired of an object.
Even if the idea behind the "Blow" armchair stems from an inflatable boat, the armchair

required that a new production technology be created, because PVC cannot be glued like Neoprene. Since the designers considered the transparency of the material paramount, numerous trials followed before the appropriate production process, electronic welding of the foil, was finally discovered.
Marcel Breuer's vision from the mid-twenties – of being able to sit on a column of air – finally came true with "Blow." *PD*

^From an article in *Il Giorno* of May 29, 1968
> Contemporary interior with "Blow"

15
Name: UP5 and UP6, Donna
Designer: Gaetano Pesce
Design: 1969
Production: 1970-3

Manufacturer: C & B Italia (Cassina & Busnelli), Novedrate, near Como, Italy
Size: 92 x 117 x 137; seat height 40, UP6 circumference 60 cms
Material: polyurethane foam, cold foam-molded, nylon-jersey

"Donna" is completely in tune with the spirit of Pop Art and the Gaetano Pesce fondness for anthropomorphic shapes. The chair was actually designed to resemble a prehistoric, female fertility figure, with a ball attached to symbolize captivity: "In this design I have expressed my idea of women. A woman is always confined, a prisoner of herself against her will. For this reason I wanted to give this chair the shape of a woman with a ball chained to her foot to use the traditional image of a prisoner."[2] The unconven-

tional nature of the shape also applies to the construction and marketing of the chair which was one of a series of six. Together they succeeded in marking a radical break from traditional upholstery production thanks to the technology developed by C & B Italia for creating oversized foam parts.

"Donna" consists of a molded monoblock of foam without any supporting structure since the "foam rubber" is dense and free-standing. First, a finished piece of furniture covered with elastic

nylon jersey is reduced in a vacuum chamber to about 10 percent of its normal volume and is then wrapped in airtight foil. The customer can easily transport the otherwise unwieldy piece single-handedly. After removal of the wrapper at the destination, the chair slowly recovers its original shape without outside help as air seeps back into the capillaries of the polyurethane foam. *PD*

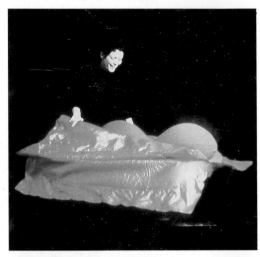

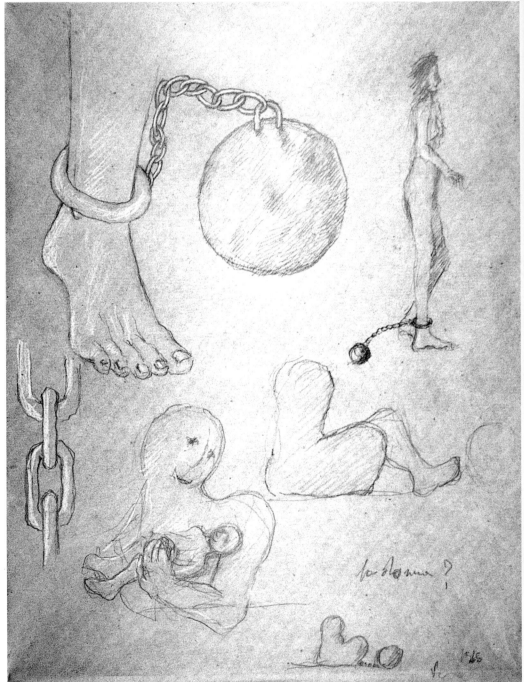

≫ The "Donna" self-inflates
≫ From a 1969 C & B brochure
∧ G. Pesce: Model for "Donna," 1969
˥ G. Pesce: Drawings for "Donna," 1968-9

16

Name: Wiggle Side Chair
Designer: Frank O. Gehry
Design: 1972
Production: 1972

Manufacturer: Easy Edges, Inc., New York
Size: 85 x 42.5 x 60; seat height 45.5 cms
Material: corrugated cardboard, fiberboard,
round timber

■

Cardboard furniture came on the scene during the sixties as a cheap and light alternative to traditional furniture. At that time attempts were made to reinforce the support of the single-layer cardboard offered by using folds, tabs, slots, and other devices. Nevertheless, cardboard was not able to compete against plastic, which was just as light.

Frank O. Gehry discovered a process that ensured cardboard furniture-making a new burst of popularity. "One day I saw a pile of corrugated cardboard outside of my office – the material which I prefer for building architecture models – and I began to play with it, to glue it together and to cut it into shapes with a hand saw and a pocket knife."[3] It was thus possible to transform

massive blocks of cardboard into cardboard sculptures.

Gehry named this material Edge Board: it consisted of glued layers of corrugated cardboard running in alternating directions, and in 1972 he introduced a series of cardboard furniture under the name "Easy Edges." The "Easy Edges" were extraordinarily sturdy, and due to their surface quality, had a noise-reducing effect in a room. The design theorist Victor Papanek, one of the first to address the ecological responsibility of designers, praised Edge Board as a useful application of a packing material to furniture. The "Easy Edges" were a great success and brought Gehry overnight fame as a furniture designer, but at the same time he was into a role he did not

like. Even sales prices were no longer consistent with Gehry's basic idea of offering furniture to suit anyone's pocketbook. "I started to feel threatened. I closed myself off for weeks at a time in a room to rethink my life. I decided that I was an architect, not a furniture designer ... and I simply stopped doing it."[4]

Gehry made an international breakthrough as an architect in the late seventies, among other things with the design of his private residence in Santa Monica, California, in 1978. Since 1986 Vitra AG has reproduced four models of his "Easy Edges." *MK*

F. O. Gehry: "Little Beaver," 1987

From a 1972 Easy Edges brochure

17

Name: LightLight
Designer: Alberto Meda
Design: 1986
Production: 1987-8

Manufacturer: Alias s.r.l.,
Grumello del Monte, Italy
Size: 70.5 x 53 x 47.5; seat height 47.5 cms
Material: epoxy resin, Nomex, carbon fiber

Materials developed for aeronautics and space technology have long been important for manufacturers of sports articles and automobiles. But only since the mid-eighties has high-tech also played a role as a material in the design of everyday objects.
Alberto Meda wanted to reduce the weight of the "LightLight" chair to a minimum and to emphasize the extremely durable nature of the material. A honeycomb structure, using rigid Nomex polyurethane foam, formed the internal structure of the seat and the back. It is enclosed on both sides by carbon fiber which gets its strength from epoxy resin. The thin legs and the armrests are also made of carbon fiber. The back and legs

are, moreover, reinforced by a layer of vertically aligned fiber, thus increasing the stability in vulnerable areas.
Carbon fibers are also used in the production of tennis rackets and fishing rods because of their lightness and unbreakableness. In the "LightLight" chair, they enable a reduction to rudimentary, fragile-looking shapes without construction details being visible.
In 1987 Meda described the development process: "During the first phase the structural problems were discussed without any consideration of economic factors. In the current second phase, a study is underway to explore the ins and outs of the industrial production of the

product. At the moment production is still by hand, even though at a high-tech standard."[5] This study resulted in fifty examples of the "LightLight" chair which were produced in 1987–8 and sold at a price of about DM 2,200. With regard to cutting the carbon fiber and its further mechanical processing, replacing work by hand involves very expensive machinery. Since this did not allow any reduction in production costs, the manufacture of the chair was discontinued in 1988. *MK*

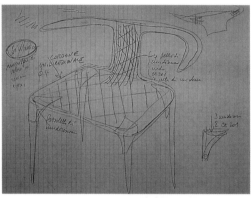

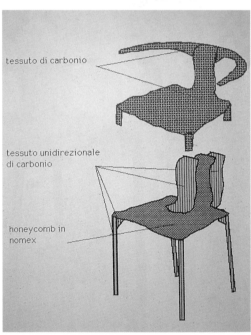

tessuto di carbonio

tessuto unidirezionale di carbonio

honeycomb in nomex

≫A. Meda: Sketch for "LightLight," 1986
^Structure of "LightLight," 1987
> Individual parts of "LightLight

18

Name: Louis 20
Designer: Philippe Starck
Design: 1991
Production: 1992 to the present

Manufacturer: Vitra AG, Basel
Size: 84.5 x 59 x 60; seat height 47 cms
Material: blown polypropylene;
polished aluminium

Philippe Starck is regarded as the leading French figure in the area of New Design in the eighties. He has achieved an international reputation and creates designs for leading companies worldwide.

Starck is fascinated by the efficiency of modern production methods which allow the manufacture of low-cost articles, and he sometimes even demands the right to determine pricing with the manufacturer.

Since the end of the eighties he has combined tubular steel with plastic. The "Dr. Glob" series of chairs, which he designed for the Italian manufacturer Kartell in 1988, involves an interplay of contrasts in material and shape. The continuous angular front legs and seat made of pastel-colored plastic developed by swaging are complemented by black- or silver-lacquered round back legs which rise up to a curved back section. The contrast in materials is also a main feature of the stackable "Louis 20" chair. Here, the voluminous hollow front legs, the seat with the characteristic Starck front curve, and the springy back section are blown from a single piece of polypropylene. The frame of the back legs is sturdily joined with an oversized fixing plate to the hollow plastic body so that the chair can be tilted on its back legs without any damage. Its subtle color scheme combined with the brilliance of the polished aluminum make this chair just as popular in private as in public spaces, and it is also suitable for outdoors. It can be easily dismantled into recyclable elements in only a few seconds by loosening the screws on the armrests and the attachment plate of the back legs.

Starck ironically named the chair "Louis 20," poking fun at the French royal tradition of distinguishing kings of the same name by numbering them from IV to XVIII, including Louis XIV, the "Sun King," and of identifying styles during their respective reigns the same way. *PD*

∧ Connection of plastic part and back legs of "Louis 20"
≻ "Louis 20" and the "Louise" table from a Vitra brochure, 1994

Construction

Technology and construction are closely related domains that reciprocally influence each other. Forms and connecting elements in furniture are thus frequently based on available materials and manufacturing processes. Likewise, certain constructions may call for specific manufacturing technologies. The designer is, however, responsible less for the technology and more for the construction. The latter is one of the central challenges for designers, for it decisively determines how the furniture can be used and how comfortable it is. New species like swivel chairs, folding chairs, or chairs with cantilever bases were the product of developments in construction.

Until the nineteenth century, the construction of furniture, like architecture, largely took a back seat to representative ornamentation which was geared to artistic styles of the day. As of the mid-nineteenth century, a belief in the unlimited capabilities of technology and engineering arose in Europe and America parallel to the growth of the steel industry. Furniture, too, was suddenly seen as a machine: functional, versatile, and easy to use. And enthusiasm for these new possibilities generated an aesthetics of its own. Ships, airplanes, and steel factory buildings were sources of inspiration for practical and formal innovations. In the twenties and thirties, the aesthetics of the machine was nurtured as the expression of a social utopia that wished to change the shape life took by means of a functional aesthetics. And even after World War II, the constructive side to furniture stood first and foremost for its modernity and utility. However, designers started handling constructive elements in a freer and more playful fashion than before. Besides this aesthetic change, fundamentally new construction ideas emerged, such as variable office furniture systems and self-assembly furniture featuring interchangeable parts. *MSC*

19
Name: Centripetal Spring Armchair
Designer: Thomas E. Warren
Design: 1849
Production: unknown

Manufacturer: American Chair Company,
Troy, New York
Size: 107 x 61 x 71; seat height 48 cms
Material: varnished cast iron, varnished
steel, wood, velvet upholstery

■

In its day, this armchair offered a unique degree of luxury due to the eight steel strips bent elliptically and connected under the seat by a funnel-shaped centerpiece. This central section supports a vertical bolt around which the seat can rotate, and at the same time is springy in all directions. Warren planned to use springy steel strips in a similar way for seating for railway cars. Only later did he apply his patented idea to chairs for residential use.

The "Centripetal Spring Armchair," several variations of which were presented at the 1851 World's fair in London, is also one of the first U.S. chairs to feature a cast-iron frame. Designed during a period full of inventive energy and a still unlimited faith in technical feasibility, this armchair is one of the first in a line of versatile pieces of furniture intended to satisfy the needs of its users like a machine. *MSC*

T. Warren: patent drawing for springy railway car seats, 1850

20
Name: No. 670 (Sitzmaschine)
Designer: Josef Hoffmann
Design: about 1905
Production: c.1905-16

Manufacturer: Jacob & Josef Kohn, Vienna
Size: 106 x 67.5 x 90; seat height 27 cms
Material: bent beechwood, turned wood, plywood, brass

■

This type of easy chair with a reclining back has been produced since the seventeenth century. After 1860 the company owned by Englishman William Morris, founder of the Arts and Crafts movement, manufactured and marketed this chair. With its stringent, no-frills design focusing only on elementary parts, it probably served as a model for the later designs of Josef Hoffmann. The Arts and Crafts movement, which greatly influenced Hoffmann and his colleagues Gustav Siegel and Koloman Moser in Austria, was opposed to mechanized mass production and what they regarded as inhuman products. The movement advocated an ethic and aesthetic motivated by social concerns, with form, function, material, and production understood as a unity. Around the turn of the century the Jacob & Josef Kohn company, which produced

bentwood furniture to an industrial standard, hired the avant-garde Viennese architects Hoffmann, Siegel and Moser to make their line more appealing to higher-end clients by means of fashionable designs.
Hoffmann's model "No. 670" was presented as part of one of his most important projects, a furnished model country home for the Vienna Art Show in 1908. The chair was distributed by Jacob & Josef Kohn until 1916. Here, the admittedly pedestrian form of the reclining easy chair is given a striking mechanical look. The frame construction made of bent squared timber with a frame filled with geometrically arranged pieces of plywood and the semi-circular curves of the rear section emphasize the constructive aspect of the object. The balls which are as functional as they are decorative – a typical detail

of Hoffmann's – balance the curved and rectangular elements. At the same time as they stabilize the chair in the corners of the structure and under the runners, they support a shiftable crossbar on the rear arches which locks the back section at different reclining angles. Additionally, they create a visual balance to the square holes in the side and back sections.
Presumably Jacob & Josef Kohn offered the "Sitzmaschine," as the model "No. 670" was later called, with loose cushions. The example shown here with a pull-out footrest was a special order or produced only in a small series. *MSC*

∧ J. Hoffmann: Entry hall, c.1908
⟩ From a J. & J. Kohn catalogue, Vienna, 1916

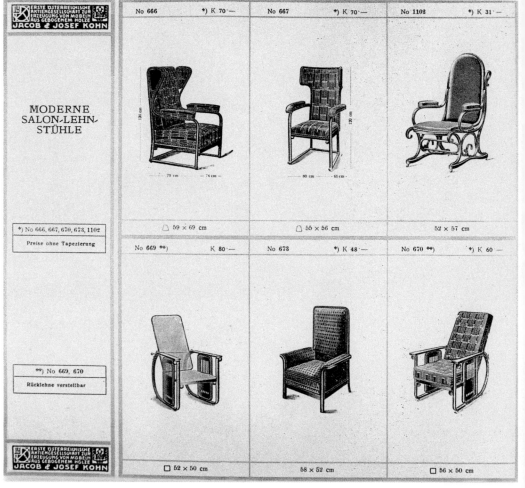

21
Name: E 1027
Designer: Eileen Gray
Design: 1927
Production: 1927-30

Manufacturer: Atelier Eileen Gray/Galerie Jean Désert, Paris
Size: height 61-100 cms, diameter 50 cms
Material: varnished tubular steel, acrylic glass

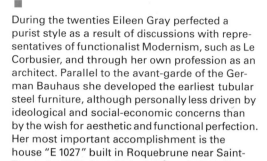

During the twenties Eileen Gray perfected a purist style as a result of discussions with representatives of functionalist Modernism, such as Le Corbusier, and through her own profession as an architect. Parallel to the avant-garde of the German Bauhaus she developed the earliest tubular steel furniture, although personally less driven by ideological and social-economic concerns than by the wish for aesthetic and functional perfection. Her most important accomplishment is the house "E 1027" built in Roquebrune near Saint-Tropez in 1927, for which she also designed a

table of the same name. Originally conceived as a night table for the sick or bedridden or simply for people who "breakfast in bed," it was later also used as a side table in living rooms and on terraces. Its origin as a night table explains the asymmetrical shape. The ring at the base could be pushed under the bed and, thanks to the opening, can fit around the foot of the bed; the height of the tabletop allows adjustment for the thickest down quilts and can double up as a tray. The structure comprised of double tubular steel mounted on the side is reminiscent of

the cantilevered chairs designed at the time and contradicts the conventional notion of a table with four legs. From the time of the production around 1930 only about twelve examples survive. Their tabletops are of glass, acrylic, or black metal. It was only after Eileen Gray's death in 1976 that the mass production of this timeless classic she had so hoped for actually started. After being produced for several years under an Italian license, the German manufacturer Vereinigte Werkstätten, today known as ClassiCon, took on production of this table in 1983. *MK*

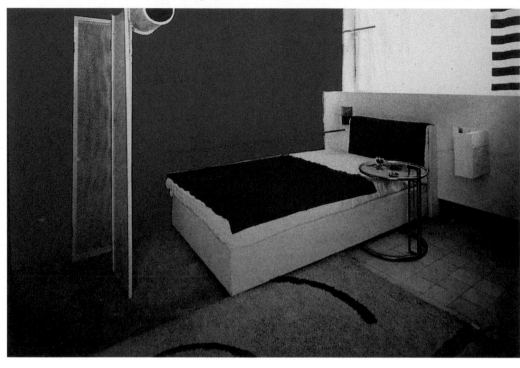

∧ Guest bedroom in house "E 1027" by E. Gray, c. 1930
> E. Gray: Side table, 1925-8

22

Name: MB 744
Designer: Pierre Chareau
Design: 1927
Production: 1927

Manufacturer: Atelier Pierre Chareau, Paris
Size: 98 x 140 x 47 cms
Material: blackened hoop iron, wood

■

While the uncompromising furniture of the German Bauhaus avant-garde erased any evidence of influences identified with the earlier "bourgeois" style in their designs, the most progressive French designers like Eileen Gray or Pierre Chareau still clearly adopted elements from traditional furniture designs from the twenties. In Paris, Pierre Chareau was an important go-between in the twenties between Art Deco and the increasingly popular function-alistic modern style. He created a memorial for himself as an avant-garde architect with his house "Maison de verre," but he considered himself primarily a craftsman: he never allowed his furniture to be mass-produced and rarely made any statements about his work.

In a series of desks which he completed individu-ally for a client together with metalsmith Louis Dalbet, he combined light wood with a flattened base of blackened hoop iron. The version "MB 744" has a fan-out tabletop on the left side, on the right a storage area, and under the top right a swivel cabinet. In contrast to the elegantly curved tubular steel, which was preferred by the Bauhaus designers and which derives its visual charm from harmonious lines, here the focal point is the skeletonlike structure and its carefully balanced volume.

The simplicity and clarity of the connections between the individual components by means of visible screws and the mechanism of the swivel-mounted parts call to mind that aesthetic of the machine world which was championed by many artists whom Chareau knew and who were members of a circle of Cubists and Constructivists. *MK*

∧Interior by Robert Mallet-Stevens with desk "MB 405" by P. Chareau
< "Maison de verre," 1930s
∨P. Chareau: Side table with adjustable top, c. 1927

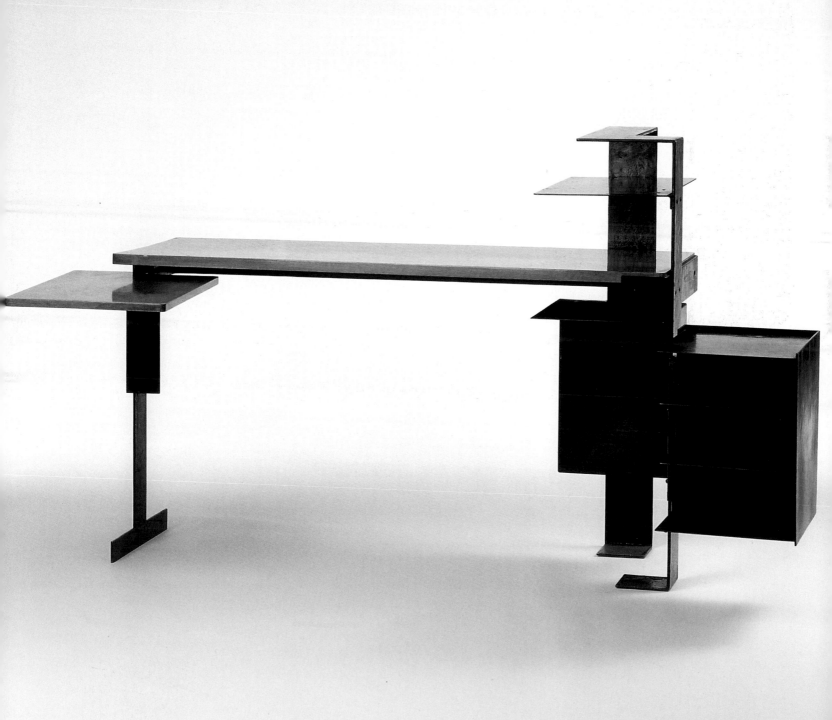

23
Name: Fauteuil à dossier basculant
Designer: Le Corbusier, Pierre Jeanneret,
Charlotte Perriand
Design: 1928
Production: c.1928
(before series production)

Manufacturer: Le Corbusier, Pierre
Jeanneret, Charlotte Perriand, Paris
Size: 64 x 64 x 67; seat height 39 cms
Material: chrome-plated tubular steel,
leather, steel springs

Le Corbusier always chose pieces of furniture with a rational structure and timeless design for the sparse and functional furnishing of his houses, such as a so-called "colonial chair" by the English firm, Maple & Co. "Indian Chair No. 1761" seems to have served as model for the design shown here but also convinced Le Corbusier, Pierre Jeanneret and Charlotte Perriand of the necessity of creating a more comfortable furniture. One important common feature is the back section, which can be tilted by two side attachments and thus supports the back in any position. The idea for this design was being developed in the Le Corbusier studio at just about the same time as the designer Eileen Gray created her "Transat" chair for the house "E-1027."

What was new about the chair by Le Corbusier, Jeanneret, and Perriand, however, was the translation of a customary basic form into an elegant piece of tubular steel furniture which emphasized the functionality of the simple tilting mechanism. Instead of straight tubes to attach the seat and to mount the back section on the legs, the back is pushed forward and supported together with the seat by a single connector which is welded from one straight and one bent tube. The complicated form intentionally departs from the right angles of the rest of the construction to emphasize the comfort of the chair, the reclined seat, and the mobile back. The back section in the early version shown here revolved freely around the central axis; later the rear suspension for the armrests was extended inwards so that the back was only partly moveable. In addition to a leather covering, the chair was also available in patterned calfskin for the back and seat. The earliest models, including one in calfskin, were produced for the library of the villa Church in Ville d'Avray in 1928 by craftsmen under Charlotte Perriand's supervision. Other models were exhibited during the 1929 Paris autumn salon at the "L'équipement d'une habitation" stand created by Le Corbusier, Pierre Jeanneret, and Charlotte Perriand. The plan was for the Peugeot company to mass-produce the "Siège à dossier basculant," along with other furniture designed by this architect team, as that firm was already experienced in using tubular steel for the construction of bicycles. However, the plan did not materialize, and the Thonet Company was approached to handle the costly production of a version that was almost identical to the 1930 version, the model "B 301." Afterward it was manufactured by the Swiss Embru Company under license from Thonet, then by Heidi Weber, and from 1965 to the present by Cassina. *MSC*

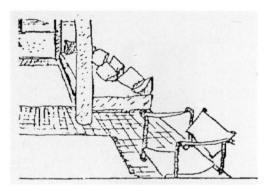

Le Corbusier: Interior sketches of the villa Baizeau, February 28, 1928 (FLC 8503)

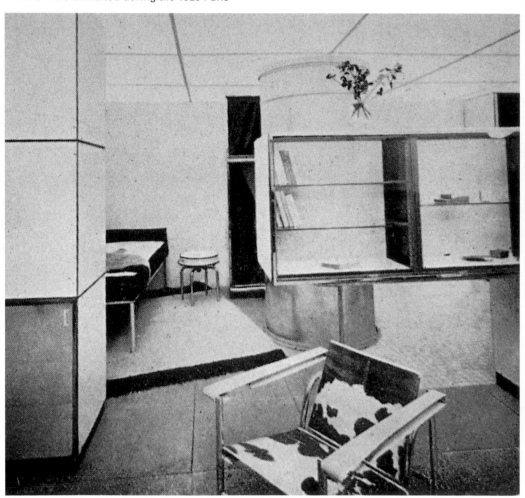

Le Corbusier, P. Jeanneret, C. Perriand: "L'équipement d'une habitation" at the 1929 Paris autumn salon

24

Name: Chaise longue à reglage continu, B 306
Designer: Le Corbusier, Pierre Jeanneret, Charlotte Perriand
Design: 1928
Production: since 1930

Manufacturer: Thonet Frères, Paris
Size: c. 70 x 56.6 x 156 cms
Material: chrome-plated and varnished steel, fabric, steel springs, rubber

■

Compared to the social ideas of the Bauhaus and its minimal designs, French tubular steel furniture, which was influenced by Art Deco, could be considered luxurious. The extravagant shapes and combinations of materials corresponded to the needs of Parisian society for a decidedly modern quality of life and comfort. The few furniture designs which Le Corbusier and Pierre Jeanneret sketched in cooperation with Charlotte Perriand included different drawings of chaises longues. However, not a single item had ever been realized; except for a few bookcases which, however, must be classified more as permanent fixtures of the open, spacious buildings that Le Corbusier furnished in a technical, functional manner and conceived of as "machines for living." His approach called for sparse and functionally related furnishing, e.g., like Thonet's armchair "No. 6009," the modernness of which was rediscovered through its predominant use in Le Corbusier interiors. Charlotte Perriand, whose nickel-plated copper furniture had just been introduced at the 1927 Paris autumn salon, joined the studio Le Corbusier shared with his cousin Pierre Jeanneret at the end of that year. Between 1928 and 1929, presumably to a great extent based on Le Corbusier's sketches, the three created different pieces of furniture such as a swivel stool, tables, armchairs, and a chaise longue. Included among these designs, which are all highly regarded today, is this chaise longue which is undoubtedly one of the most famous items of twentieth-century furniture. In 1928, in a perspective interior view, Le Corbusier sketched the chaise

longue which consists of a padded surface bended sharply twice and resting on the edge of the foot section, supported at the head by a column. In newspaper advertisements of the same year, the Paris physician Pascaud publicized an anatomically shaped lounge chair with an adjustable back piece and neckrest, the so-called "Surrepos." Surely Le Corbusier was also familiar with a rocking chaise longue, equipped with an adjustable back: Thonet's "Rocking Sofa No. 7500." But Le Corbusier, Jeanneret, and Perriand did not wait until the "Surrepos" was on the market and approached the idea from an entirely new perspective. They designed a multifunctional structure which made the reclining surface, fixed on a pair of bows, independent of the base. Since this section rests loosely on the H-shaped supports of the base, its inclination can be adjusted continuously. The rubber sleeves around the crossbeam of the support prevent slipping when someone uses the chaise longue. When the reclining surface is lifted off the base, the bows serve as runners for a rocking recliner.
The different parts of this chaise longue also visually communicate the dynamic of its versatility, even with regard to such details as the inclination of the H-shaped supports, whose oval crosssections are similar to the wings of an airplane. (They were tear-shaped in the original model.) Le Corbusier, who was fascinated by the aesthetics of machines, also called this chaise longue a "relaxing machine."
In the first model, which was produced by craftsmen under the supervision of Charlotte

Perriand for a library of the villa Church in 1928, the ends at the foot and head sections of the chair were still welded on and thus interrupted the continuous line of the tubular steel frame. An example of this type of chair was exhibited by Le Corbusier, Jeanneret, and Perriand at their "L'équipement d'une habitation" stand at the 1929 Paris autumn salon. In the next model, designed for the gallery in the villa La Roche in 1928, this formal inconsistency was corrected. The original scale drawings of this model, which the three designers passed on to Thonet, coincide with the contract signed in 1929 and formed the basis for production, which began in 1930. The example shown here was probably a Thonet prototype. The elliptical profile of the bar between the front and back sections of the base is already like those used in the Thonet mass-produced versions. Unlike here, in the original as well as with the mass-produced design, the front and back sections of the base were at the same height. Thonet advertised this piece of furniture in a 1930 catalogue with a canvas or calfskin covering. In the meantime the chaise longue was produced again by the Swiss Embru Company under license from Thonet and from 1965 until the present by Cassina. *MSC*

Le Corbusier: Sketch for the interior of "Immeubles villas," 1922-3 (FLC 19097)

Sketch for the interior of the villa Baizeau, 1928 (FLC 8503)

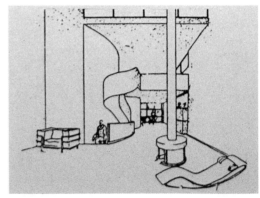

Sketch for the interior of "Canneel," July 1929 (FLC 8529)

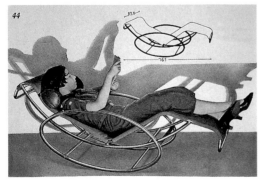

Chaise longue "B 306/0" from a 1930 French Thonet catalogue (taken off the market by Le Corbusier, Jeanneret, and Perriand)

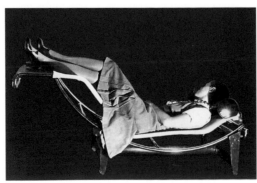

C. Perriand on "B 306," c. 1930

"B 306" as a rocking recliner

25
Name: B 35
Designer: Marcel Breuer
Design: 1928–9
Production: c.1930 to the present

Manufacturer: Gebrüder Thonet AG,
Frankenberg on Eder, Germany
Size: 82.5 x 60 x 80; seat height 35 cms
Material: chrome-plated tubular steel,
polished-yarn fabric, varnished wood

■

Marcel Breuer is widely recognized as one of the most important furniture designers of the twentieth century. In 1930, following an undeniably successful period as head of the Bauhaus furniture workshop in Dessau between 1925 to 1928, together with Walter Gropius and Herbert Bayer he set up the section for the Deutscher Werkbund as a part of an exhibition of the French Society of Decorative Artists in the Paris Grand Palais. At this much acclaimed premiere of German design in France following World War I, he for the first time presented his club chair "B 35," which he had designed in 1928-9. With this ingenious design, Breuer succeeded in integrating all the functions of a cantilever tubular steel chair into the structure of a single continuous line. This afforded an extremely comfortable doubling of the cantilever effect, because the armrests, which swung independ-

ently of the seat, balance the bounce of the seat and back frame which cantilevers toward the back; in addition they pleasantly give way when leaned upon while standing up or sitting down. The steel tubing, which runs from the armrests through to the runners and then shapes the seat and back, actually consists of three parts which are joined and screwed together beneath the covering sewn around them. Making the many bends in a single piece of continuous tubing might have been technically possible at that time but would still have been very complicated. Crossbars in the front and back as well as a spreader bar under the seat offer greater stability.
Breuer combined the technical coolness of tubular steel with wooden armrests and the polished-yarn fabric, "Eisengarn," for covering the seat and back. The exact positioning of these

elements ensures that the user does not come in contact with the cold steel. "Eisengarn" is a stiff cotton fiber which glistens like metal due to treatment with wax (in the chair shown here, it has already bleached out). The fiber was developed in 1926 at the Bauhaus in Dessau specifically for covering Breuer chairs after the horsehair fiber which was originally used proved to be too expensive and insufficiently resilient.
The first known version of the "B 35," for a Berlin town apartment, was upholstered; the 1930 version exhibited in the Grand Palais was covered in leather. From 1930-7 Thonet produced the chair with leather, iron wool, or wicker coverings and from 1971 to the present with leather or wicker. The position and the type of attachment for the crossbars already varied in the first models. *MSC*

∧ Exhibition room of Deutscher Werkbund in the Grand Palais, Paris, 1930
> "B 35" frame

26

Name: Grand Repos
Designer: Jean Prouvé
Design: 1928-30
Production: c. 1930

Manufacturer: Atelier Jean Prouvé, Nancy
Size: 99 x 70 x 172; seat height 33/15 cms
Material: varnished steel, steel springs,
ball bearings, canvas

■

Jean Prouvé, son of the director of the École de Nancy, the school that so influenced Art Nouveau, worked from 1926 until his death in 1984 primarily as an architect and designer. The use of industrially prefabricated metal structures for his buildings contributed significantly to the introduction of light construction work in modern architecture. In 1926 he began to make architectural elements out of molded and welded metal, using a technique also employed in automobile construction at that time. Up until 1954 he had developed and built numerous models using this process. "Grand Repos" is one of his earliest designs. It was presented to the public in 1930 in Paris at his first exhibition at the Union des Artistes Modernes, of which he was one of the founding members. In traditional chaise longues the back can be adjusted separately from the seat; here, however, a single seat/back element is pushed continuously on ball bearings along a steel supporting slat, which is hollow on the inside. The armrests welded to the side sections serve as braces with which to push oneself backward or pull oneself forward and are supported by two steel springs attached under the seat. The shape of the rigid steel frame covered with canvas – comfortable both in a sitting or reclining position – is reminiscent of the similarly rigid but continuously adjustable surface of the famous chaise longue designed by Le Corbusier, Charlotte Perriand, and Pierre Jeanneret.

Prouvé never mass-produced the "Grand Repos" and only two original models are known. Today it is being manufactured again by the Tecta Company in Lauenförde, Germany. *MSC*

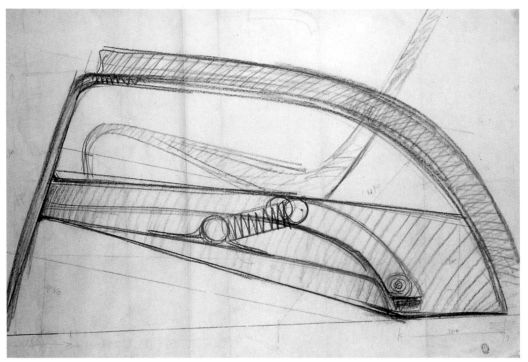

∧ "Grand Repos" as a chaise longue
< J. Prouvé: drawing for "Grand Repos," 1928-30

27

Name: (Folding Chair)
Designer: Jean Prouvé
Design: 1930
Production: 1930

Manufacturer: Ateliers Jean Prouvé, Nancy
Size: 102.5 x 45 x 51; seat height 43.5 cms
**Material: varnished steel, varnished tubular
steel, canvas**

Jean Prouvé did not look to the work of other designers for inspiration for his own projects. Rather, he consistently used the technology of the day and developed special structural solutions to each new problem and detail. This sovereign attitude sets him alongside the other great designers of this century, such as Marcel Breuer, Alvar Aalto, or Charles and Ray Eames. All Prouvé's furniture has a unique style and undeniably bears the signature of the engineer. "For me pieces of furniture are comparable to a machine frame which is exposed to much wear and tear, and this has prompted me to design

furniture with the same care, according to the same laws of statics and even using the same materials,"[6] he explained.
Prouvé's folding chair was created at about the same time as another design with an almost identical shape. Here, the seat and back create one rigid unit which can be slightly inclined backward around an axis at the upper end of the legs. The model shown here by contrast, which looks like emergency, theater or airplane seating, is an unusual version of a stackable chair. While the folded chair fits exactly into the rectangular frame of the back, the placement of the front feet,

which face inward, allows an endless row of the chairs to be positioned snugly one after the other. The chair is both light and stable due to the frame of hollow steel tubes and tautly stretched canvas; moreover, it requires only a minimum of material. Although it looks as if it would tip over backward if weight were exerted against the back, the angle of the rear legs is large enough to guarantee a solid standing position. *MSC*

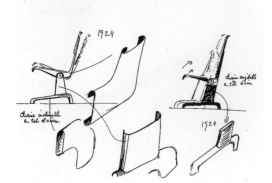

┌ J. Prouvé: Facade for the Lille trade fair building, 1950
∧ J. Prouvé: School furniture, c. 1950
< J. Prouvé: Drawing for folding chairs, 1924

28

Name: Siesta Medizinal
Designer: Hans and Wassili Luckhardt
Design: 1936
Production: since 1937

Manufacturer: Gebrüder Thonet AG,
Frankenberg on Eder, Germany
Size: 113.5/84 x 67 x 90.5/163;
seat height 41 cms
Material: wood, leather upholstery

■

When Le Corbusier, Charlotte Perriand, and Pierre Jeanneret first presented their anatomically shaped, adjustable chaise longue at the end of the twenties, Hans Luckhardt designed, first alone and after 1933–4 together with Anton Lorenz, the so-called "movement chairs." At the time, Lorenz concerned himself especially with medical problems associated with sitting. Around 1935 the first trial models were produced by Thonet. On the basis of these trials, Luckhardt developed numerous examples in a line of chaise longues which Thonet marketed as of 1937 under the name "Siesta Medizinal." The chair's true innovation lay in the mechanics of its so-called "steering mechanism," which synchronously moved the three separate supports for the back and the upper and lower thighs, ensuring adjustment to each movement of the body automatically by a mere shifting of weight, and keeping the chair stably balanced at all times. If the user stretches out, the chair stretches with him, extending into a lightly wavy chaise longue or, in the opposite direction, retracting back into a chair position. It can be fixed in any position by a screw attached to the side. The space available is generously proportioned on anatomically shaped slats; armrests and an adjustable headrest round out the comfort of the chair. Underwater trials, which Lorenz conducted in 1938 at the Kaiser Wilhelm Institute for Industrial Physiology in Dortmund, proved after the fact that the user is in an optimal position for relaxation on the stretched out, slightly wavy surface of the "Siesta Medizinal." Luckhardt also created his prototype for the first automatically adjustable airplane seat at the same time as the "Siesta Medizinal." It was tested by Air France in 1938 but, due to the outbreak of the war, did not go into mass production. In addition to numerous other versions and further refinements, e.g., as a folding chair, the construction was also marketed by Thonet as a chair for medical use made of tubular steel with metal springs for cushioning and armrests which could be adjusted upward. In the fifties, the U.S. patent granted to Anton Lorenz for the mechanism of the chair sparked a huge industry which specialized in the production of so-called reclining chairs. *MSC*

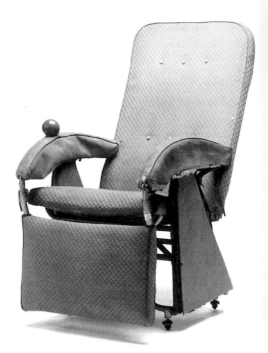

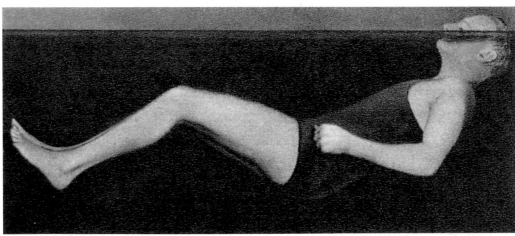

≫"Siesta Medizinal" extended
⌃ Underwater experiment by the Kaiser Wilhelm Institute, from a Thonet catalogue, c. 1940
⌐ H. and W. Luckhardt: Airplane seat for Air France, c. 1938

29

Name: (Aluminum Armchair)
Designer: Gerrit Thomas Rietveld
Design: 1942
Production: 1942

Manufacturer: Gerard van de Groenekan
and Wim Rietvelt, Utrecht
Size: 71 x 70 x 65; seat height 33 cms
Material: sheet aluminum

Gerrit Rietveld often utilized standardized semifinished industrial material to produce furniture using minimal labor and material inputs. Plywood and sheet metal were especially suitable, because it was possible to bend them into complex, self-supporting shapes without additional structural parts. In 1927 Rietveld began his experiments with thin plywood which he bent into the shape of a chair. In the same year he also built his "Birza" armchair consisting of a single sheet of fiberboard which was cut, bent, and screwed together. The most famous outcome of his idea of developing a chair from a single sheet was the "Zig-Zag" chair completed in 1934. In a later version of the "Zig-Zag," Rietveld used a perforated wooden board as a back for decorative purposes. In the aluminum design shown here, the perforations are,

however, necessitated by the construction. The turned down edges, just like the bent outer edges of the chair, stiffen the larger expanses of metal. Two drawings for the design support the notion that the original intention was to make the chair out of folded fiberboard. Since this material was not available, Rietveld adapted the original design and used aluminum for the prototypes, which is structurally a completely different material. He was presumably familiar with Hans Coray's "Landi" chair, made of perforated aluminum and introduced in 1930; however, he created a completely unique construction which even today seems futuristic. As the conical feet and crossbeams in the front legs show, he was not completely successful in shaping the chair out of a single piece. Furthermore, the metal in the corners cracks easily when exposed to wear

and tear, just like Coray's "Landi." Rietveld continued to develop his ideas further. One year prior to his death he wrote:
"We are just at the beginning of the production and acceptance of purely industrial products. In the future I envisage, for example, a piece of material which, after a series of mechanical functions, leaves the machine as a finished chair in only 10 minutes and in such a neutral form that it can fit into any interior because it is such a simple element."[7]
Concurrent with the aluminum chair Rietveld also designed furniture of folded wicker: a chair, dining room chairs, and even a bed. *MSC*

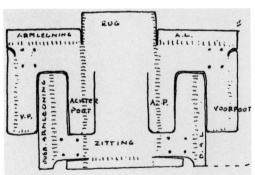

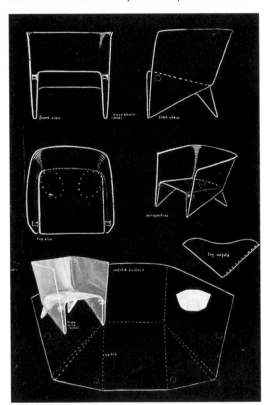

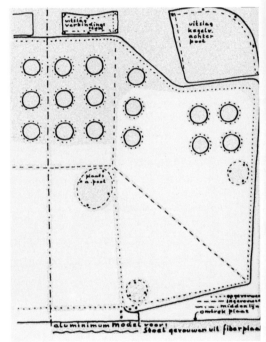

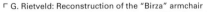

⌐ G. Rietveld: Reconstruction of the "Birza" armchair
< G. Rietveld: Schematic drawing for the "Birza" armchair
∧ G. Rietveld: Drawing for a folded armchair, 1930-40
⌐ G. Rietveld: Schematic drawing for the aluminum armchair, 1942

30

Name: ESU (Eames Storage Unit) 421-C
Designer: Charles and Ray Eames
Design: 1949-50
Production: 1950-2

**Manufacturer: Herman Miller Furniture
Company, Zeeland, Michigan**
Size: 149 x 120 x 43 cms
**Material: varnished steel, coated plywood,
wood, plywood, fiberglass, masonite,
rubber**

The Eames storage units represent a further development of the model furniture created at the beginning of the century in the Deutsche Werkstätten and at the Bauhaus. These, too, were made up of standardized elements joined together as building blocks. The stringently geometric construction and the use of dominant primary colors in the Eames storage units bring to mind the design principles of the De Stijl group.

Eames repeatedly worked on modular wall units after his participation in the New York Museum of Modern Art competition "Organic Design in Home Furnishings." One of his prize-winning designs was a wall unit developed jointly with Eero Saarinen in 1940-1 consisting of interchangeable elements with a bench as the basis upon which different boxlike elements could be freely arranged and stacked. Eames lent a more pleasant appearance to the system in his "Modular Storage Units" of 1946, especially by using plywood with an imprinted pattern of circles for the first time.

After the construction of their "Case Study House No. 8" in 1949, Charles and Ray Eames reworked the concept of modular wall units from the ground up. In keeping with the construction and design pattern of their house, they developed a system of freestanding shelves which is assembled according to the principles of industrial mass production. As a variable construction set, the system offered nearly unlimited possibilities for combining prefabricated individual parts according to practical and decorative needs. The basic element in the system is a self-supporting iron L-bar which was available in five sizes and optionally with a black lacquer, zinc, or chrome finish. The shelves were plywood, veneered with birch, walnut, or plastic laminate. The back and side sections of the compartments were available either in plywood, perforated metal, or masonite painted in eight different colors. Welded iron rods in cross form substitute for the colored pieces in some places to stabilize the supporting framework. The compartments can be closed off with sliding doors of ebony-colored fiberglass, black plastic laminate, or plywood with an imprinted pattern. The system

also comprises compartments with three drawers each. Four desk versions were offered separately to match the shelves. Although the reasonably priced building set was suitable for homes as well as offices and went on display in 1950 in six different variations at the influential exhibit "Good Design" cosponsored by the Museum of Modern Art, it was still difficult to sell. Because of the complicated assembly involved, the furniture was later offered in the form of finished shelves, and the feet, which frequently broke off during transport, were replaced by screw-on tubes. Despite this, the "Storage Units" were not a market success and production was discontinued in 1955. *MSC*

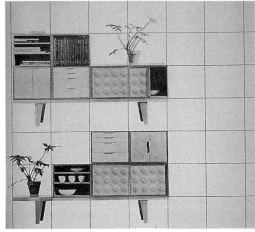

^"Case Study House No. 8," 1945-9
‹ Eames and Saarinen: furniture for the "Organic Design in Home Furnishings" exhibition
⌐ From an article in *Arts and Architecture,* September 1946
› From a Herman Miller catalogue, 1952

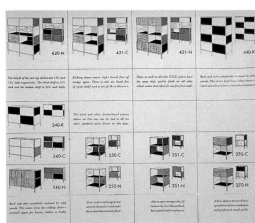

31

Name: No. 422, Diamond Chair
Designer: Harry Bertoia
Design: 1952-3
Production: 1953 to the present

Manufacturer: Knoll Associates, Inc.,
New York
Size: 71 x 110.5 x 81; seat height 36.5 cms
Material: varnished steel wire, round iron,
rubber

■

Harry Bertoia, who came from Italy, originally dedicated himself to sculpting. While heading the metal workshop of the Cranbrook Academy in Michigan from 1939–43, he began to experiment with flowing, three-dimensional shapes. At Cranbrook he became acquainted with Eliel and Eero Saarinen, with Charles Eames and his later wife, Ray Kaiser, as well as Florence Schuster, later wife of the furniture producer Knoll. In 1943 Charles and Ray Eames persuaded Bertoia to move to California, where he cooperated on the development of their first pieces of furniture. Disappointed that his contribution to these joint designs was not recognized, he left the studio in 1946. Hans Knoll, director of the company, whose program already included the designs of well-known architects and designers, equipped him with a studio of his own in 1950 as well as a monthly allowance and the possibility of freely developing his creativity without any special constraints. Bertoia thereupon created a series of chairs and seats using techniques he was familiar with from gold work and sculpting with iron wire. Until 1953 he developed these ideas together with specialists from the Knoll company until they were ready for mass production. At the same time, the first wire chairs were created by

Charles and Ray Eames but were presented nearly a year earlier. Bertoia's series consists of a small and large version of the "Diamond Chair," a "Diamond Chair" with an extended back, a foot stool, a children's chair, two other chairs, and a bar stool. Knoll marketed these pieces, which were suited for indoor and outdoor use, first in painted black metal and later with a black or white plastic coating, as well as in chrome and with removable pads. The structure of the "Diamond Chair" clearly separates the different functions of the chair: the transparent wire shell is bent out of a quadratic lattice into an organically shaped diamond like a net frozen in space, and the base of round iron embraces it like a polished diamond. Bertoia considered his furniture to resemble his sculptures and explained: "In sculpture I am primarily interested in the relationship between form and space and the characteristics of the metal. In chairs many functional problems have to be solved first... but basically chairs are also studies in space, form and metal. On close inspection it becomes clear that they are mostly made up of air.... Space flows right through them."[8] The generous dimensions of the "Diamond Chair," with its projecting armrests and hard rubber connections

that noticeably give way with pressure, definitely lent an element of comfort to the mathematical coolness of the construction. But the cushioning still does not make any formal sense despite the comfort it affords, since it interferes with the transparency of the chair and gives it the look of a common shell. The "Diamond Chair" was designed to be viewed from all sides like a sculpture and thus fits perfectly into the elegant, sparsely furnished interiors of the fifties. The chair was, however, quite expensive even though Bertoia had developed a machine for bending the wires three-dimensionally; production was difficult because the preshaped wires had to be individually welded together. The susceptible rubber pieces were later replaced by screwed metal tracks. Bertoia wrote: "I was never satisfied with my own designs, no matter whether they were flops or masterpieces,"[9] and, after completing his line of furniture for Knoll, dedicated himself exclusively to art, including numerous large-scale sculptures which graced the buildings of famous architects. *MSC*

^H. Bertoia in his studio in Bally, Pennsylvania, 1976
< H. Bertoia: Wire model for seats, c. 1950

32

Name: Coconut Chair
Designer: George Nelson
Design: 1955
Production: 1956–64

Manufacturer: Herman Miller Furniture Company, Zeeland, Michigan
Size: 84 x 104 x 86; seat height 34 cms
Material: polished aluminum, sheet steel, foam rubber, artificial leather, chrome-plated round steel

Like his "Marshmallow" sofa, Nelson's "Coconut" armchair already alludes to the spontaneous lifestyle of the sixties, which was created by a popular everyday culture. Instead of looking for a shape functionally equivalent to the human body, Nelson made a memorable symbolic statement that introduced a new, deliberately easy-going type of sitting. He found a crucial impulse for his shapes in the expansive gestures of popular fifties art such as the abstract-surrealistic work of Joan Miró, or Alexander Calder.

In the original version, the shell looked like a coconut and consisted of a piece of bent steel with foam rubber padding available in artificial leather, fabric, or leather upholstery. The frame was made of a piece of steel tube bent along the length of the shell for the two front legs, with a second piece for the back legs, whereby the legs which stuck out were stabilized additionally by welded crossbars. Thus, the frame seemed to stretch across a floating curved form and to be attached to the floor. Herman Miller later produced the shell using fiberglass-reinforced

polyester and screwed aluminum tube legs singly onto the form; the crossbars were also screwed on. The initial production of a footstool to match the chair was later discontinued. The "Coconut" shown here represents a mixed form in the history of the chair, and the new stand supports a shell made of steel. Vitra has been producing the "Coconut" since 1988. *MSC*

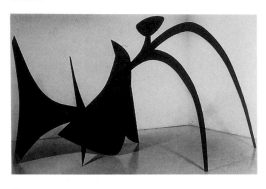

^From a Herman Miller brochure
ⵊAlexander Calder: "Black Widow," 1959
ⵊ "Coconut Chair," with footstool

33
Name: No. 670 and No. 671,
Lounge Chair and Ottoman
Designer: Charles and Ray Eames
Design: 1956
Production: 1956 to the present

Manufacturer: Herman Miller Furniture
Company, Zeeland, Michigan
Size: 82 x 83 x 84;
seat height 35 cm/42 x 65 x 53.5 cms
Material: bent plywood, rosewood veneer,
blackened and polished cast aluminium,
leather cushions, plastic, rubber

■

Like many of the Eameses' furniture designs, the club chair "No. 670" was the result of Charles Eames's cooperation with Eero Saarinen in 1940, when both participated in the New York MoMA's "Organic Design in Home Furnishings" competition. Based on the arm chair exhibited there made of a single piece of three-dimensionally shaped plywood for the seat and back, Eames Office prototypes were created in 1946 using three separate bent plywood elements for shoulders, back, and seat; these were connected by hard rubber discs. Tubular steel and plywood structures were tried out as supports. Don Albinson, who had worked with Eames since 1946, was involved in these earlier experiments as well as on the final version shown here, which was created ten years later.

Although it can be easily and completely dismantled using only a monkey wrench, the construction of the chair is more complex than any other chair designed by Charles and Ray Eames. Moreover, it is the most comfortable and

most expensive piece of furniture the couple created. The plywood shells, bent two-dimensionally for the shoulders, back, seat, and ottoman were veneered in the early version with rosewood and later with walnut or rosewood. The leather upholstery, originally filled with goosefeathers and later with soft foam, is completely removable. One special feature of the construction is the connection of the seat to the back. While both back sections are held together by two cast aluminum supports and hard rubber discs, the armrests provide the only connection of the back with the shell and feature washers made of Neoprene. The chair can be rotated on the star-base, but its individual elements are firmly connected to each other. Its inviting soft padding and the generous, well-shaped dimensions offer, at least in conjunction with the ottoman, nearly optimal sitting comfort. The Eameses' "Lounge Chair," taking its cue from the club chairs of the last century, owes its striking appearance first to its impressive size, which

gently embraces the user. Also worth mentioning are the high-grade materials; even the aluminum is enhanced by expensive finishing on the polished outer side and blackened side parts. At the same time, the division between the individual functions through the segmentation of the structure and the use of different materials gives the chair a technical appearance. This linking of a technically mature modern structure with luxurious sitting comfort soon turned the chair into a beloved (and expensive) status symbol. In 1957 it was awarded first prize at the Triennial in Milan. Far more than 100,000 of this model have been produced to date by Herman Miller, and after 1958 also by Vitra, and the chair is considered one of the great design classics. *MSC*

∧ Production of the "Lounge Chair," from a
 Herman Miller brochure
> C. and R. Eames in their living room, 1960s
⌐ Components of the "Lounge Chair"

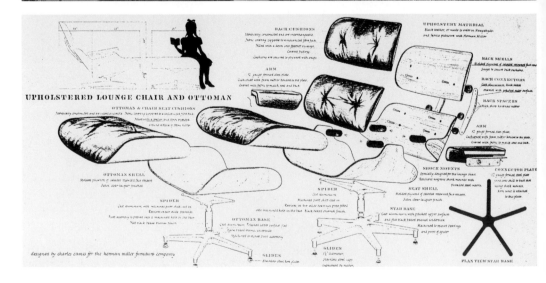

Name: No. 64916/No. 64940, Action Office
Designer: George Nelson
Design: 1964
Production: 1964-1971
Manufacturer: Herman Miller, Inc., Zeeland, Michigan; Herman Miller AG/Vitra AG, Basel

Size: 110 x 167 x 83 cms/102 x 50.5 x 54; seat height 77.5 cms
Material: polished aluminum, chrome-plated tubular steel, oiled and varnished wood, plastic, vinyl/chrome-plated and varnished steel, leather, latex foam, polished cast aluminum

In an initiative unusual for the furniture industry, Herman Miller, the American manufacturer, set up a research department in 1960 headed by Robert Probst. One of its central tasks was a long-term study of the problems associated with office work. Based on the insights this yielded, George Nelson as the designer responsible for the project developed a completely new system of office furniture based on modular components and offering versatile configurations that could be adapted to the changing requirements of people and their work in office environments. The system consists of different tables, a lectern with a footrest, a stool-like chair on wheels, a screened-off table for telecommunications equipment, stackable shelf sections that are open, lockable, or equipped with working surfaces, as well as a variety of accessories. The common denominator here is a U-shaped cast

aluminum base which can support shallow elements like a shelf and, if doubled up, forms an H-shaped base for wider elements such as a work or conference table. One particular innovation of the "Action Office" was the combination of desk and lecterns which is appropriate for the most diverse types of office work. Without limiting working surfaces or restricting freedom of movement, the system offers – for example by means of a hanging file attached at the front end – direct access to materials which are in view at all times. There is a flat drawer under the lectern tabletop for writing utensils. Materials left lying on the table and hanging files can be covered over at the end of the task with a pull-down shutter.

It was intended that the stand-alone furniture ideally create a semiopen "Arena" as a versatile working space.

Several important requirements outlined by Probst suffered under the impressive aesthetic features which Nelson refused to do without. In addition the system proved itself to be too complicated and expensive from a technical and production standpoint. Based on Nelson's "Action Office," Probst later designed the more economical "Action Office II" in 1968; this combined the modules with stand-alone and interchangeable walls. This enabled rooms to be laid out for single or group work either with enclosed or open spaces. The system, which was particularly suitable for the flexible organization of office environments, was enormously successful and strongly influenced office design and work in the seventies. *MSC*

"Action Office" modules create an "Arena," from a Herman Miller catalogue, 1965

Herman Miller advertising photograph for "Action Office"

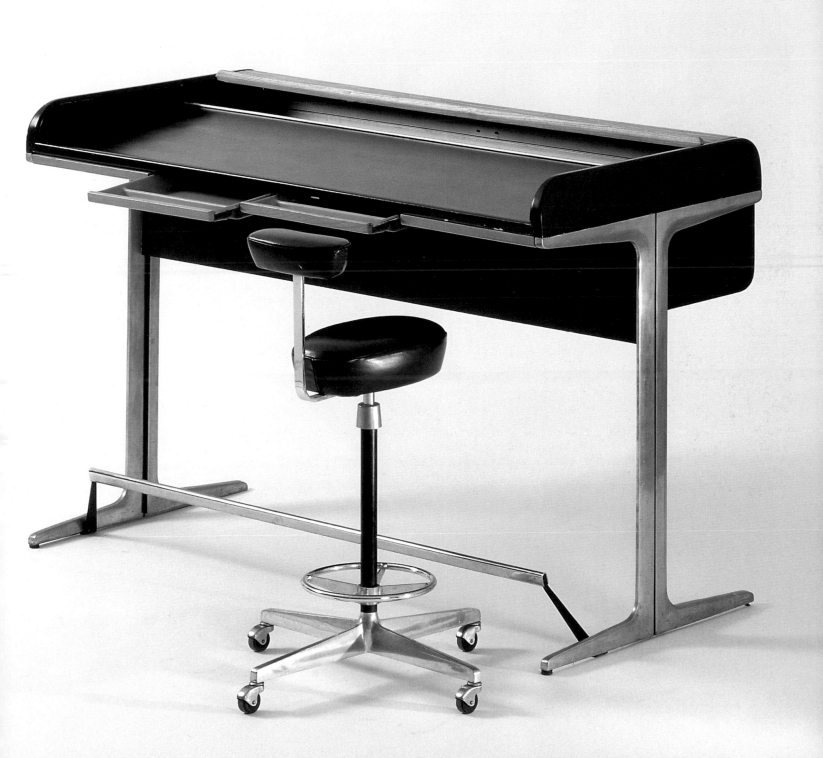

Name: Chaise Longue PK 24
Designer: Poul Kjaerholm
Design: 1965
Production: since 1965

Manufacturer: E. Kold Christensen,
Copenhagen
Size: 87 x 66.5 x 155 cms
Material: stainless steel, wicker, leather

■

Until his death in 1980, Poul Kjaerholm made a large contribution to the international reputation of Danish furniture design. He broke with the Scandinavian tradition of solid wooden furniture and took up aspects of the classical European Modern style in his simple, purist designs. Characteristic of his work was the combination of both crafted and industrially finished elements, and the use of superior materials.
The continuously adjustable structure of his "PK 24" chaise longue is reminiscent of the famous one created by Le Corbusier. But while Le Corbusier emphasized the functionality of the chaise longue, Kjaerholm reduced the construction to an unobtrusive frame made of steel strip. This material is also to be found in the designs of Mies van der Rohe, but it is not otherwise commonly used. For the reclining surface Kjaerholm chose a rattan cover, and the only padding is a neckrest which hangs loosely over the back section and is held in place by a counterweight. This gives the chaise longue a flat, delicate look which derives its visual charm from the elegant lines of the reclining surface. With its open, transparent structure and lack of simulated coziness, the chair achieves Kjaerholm's goal of creating simple and honest furniture. This model is being produced today by the Danish company Fritz Hansen, in Allerød. *MK*

< From a Christensen brochure
└ Bruno Mathsson: Chaise longue with bookstand, 1934

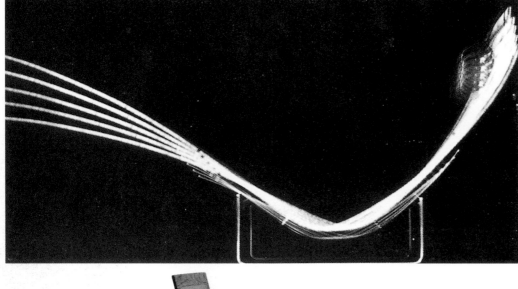

37

Name: AEO
Designer: Paolo Deganello with Archizoom
Design: 1973
Production: 1973 to the present

Manufacturer: Cassina s.p.a.,
Meda, near Milan
Size: 106 x 79 x 70; seat height 50.5 cms
Material: plastic, varnished steel,
fabric covering

■

When Paolo Deganello, cofounder of the Archizoom group from Florence, Italy, presented the "AEO" chair in 1973, it attracted great attention. The chair is undeniably comfortable, but opinions differ on its unusual appearance. One side regards it as a caricature of the robust television chair, the other as an icon of a new functional aesthetic.
Deganello investigated the demands on the back, seat, base, and frame and strictly separated these elements by function and material used. The base made of plastic with an organic curve supports an iron framing which distributes forces smoothly and is only partially covered by the seat cushion and the back section. An extremely thick cushion resting on a piece of stretched cloth serves as the seat. The back is made of two-ply canvas and is loosely stretched over a springy back-base, creating sharp folds. In his synthesis of these elements, Deganello does not comply with a particular aesthetic convention but instead sets the different qualities off against each other. Deganello hoped a network of small suppliers would produce the individual parts of the chair and thus link mass production to craftsmanship. This additive concept is reflected in the fact that the chair was available as a "build-it-yourself" kit. "AEO" stands for Alpha and Omega, the first and last letters in the Greek alphabet: the original material and its functionally dictated use are equal aspects of the object. Several years after its eye-catching launch, "AEO" established itself on the market. *MK*

Individual parts of "AEO"

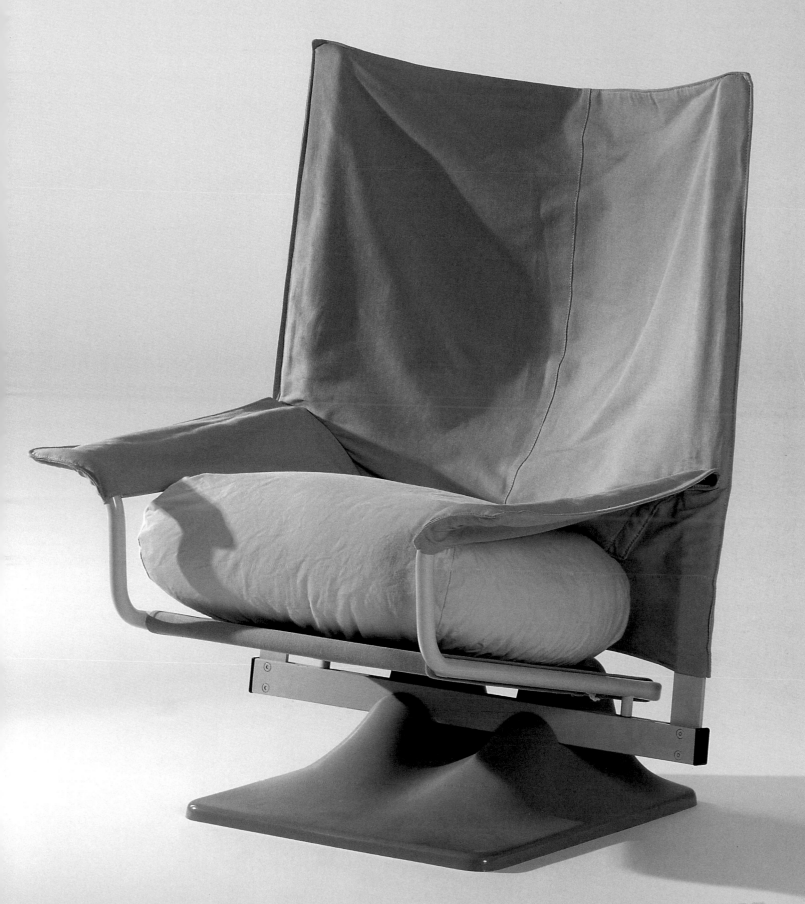

38
Name: Cab, No. 412
Designer: Mario Bellini
Design: 1976
Production: 1977 to present

Manufacturer: Cassina s.p.a.,
Meda, near Milan
Size: 81 x 51.5 x 46; seat height 44 cms
Material: tubular steel,
butted leather cover, plasti

Bellini's "Cab" essentially consists of two elements that are completely distinct. A leather cover is stretched over a bare tubular steel chair frame like a tight skin. The cover can be opened or closed via four zippers running along the inside of the legs under the seat. The only reinforcement to the structure is a plastic plate which supports the seat. The innovation here consists in Bellini's applying the principle of mounting the cover onto the frame of the metal chair using zippers, which had previously only been used for upholstered furniture. In contrast to the typical aesthetics of tubular steel furniture, which stresses the visual contrast of construction and cover material, Bellini opted here to completely envelope the supporting structure. The chair is thus lent a uniform appearance enhancing the quality of the natural leather. *PR*

"Cab" and its individual parts

Reduction

■

There are numerous factors prompting the reduction of a design to what is absolutely necessary.

In times of economic distress, it is caused by a lack of materials, and in a rosy economic climate it is sometimes self-imposed by designers and serves to give the qualities of an object's concentrated form, such as in Ludwig Mies van der Rohe's claim that "less is more".

Reduction often has a socially critical edge to it, by implicitly abstracting away from surfeit. A reduced design generates pure, i.e., unfalsified, forms, alludes to structural aspects, and frequently emphasizes an aesthetic exuded by the materials themselves.

Early examples date from the first quarter of the nineteenth century and stem from secluded American Shaker communities, which created simple forms based on craftsmanship as an answer to emerging industrialization.

The Arts and Crafts Movement of the outgoing nineteenth century, especially in the wake of the thought of English social reformer John Ruskin, culminated in Ludditism and a refocus on simple, traditional production technologies.

Only after the renewal of this mood by the international spread of Art Nouveau did a conciliation appear possible between industrial mass production and structural purity, in a phase between the wars which is generally termed Rationalism. It is noteworthy here that in times of postwar poverty, a short economic recovery, and international economic crisis, the first tubular steel furniture saw the light of day, only fourty years after the development of seamless tubes by the Mannesmann brothers.

The improved quality of materials and technological innovations thus did not act as the decisive trigger for design using reduced forms, even if the latter certainly made use of the former. It is the fine arts that have had the decisive influence such as Constructivism, De Stijl, Bauhaus, New Objectivity, Concrete Art, Minimal Art, and Arte Povera. Different stylistic ascriptions, or the most recent terminological descriptions, such as New Modesty, may pin-point individual phenomena, but they do not emphasize the general significance of this design approach. *PD*

39

Name: MR 10
Designer: Ludwig Mies van der Rohe
Design: 1927
Production: 1927-30

Manufacturer: Berliner Metallgewerbe
Josef Müller, Berlin
Size: 79.5 x 46.5 x 71; seat height 40 cms
Material: nickel-plated tubular steel,
iron wool

■

As vice president of the Deutscher Werkbund from 1926–32, Mies van der Rohe was entrusted with the realization of the overall Weissenhof Settlement project near Stuttgart when the Werkbund exhibition opened there in 1927. In the course of the preparations he met with Heinz Rasch, Mart Stam, and others in Stuttgart on November 22, 1926.
During this meeting, Mart Stam explained his design of a chair without back legs and sketched the same. Since Stam was interested in a cubist, geometrically stringent look, he chose to use lengths of gas piping which were screwed to each other with angle fittings with small radii. "Mies came back from Stuttgart in November 1926 and talked about Mart Stam and his idea for the chair. We had a drawing board on the wall on which Mies drew the Stam chair, as right angles from top to bottom. He even added the sockets and said: 'Ugly, these sockets are so ugly. If he had only rounded them off – that would have been much more attractive' and sketched a curve. The single curve he drew on the Stam sketch gave birth to the new chair."[10] Several

Stam chairs were manufactured in the Eisen-möbelfabrik Arnold in Schorndorf near Stuttgart for the interior of a Stam house in the Weissen-hof Settlement, but without any sockets of hot-molded iron piping. As the sockets were too soft, the first prototype Stam sat on gave way under his weight. Reinforcements of round iron inserts created a sufficiently stable yet resilient structure.
Meanwhile, Mies van der Rohe was experimenting with Mannesmann precision tubular steel, which he bent cold to retain the elastic quality of the thin-walled tubular steel. The semicircular curves of the "front legs" enhance this effect, since they optimally support the springy function of the tubing.
Just after Mart Stam, Mies van der Rohe also exhibited his chairs, the first cantilever-based chairs in the Weissenhof Settlement. The flexibility of the structure afforded the same seating comfort otherwise only afforded by upholstered chairs and armchairs, without any of their associated coziness. The delicate lightness of the tubular steel furniture predestined them

for the interiors of the New Building movement. In the year of their launch, Mies van der Rohe also applied for a patent for the cantilever in the United States. His application was at first turned down with reference to the American patent Harry E. Nolan had taken out in 1924 (applied for in 1922) which already planned a cantilever-based garden armchair with spiral springs. Only after Mies van der Rohe was able to prove that this solid chair made of steel round rods could never be springy – he built a prototype for the model, which was never produced – did he receive the patent. A wave of adaptations, improvements and also curios in tubular steel soon appeared as a reaction to the Werkbund exhibition in the Weissenhof Settlement. Today, Mies van der Rohe's cantilever-based chair is marketed in different versions by Tecta (Lauenförde), Thonet (Frankenberg) and Knoll International. *PD*

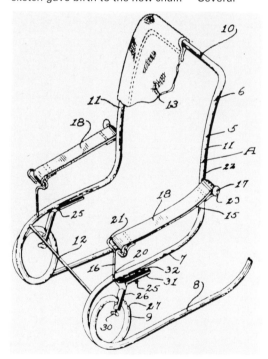

⌐ Harry E. Nolan: Drawing for the U.S. patent of a spring-based chair without back legs, 1922
∧ Mart Stam: Tubular steel furniture for the Weissenhof Settlement, 1927
> A "MR 20" armchair in the Luckhardt residence, Berlin, 1937

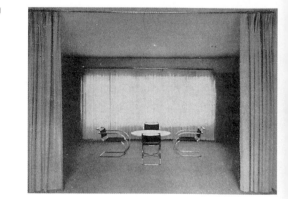

40

Name: Chaise sandows
Designer: René Herbst
Design: 1928–9
Production: since 1929

Manufacturer: Etablissements R.-H. (ed.), Paris
Size: 81.5 x 46.5 x 44.5; seat height 46 cms
Material: varnished tubular steel,
rubber stretcher belt (expander)

■

René Herbst is considered one of the first designers in France to use tubular steel for furniture construction. His most important furniture designs using this material were made between 1927 and 1937. In addition to tubular steel, he also worked with new materials such as rubber, Bakelite, and plastic.

René Herbst explained that he believed the most important criterion in designing an armchair was that it could stand on four feet and look as simple as possible. Thus, the armchair belonged to a series of seating whose designs were characterized by simple, clear lines and offered great sitting comfort with a minimum of material.

The seat and back sections were made of elastic rubber stretcher belts (*sandow* in French) which were known from expanders. Herbst was accordingly one of the first to introduce the motif of the *objet trouvé* into furniture design.

The belts are hooked onto the frame of the chair, a type of connection that is also reminiscent of an expander.

The chair's transparency and adaptability to body contours predates fifties design methods. The visible structural work and the purity of the lines are essential elements in the timeless designs of René Herbst. *PD*

⌐ R. Herbst: "Fauteuil de repos," 1928-9
∧ R. Herbst: "Appartement de jeune homme," at the Brussels exhibition for the applied arts in 1935
〉 Cabin on a passenger steamer, as part of the Union des Artistes Modernes exhibition at the 1934 Paris autumn salon

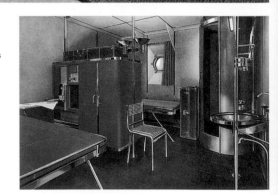

41

Name: ST 14
Designer: Hans and Wassili Luckhardt
Design: 1931
Production: 1931-2

Manufacturer: Desta
(Deutsche Stahlmöbel), Berlin
Size: 87.5 x 53.5 x 61; seat height 44 cms
Material: chrome-plated tubular steel,
molded and varnished plywood

■

Hans and Wassili Luckhardt belonged, as did the Taut brothers, Hans Scharoun, Ludwig Mies van der Rohe, and Walter Gropius, to a group of young architects who met with the established architects Hans Poelzig and Peter Behrens after World War I in Berlin and Dessau. In this circle visionary, socially critical ideas were exchanged; artistically these men felt an affinity to Expressionism and Cubism. The architect, they believed, should be a creative protagonist in redesigning society. While these ideas later found a Rationalist expression in the Bauhaus, the work of the Luckhardt brothers always suggested a freer attitude toward form which Wassili Luckhardt described in the year 1921: "Putting aside pencil and ruler, I take clay and plasticine and begin to knead directly and without outside influences."[11]
With this approach, the Luckhardt brothers also took advantage of the qualities of tubular steel

for building furniture. The unusually elegant shape of the cantilever-based "ST 14" which was produced from 1931 on by the Desta Company, extends far beyond the geometrical, Cubist forms of the Bauhaus school to achieve a streamlined aesthetic. In contrast to Mies van der Rohe's cantilevered "MR 10," with its curves in precise semi- and quarter-circles, the tubular steel here is bent into an organically flowing line. The back is completely adapted to the rounding of the tubular steel and the seat appears to float freely in the form. The chair comes close to the aesthetic ideal of tubular steel furniture as Hans Luckhardt formulated it in 1931: "The quiet, attractively taut line predominates."[12]
Hans Luckhardt compared the stylistic influence of tubular steel in furniture making with the influence of the skeletal steel manner of building high-rises, Luckhardt's main interest in the latter half of the twenties. At the 1928 "Home and

Technology" exhibition in Munich, they presented a miniature flat built in a skeletal steel manner and fitted out with tubular steel furniture. After the beginning of 1931, the Luckhardt brothers had a stake of RM 0.60 per unit in the sales of their models under a license agreement with Anton Lorenz, the founder of Desta. In the so-called Desta-Haus at the 1931 Berlin Building Exhibition, they put the "ST 14" on show, which was also available with a seat that could be flipped up.
When Thonet took over the Desta company in 1932, only those chairs still in stock were taken on. In 1984 Thonet relaunched production of the "ST 14." *MK*

⌐ Alfred Zeffner: "GT 74" liqueurs trolley, 1931
∧ Luckhardt brothers: Desta-Haus at the Berlin Building Exhibition, 1931
‹ H. & W. Luckhardt: "ST 15," 1931

42
Name: (Plywood Armchair)
Designer: Gerald Summers
Design: 1933-4
Production: since 1935

Manufacturer: Makers of Simple Furniture,
Ltd., London
Size: 74 x 60.5 x 91.5; seat height 32 cms
Material: bent plywood

■

In the history of industrial design there have always been attempts to shape everyday objects in only one piece of semifinished industrial material like rods, tubing, wire, or sheets. There is hardly a design that better illustrates the ideal unity of material, production and form, however, than this armchair by Gerald Summers. His admirably simple construction dispenses with connectors and almost with off-cuts, using one single sheet of plywood. Following a simple pattern, Summers separated the back legs from the back and armrests and bent the segments

thus created in different directions. The result was an organically shaped armchair, comfortable even without cushions, involving low material and labor inputs.

Possibly the chair was conceived for use in the tropics. With its smooth surface and lack of metal connectors, it is hygienic and deteriorates only gradually. Its unusual shape probably stems from Alvar Aalto's furniture, especially the spectacular "Paimio" chair, which was shown in London in 1933. In his own company, Makers of Simple Furniture, Ltd., founded in 1929,

Summers produced only 120 units of the chair. Despite the constructive advantages, the production costs of the chair and thus the sales price were higher than the designs of the popular Scandinavian. It was certainly also a disadvantage that the back legs could not withstand great stress and snapped easily. *MSC*

∧Pattern of the Summers chair
⌐ Hans Pieck: Chair, 1946-7

43
Name: Zig-Zag
Designer: Gerrit Thomas Rietveld
Design: 1932-34
Production: 1935 to c. 1955

Manufacturer: Metz & Co., Amsterdam
Size: 75 x 37 x 44.5; seat height 42.5 cms
Material: red-stained elm, brass screws

■ As a variation on the model of a chair without back legs first developed by Mart Stam, Gerrit Rietveld's "Zig-Zag" chair remains one of the most radical formulations in furniture design. Presumably the immediate forerunner was Heinz and Bodo Rasch's eye-catching "Sitzgeiststuhl" (sitting spirit chair) of 1927. Its shape, which the Rasch brothers fashioned to match the posture of a person sitting, consisted of a base and a curved surface bent twice for the back and the upper and lower thighs. Comparable to tendons in human limbs, the construction of the rounded side sections is thus stabilized. Rietveld abstracts from the quite complicated but structurally correct form to create a simple zigzag, but the logic of the construction suffers. Actually a whole series of tests were necessary to achieve a practical solution. "Zig-Zag" appears to completely contradict our ideas of a usable piece of furniture since its free-standing surfaces appear to collapse as soon as any weight is placed on them. However the chair is stabilized by dovetail joints between the seat and back, reinforcements

with screws and nuts, as well as wooden wedges in the corners. Rietveld was very much aware of the discrepancy between the simple shape and the relatively complicated construction and said himself, it is not a chair but a "designer joke." The actual goal of the design was to create a functional form which does not displace space but allows it to be perceived as a continuum; indeed, of Rietveld's entire body of work the "Zig-Zag" represents the most economical example of such a form. It is an uncompromising transposition of minimal requirements onto a chair, reduced to such an extent that even the screws appear to be decorative.

An idea that always accompanied the history of furniture design – of mechanically producing a chair from a single continuous form – led Rietveld to his first experiments with bent, spliced plywood in 1927. In 1932 he began designing what later became the so-called "Zig-Zag" chair for the Amsterdam furniture manufacturer, Metz & Co. Plywood or chip wood on a metal frame was a failure, however. Not until 1934 did he

succeed in creating a stable, very comfortable, and even stackable version. From 1935 this was produced with somewhat differing proportions, connections, and surface treatments by both Rietveld's master cabinetmaker and Metz & Co., in great numbers up until the fifties. The model shown here stems from such a production in the thirties. The producer of today's version of the "Zig-Zag" is the Cassina Company which purchased the rights to manufacture all of Rietveld's furniture designs in 1971. Rietveld used the "Zig-Zag" together with a matching table in many of his later interiors and also created an armchair version with and without a perforated back, as well as a "Zig-Zag" children's highchair. *MSC*

^ Metz & Co. showroom, Amsterdam, 1947
≪ Heinz and Bodo Rasch: "Sitzgeiststuhl," 1927
< G. Rietveld: "Zig-Zag," with armrests, 1934

44

Name: B.K.F. (Hardoy Chair)
Designer: Grupo Austral
Design: 1938
Production: since 1938

Manufacturer: Artek-Pascoe, Inc.,
New York
Size: 93 x 71.5 x 75; seat height 31.5 cms
Material: varnished steel, leather

■

This piece of furniture was probably modeled on a folding chair from England patented in 1877. There, four wood crosses connected by joints create a foldable frame over which canvas was stretched for the seat and backrest. Since the chair can be compactly folded and is easy to transport, it was very popular for travel, leisure, and also for homes; and due to its famous owners such as Thomas Alva Edison and Theodore Roosevelt, it soon became famous. From 1905 to the present it has been sold in nearly unchanged form by the American folding and camping furniture producer, Gold Medal, Inc. The Argentineans Bonet, Ferrari-Hardoy, and Kurchan adapted the 1938 design to create a rigid construction made of two loops of bent steel rods welded to each other with leather or fabric covers. In the previous year the three had been apprentices in France with Le Corbusier. It is possible that he became familiar with traditional English folding furniture at that time, for the tubular steel chair "Siège à dossier basculant" created in 1928 was also modeled on an English folding chair. With their design, which won a prize in 1940, Ferrari-Hardoy, Kurchan and Bonet succeeded in creating an unusual, timeless piece of furniture: Although the signlike shape has the feel of an abstract improvisation, one reason why the model was very popular in interiors in the fifties, it is simultaneously convincing, given the clear logic of its structure. This bodiless, light chair, which even offers some of the comfort of a club armchair, is one of the most successful furniture designs of this century. *MSC*

∧ "Camp Chair" by J. B. Fenby in Mukden, China, c. 1900
> Knoll catalogue, c. 1950

45

Name: (Plywood Chair)
Designer: H. V. Thaden
Design: 1947
Production: unknown

Manufacturer: Thaden Jordan Furniture
Corporation, Roanoke, Virginia
Size: 109/98 x 50 x 69/84;
seat height 29/22,5 cms
Material: bent plywood, wood, metal

■

This chair was presumably intended as an experiment and was never produced in a large series. The back and seat consist of a single bent plywood panel, the front edge covered with a protective rod to prevent the edge from being broken. A second plywood panel, its edge similarly protected, serves as a rear support that can be locked at two different heights. It is reinforced by a third, thinner piece of plywood, which is braced between the seat and the rod in back.

As early as 1874, Isaac Cole registered a patent on a chair made of bent plywood with a shape nearly identical to the one shown here. It was followed by similar designs by August Thonet around 1900 and by Alvar Aalto in the thirties. Because the material is not particularly strong, it is doubtful whether Thaden's construction could have withstood normal use. However, it was certainly more than mere aesthetic considerations that led to this spectacular design. The construction is extremely clever, even if it is not practicable in this form. Particularly original is the use of slot-in connectors for the height-adjustable joint between the backrest and the supports. In those days, this kind of fastener was found primarily in airplanes, boats, or automobiles, where it was used to secure tarpaulins or convertible tops. During the forties, aviation was the source of many innovations in furniture design. The shape of the chair, which seems to hover in the air much like an airplane wing, suggests that it may indeed have derived its inspiration from this source. *MSC*

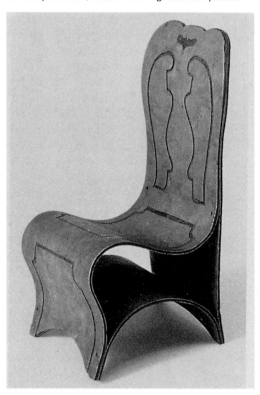

Isaac Cole: Chair made of bent plywood, c. 1874

August Thonet (?): Chair made of bentwood, 1880-85

46
Name: (Bellevue Chair)
Designer: André Bloc
Design: 1951
Production: unknown

Manufacturer: André Bloc, Meudon, France
Size: 82.5 x 39.5 x 49; seat height 42 cms
Material: bent plywood, varnished steel

■

Furniture designs by architect André Bloc were greatly influenced by the works of sculptor Jean Arp. Arp's flowing forms, which are often abstractions of the human body, served as Bloc's inspiration for this design as well.

There are only a few copies of the chair, which was most likely produced expressly for his Bellevue house in Meudon. Some of them feature a V-shaped metal construction which makes up the rear legs, while others are supported at the back by two separate metal legs. All models have a backrest and seat made of a single piece of material – an S-shaped curve.

Attempts to create the front legs, seat and back of a chair using just one piece of bent wood had already met with success. The first was Isaac Cole in 1880, and then, at the turn of the century, August Thonet. To create a visual unity, Cole and Thonet glued the separate back support to the backrest to engender one single form. Rietveld's "Zig-Zag" chair combined a wooden back, seat, and frame into a unit that was visually excellent, but a failure as a structure. Bloc, on the other hand, believed that function transformed into pure form would no longer possess any superfluous features. As he could not make all of his chair parts from one casting, he let the contrasts remain and instead minimized the difficulties involved in the construction.

A desk designed by André Bloc at around the same time similarly involves a simple, sculptural construction. *PR*

^ Interior of the Bellevue house in Meudon
‹ Advertising section from *L'Architecture d'Aujourd'hui*, 1951

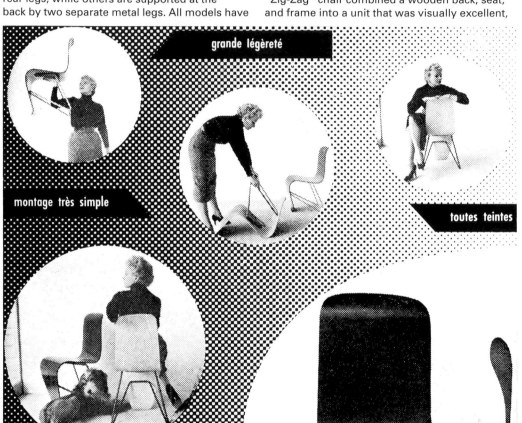

grande légèreté

montage très simple

toutes teintes

contreplaqué moulé et piètement acier

commandes à l'a. a., 5, rue bartholdi, boulogne, seine

47

Name: No. 3100, Ant
Designer: Arne Jacobsen
Design: 1952
Production: 1952 to the present

Manufacturer: Fritz Hansens Efa. A/S,
Copenhagen, Denmark
Size: 77 x 52 x 51.5; seat height 44 cms
Material: formed plywood,
chrome-plated tubular steel, rubber

■

In the early fifties, the Danish furniture industry adopted a new manufacturing process. Solid wood was increasingly replaced by materials such as steel and plywood, significantly reducing the need for complex structures.
Arne Jacobsen's chair is an outstanding example of this newfound simplicity. It consists of only a few parts, can be produced at low cost, and is extremely lightweight. The seat and back are made up of an ordinary piece of plywood, while the arrangement and form of the three steel tube legs attached to the underside of the seat in the center enable the chair to be stacked.

Charles Eames and Eero Saarinen had already produced a three-dimensional chair shell in the few prototypes of their "Organic Armchair" back in 1940–1. They had tried to prevent breakage between seat and backrest – where three-dimensional distortion was the greatest – by leaving a gap in the material, whereas Jacobsen approached the problem from the outside. He narrowed and reinforced the conjunction of the differently arched surfaces of seat and back by means of additional layers of veneer. This guaranteed that the backrest was both stable and flexible.

Jacobsen's chair, which played an important part in the modernization of Scandinavian furniture design, was given the popular epithet "Ant" owing to its characteristic curved waistline and the thin legs. In 1955, "No. 3107" emerged, a variation featuring a less segmented outline and four legs. This successor was available in a multitude of colors and became highly popular. After Jacobsen's death, a four-legged version of the "Ant" was also produced. *PR*

∧ From a Fritz Hansen catalogue, 1952
< A. Jacobsen: Chair "No. 3107"
⌐ Interior of a terrace house by A. Jacobsen in Søholm, c. 1955

48

Name: (Garden Chair)
Designer: Willy Guhl
Design: 1954
Production: 1954-80

Manufacturer: Eternit AG,
Niederurnen, Switzerland
Size: 54,5 x 54,5 x 76.5 cms;
seat height 11 cms
Material: fibrated concrete,
subsequently given a surface seal

■

Willy Guhl was a pioneer of industrial design in Switzerland, both as a result of teaching for many years at the Technical College in Zurich and through his many-sided practical work. He created a number of designs for Eternit: window boxes, a spindle-shaped standing ashtray, and a beach and garden chair, which is unique in the history of furniture design.

After participating in the 1948 MoMA competition entitled "Low-Cost Furniture Design," he began working with casts of the human body and ergonomically shaped shells for reclining chairs. While previous work with laminated wood had already yielded two-dimensionally shaped chair shells, fibrated concrete – not a material typically associated with furniture-making – afforded new possibilities that Willy Guhl turned to his best advantage.

Fibrated concrete was manufactured in slabs with machines and was used for building houses. The method of processing the chair corresponds to the dimensions of these slabs, which were shaped directly after they had been pressed while still moist. Thus, production was inexpensive and required fewer materials.

Because the composite material offered great resistance to breakage and exceptional tensile strength, supporting structures were no longer required, and thanks to statics there were few limitations on the form. So the design could be minimalist, rendering the elegantly curved, absolutely weatherproof chair nearly an abstract sculpture.

The new leisure culture of the postwar era gave rise to the need for inexpensive, practical

outdoor seating. At the same time, the chair is suggestive of interiors of the sixties and seventies, with their similar curved forms.

Fibrated cement has not been used since the end of the seventies, when it was discovered that the asbestos it contains is a carcinogen. Willy Guhl's chair was also affected by this discovery: one of the last known copies was to be included in the MoMA design collection, but was promptly sent back following the discovery that the chair contained asbestos. The Vitra Design Museum has sealed the surface of its copy so that a piece of design history may be preserved. *MK*

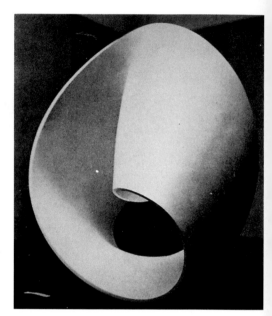

┌ Development of "Garden Chair" (plaster cast), 1954
⩓ Use as a beach chair
⌃ Pierre Paulin: "Ribbon Chair," 1965
⌐ Max Bill: "Unendliche Schleife" (endless loop), 1953
< Nathan Lerner: "One Piece Chair," 1940

49

Name: Superleggera, No. 699
Designer: Gio Ponti
Design: 1951-7
Production: 1957 to the present

Manufacturer: Figli di Amedeo Cassina,
Meda, near Milan
Size: 82.5 x 40 x 44.5; seat height 45.5 cms
Material: varnished ash wood, Spanish cane

■

Ponti himself describes this chair as the "normal," "true" chair, the "chair-chair devoid of adjectives."[13] With it, the architect pursued his own standard of keeping things to a bare minimum. At the same time, Ponti's interest in classic forms finds expression in the chair, just as it does in his buildings. Ponti borrowed the concept for "Superleggera" (super-lightweight) from a series of simple, traditional chairs that have been produced since the nineteenth century in a plant near the Ligurian fishing village of Chiavari. Their stable, lightweight construction and low price made them extremely popular. Ponti was inspired to optimize the qualities of

this model during the postwar era, when furnishings were out of necessity frugal.
In his first drawings from 1949, he altered the basic form of the Chiavari chair with an ergonomic bend in the backrest and tapered the legs toward the bottom. He then designed the "Leggera" for Cassina in 1951, which reduced the structure of the Chiavari chair to only what was absolutely necessary. It was very similar to the "Superleggera," but with rods for legs and struts in the backrest. Although the model met with great success among consumers, Ponti strove for even greater perfection and designed the "Superleggera" for Cassina in 1957, using

light, stable ash wood and a seat that was either upholstered or covered with a weave of cane or colored cellophane. Ponti reduced the round cuts of wood to a triangular cross section with edges only 18 mm long, and devised an ingenious system of slot-in connectors in which the individual struts are inserted firmly inside one another: the result is a stable chair weighing a mere 1.7 kilo. To put these to the test, Ponti threw the chair from the fourth story of an apartment building into the street, where it bounced like a ball without breaking. *MSC*

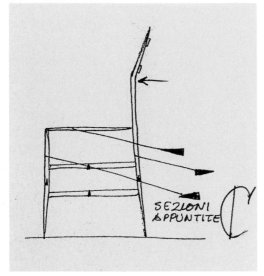

≪ G. Ponti: Drawing of the "Superleggera," 1957
⌃ Corner joints of the "Superleggera"
⌐ Demonstration of the lightness of the "Superleggera"

50

Name: Sacco
Designer: Piero Gatti,
Cesare Paolini, Franco Teodoro
Design: 1968
Production: 1968 to the present

Manufacturer: Zanotta s.p.a., Nova
Milanese, near Milan
Size: 68 x 80 x 80 cms; variable seat height
Material: removable cover made of lancio,
polystyrene filling

■

"Sacco," or the anatomic chair, as it is still called today in the Zanotta sales catalogues, symbolizes an unprecedented break with tradition. In an era characterized by the hippie culture, apartment sharing and student demonstrations, the thirty-something designers created a *non-poltrona* (non-chair) and thus launched an attack on good bourgeois taste.

After negotiations and rejections from the chemical industry, the designers turned to Zanotta with their purist solution of filling a transparent non-rigid PVC envelope with countless pieces of white polystyrene popcorn, resulting in a transparency similar to that of "Blow," the chair developed at Zanotta the previous year by designers De Pas, D'Urbino, Lomazzi, and Scolari. However, the shell was still not tough enough despite measures such as reinforcing it with synthetic fabric and sewing several segments of it together. Only then did the designers consent to using opaque materials, such as canvas (lancio), imitation leather, and leather. Because "Sacco" has no fixed form and its loose filling allows it to take on just about any shape, it molds itself to the contours of the body. "Sacco" can be used as a stool, an easy chair, or a chaise longue; it is lightweight and therefore extremely mobile. This unorthodox "furniture" is especially popular among the young and is an expression of unconstrained, relaxed living. The simplicity of the construction has prompted numerous commercial imitators to create more or less successful plagiarisms, and inspired a few hobbyists to dust off their sewing machines; polystyrene pieces used for packaging serve as the material for the filling. The popularity of "Sacco" helped found Italian design's pioneering reputation in the field during the sixties and seventies. *PD*

Piero Gatti with a prototype of "Sacco," 1968

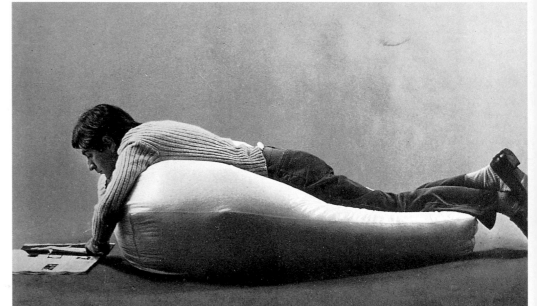

"Sacco" as a chaise longue

51
Name: Plia
Designer: Giancarlo Piretti
Design: 1968
Production: 1969 to the present

Manufacturer: Anonima Castelli s.p.a.,
Ozzano, near Bologna
Size: 75 x 47 x 50.5; seat height 45.5 cms
Material: polished die-cast aluminum,
oval tubular steel, cellidor plastic

■

Lightness, flexibility, and technical precision are the obvious advantages of this design by Giancarlo Piretti.
The folding mechanism of the chair was completely novel in its day. The chair rests on a joint made of three metal disks which connect the back, legs, and seat in such a way that they can be folded up into a flat compact form barely five centimeters thick.

The elegant chair, which is also suitable for outdoor use, has clear rounded forms, an oval-in-section tubular steel frame, and transparent plastic surfaces. When folded up, it can be hung on a wall hook made specially for this purpose, but can also be stacked when folded out.
Due to its straightforward construction and simple manufacturing, "Plia" can be produced at low cost and offered at correspondingly favor-

able prices. Over four million chairs have been sold since 1969.
In 1971, this exemplary design won the BIO 5 award at the Lyublyana Biennial and the Gute Form prize of the Federal Republik of Germany in 1973. *PR*

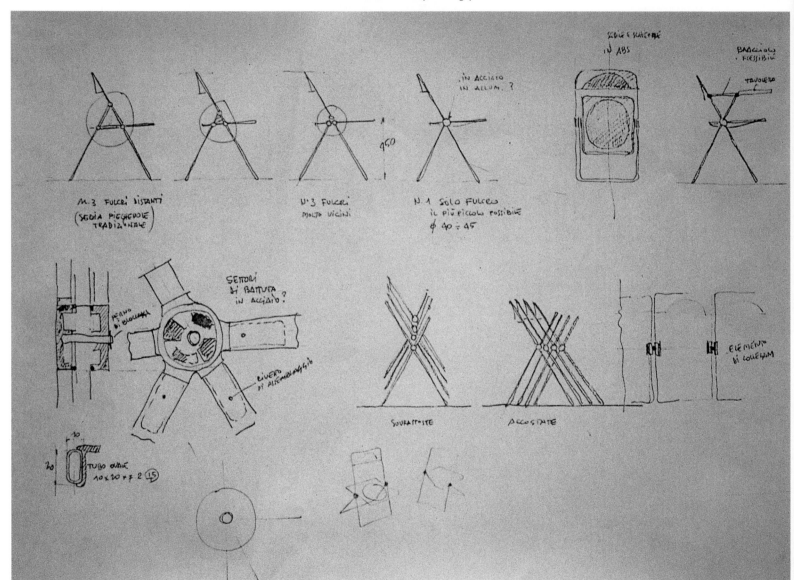

G. Piretti: Sketches of the "Plia" construction, 1968-9

52
Name: Well Tempered Chair
Designer: Ron Arad
Design: 1986
Production: 1986-93

Manufacturer: Vitra AG, Basel
Size: 80 x 98.5 x 80; seat height c. 48 cms
Material: high-grade sheet steel,
thumb screws

■

In his seemingly surrealist furniture, Ron Arad favors materials and objects from areas outside the domain of traditional furniture production. Since the mid-eighties his London studio has increasingly produced individual pieces made of sheet steel, and he always mischievously exploits their formal and functional possibilities to the full. The sculptural forms often have an unexpected impact which first emerges during use, and are just as much a result of graphic design as the experimental work that goes on in the workshop. The sort of minimalist attitude expressed by the "Well Tempered Chair," designed for the "Vitra Edition," is quite a novelty in comparison to Arad's earlier works. Here, Arad reduces the massive volume of the classic armchair, leaving only the pure surface of its rounded forms. At first glance, the cool gleam and the sharp-edged cut of the metal raise doubts whether the object can actually be used. But the "Well Tempered Chair" offers a unique kind of seating comfort: sitting amidst the steel loops, which after some time take on the body temperature of the user, you waver between coziness and uncertainty. *MSC*

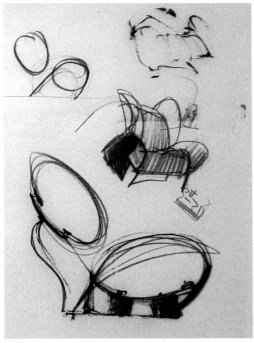

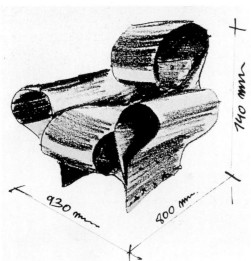

⌐ R. Arad: Sketches for the "Well Tempered Chair," 1986
< R. Arad: Drawing of the "Well Tempered Chair," 1986
∧ R. Arad: One Off showroom, 1988

53
Name: Ply-Chair
Designer: Jasper Morrison
Design: 1988
Production: 1989 to the present

Manufacturer: Vitra AG, Basel
Size: 84.5 x 39,5 x 47; seat height 47.5 cms
Material: plywood, birch veneer

■

The work of English designer Jasper Morrison is characterized by simplicity and clarity. His ideas are the very opposite of so-called Postmodern products which, with their daring combinations of patterns, colors, and materials, contributed to the downfall of Functionalism.
In the skeletal construction of the "Ply-Chair," formal complexity has been reduced to a minimum. Here, the designer as *auteur* steps out of the limelight, completely eclipsed by the object's functionality. Morrison uses his materials unpretentiously but with great precision. A wooden cross with edges that taper toward the middle is attached underneath the seat for support, but at the same time allows the seat to yield during use. This feature, together with the gently curved backrest, make the "Ply-Chair" unexpectedly comfortable in comparison to many expensive wood chairs.
The backrest of the chair is either open or slat-paneled, with a gently arched plywood leaf. Formal austerity and straightforward materials also characterize the "Ply-Table," which came out a year later. However, both table and chair are produced at relatively high cost in order to guarantee aesthetic perfection. *MSC*

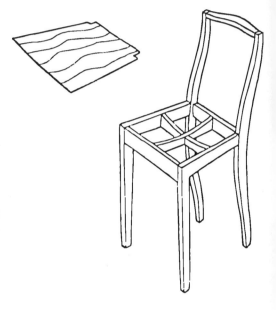

^J. Morrison: Installation "Some New Items for the House" (Part I), Berlin, 1988
⌐ J. Morrison: Drawing for the "Ply-Chair," 1988

Organic Design

■

This is not a scientifically defined concept and therefore is encountered in all sorts of contexts. In architectural reviews in the twenties it was used to refer to the functional sequence of rooms which might, nevertheless, be shaped by a Cubist notion of space. By contrast, in the domain of 3-D design within the fields of fine and applied art it is used to mean a setting in which the parts are linked together in one overriding whole so that they interact and supplement one another. Formally speaking, this is emphasized by means of fluid transitions, smoothed edges, things blending in with each other, and a design that stresses rounded forms, in order to show that, as with a plant or an animal, the functional raison d'être of an organ does not have to do with itself, but with its becoming part of the whole organism.

Designers have been acquainted with an organicist formal idiom at the least since Art Nouveau. The abstract depiction of natural phenomena like that undertaken by Henry van de Velde, probably Art Nouveau's most influential theorist, led via the dynamic conception of shapes to the development of an organicist/expressionist architecture like that practiced by Erich Mendelsohn and Rudolf Steiner, as well as to the international streamline style.

The concept achieved great popularity with a design competition initiated in 1940 by the New York Museum of Modern Art and the exhibition of the same name held in 1941 of the prize-winning entries entitled "Organic Design in Home Furnishings" and with the debates on Functionalism triggered in 1951 by essays such as *Geometry and Organicism,* by the architect Hugo Häring.

Criticism of the Bauhaus, the rediscovery of Art Nouveau, and the general mood of upheaval in the postwar era led to a uniform formal idiom in most areas of painting, sculpture, architecture, and design in the fifties. Ultimately, organic design also influenced industrial design with the growing significance of ergonomics and aerodynamics in the seventies. *PD*

Name: Armchair 41, Paimio
Designer: Alvar Aalto
Design: 1930-1
Production: 1932 to the present

Manufacturer: Oy. Huonekalu-ja
Rakennustyötehdas AB, Turku, Finland
for Artek Oy. AB, Helsinki
Size: 62.5 x 61x 88; seat height 34 cms
Material: bent plywood,
bent laminated birch wood frame

In 1928 Alvar Aalto and his wife Aino won the architectural competition to build a tuberculosis sanitarium near the Finnish city of Paimio; construction (1929-33) had just begun when they were also commissioned to do the building's interior design. They initially considered using the new Bauhaus tubular steel furniture – they already owned the "B 3" (Wassily) club chair designed by Marcel Breuer – but then quickly decided in favor of wood, "for much of this nickel and chrome-plated steel furniture seemed to us to be psychologically too hard for an environment of sick persons. We thus began working with wood, using this warmer and more supple material in combination with practical structures to create an appropriate furnishing style for patients."[14] The first examples of these attempts were shown 1929 at the 700th anniversary celebration of the city of Turku. In 1933 work on

the Paimio sanitarium was completed, and at the suggestion of *Architectural Review*, Aalto's architectural projects and furniture designs were shown in the London department store Fortnum and Mason's. The following year, the new furniture was already a part of the standard program at Wohnbedarf AG in Zurich.
As the manufacturer's export marketing left much to be desired, Alvar and Aino Aalto opened their own gallery and distributing company in 1935, inspired by Wohnbedarf AG in Zurich. The enterprise, which they called Artek (Art-Technology) was to be a "center for contemporary furniture, interior decoration, art, and industrial art." Aalto soon enjoyed worldwide fame after presentations at the VI Milan Triennial in 1936, and having designed the Finnish pavilion for the 1937 world's fair in Paris and the 1939 world's fair in New York, preceded by a solo

exhibition of his work at the MoMA in 1938. The "Paimio" chair quickly became popular and was produced in large quantities. It is made of bent laminated veneer and is the result of numerous bending trials using birch wood that is in part naturally damp. As birch wood is plentiful throughout Finland and the production method required no expensive technology, it was possible to manufacture the chair at relatively low cost. Despite its lack of upholstery, the springy seat afforded comfortable sitting, and was suited for modern interiors with its contemporary, natural, and unobtrusive form. It paved the way for the Scandinavian-influence furniture design which lasted until the sixties. *PD*

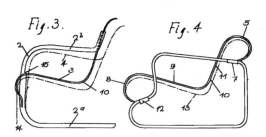

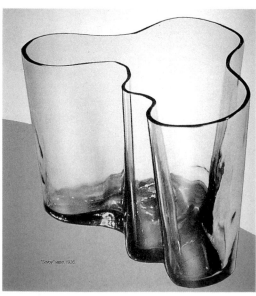

⌐ Interior of the tuberculosis sanitarium in Paimio, 1933
∧ A. Aalto: Finnish pavilion at the world's fair in New York, 1939
≪ A. Aalto: Drawings of "Armchair 31" and "Armchair 41," c. 1930-2
⟨ A. Aalto: "Savoy" vase, 1936

55
Name: Chaise Longue 39
Designer: Alvar Aalto
Design: 1936
Production: 1936 to the present

Manufacturer: Oy. Huonekalu-ja Rakennustyötehdas AB, Turku, Finland, for Artek Oy. AB, Helsinki
Size: 69 x 61x 161.5 cms
Material: bent, laminated birch wood, tensioned belts

■

"Chaise Longue 39" combines several different aspects in one piece of furniture. It is no doubt a reaction to "Chaise longue à réglage continu," Le Corbusier's tubular steel recliner from 1928. Aaltos chaise longue gives equal consideration to the S-curve, a feature which promotes relaxation, as was confirmed after clinical trials at Dortmund's Kaiser Wilhelm Institute in 1938. Its cantilevered form, which Aalto had already developed in chairs dating from 1930-1, introduces the spring principle of tubular steel furniture in a wood construction. Although Aalto also designed metal furniture on occasion, he felt that its tactile characteristics and psychological effect were cold and uninviting, while wood struck him as being more pleasant. He was already aware of this in 1929, when he created the furniture for the tuberculosis sanitarium in Paimio.

Wood was also the material preferred by architects, and it had enjoying a long tradition in rural Finland with its seemingly endless forests. In Finland, weaving textiles and carpets out of paper-twine is one of the oldest crafts. The first versions of the recliner were covered with paper-twine fabric due to the wartime dearth of raw materials. Later versions use fabric covering or leather.

Although the construction of "Chaise Longue 39" heeds the lessons of previous developmental stages, it takes laminated wood almost to breaking point, since the chair's center of gravity is extremely far away from the leg struts. In other models, Aalto reinforced the points subject to the greatest bending with additional layers of veneer, so that the parts bearing less weight remained slender. However, in the recliner, the supporting elements have the same diameter throughout, and it thus appears more uniform and continuous.

The reclining chair went on public show in 1937 at the world's fair in Paris, in the Finnish pavilion designed by Aalto. The dynamic form of superimposed waves of the armrest and reclining surface anticipates Aalto's "wavy wall" motif, with which he won the competition to design the Finnish pavilion for the New York's world fair in 1939. This motif had an influence on architecture and design until the fifties. *PD*

A. Aalto: Interior of the Finnish pavilion at the world's fair in Paris, 1937

Experiments with wood by A. Aalto, 1933

56
Name: Organic Armchair
Designer: Charles Eames and Eero Saarinen
Design: 1940
Production: 1941

Manufacturer: Haskelite Corporation, Chicago, Illinois together with Heywood-Wakefield Company, Gardner, Massachusetts, and Marli Ehrman
Size: 92.5 x 75 x 62.5; seat height 40 cms
Material: molded plywood, birch wood, foam rubber, fabric

On October 1, 1940, the Department of Industrial Design at the Museum of Modern Art in New York announced a nationwide design competition, with the goal of enhancing the level of private interiors of all classes of society through a cooperative effort between designers, manufacturers, and dealers. The theme of the competition was "Organic Design in Home Furnishings," with organic design defined as follows: "A design can be called organic if, within the object as a whole, there is a harmonious relationship between the individual elements as regards structure, material, and purpose."[15] The competition was supported by twelve renowned American department stores, who promised to sign contracts with manufacturers; one of the conditions of the competition was that the design be feasible on an industrial scale.

The jury members included, among others, Marcel Breuer and Alvar Aalto, whose chair made of two-dimensionally formed plywood was exhibited at the MoMA in 1938. Charles Eames

and Eero Saarinen won two first prizes within the six furniture categories. Especially noteworthy were chair and armchair designs in the category entitled "Seating for a Living Room."

Starting in July 1941, Charles and Ray Eames began developing a process for the three-dimensional molding of plywood in their Los Angeles apartment with the intention of producing first-class models with it. They fashioned a plaster inverse chair shell, which could be heated with electric heating elements. They covered this shell with several layers of veneer, the fibers running in alternating directions, and between each of these they placed a foil made of hot-melt adhesive. After sealing the mold, which they called the "Kazam! machine" owing to the noise it made, a bicycle pump was used to press a membrane against the veneer layers so that these clung to the inverse shell and melted the adhesive. Within four to six hours, the pressing procedure was finished. By making incisions in and cutting out pieces of the

veneer, a three-dimensional form emerged. In keeping with the competition guidelines, Haskelite was entrusted with producing the shell, while Heywood-Wakefield was in charge of lining it with a thin layer of foam rubber. Fabric designer and Bauhaus student Marli Ehrman created the cover.

In the intervening time before the inauguration of the exhibition in September 1941 at the MoMA, several chairs and armchairs were produced. The legs were made of solid birch wood instead of aluminum as intended, for the latter was not available due to the war. The backs of the chairs were not, as originally planned, a bare wood shell, since at this stage the veneer was invariably susceptible to damage.

Because of the war, and the fact that production costs were still high, the prototype did not go into serial production, thus missing the original point of the competition. *PD*

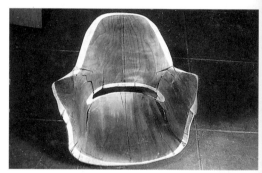

∧ C. Eames and E. Saarinen: Furniture in the "Organic Design in Home Furnishings" exhibition
◁ Plywood mold of the 'Organic Armchair'
> C. Eames and E. Saarinen: Three versions of the "Organic Armchair," 1941

57
Name: LCW (Lounge Chair Wood)
Designer: Charles and Ray Eames
Design: 1945
Production: 1946-57

Manufacturer: Molded Plywood Division of the Evans Products Company, Venice, California, for Herman Miller Furniture Company, Zeeland, Michigan
Size: 68 x 56 x 62; seat height 39 cms
Material: molded plywood, rubber

Following the MoMA's "Organic Design in Home Furnishings" exhibition, Charles and Ray Eames continued to advance the three-dimensional molding of plywood. In December 1941, an acquaintance of theirs, Dr. Wendel G. Scott, called to their attention the fact that the Navy had no suitable leg splints for injured soldiers. In just over a year, Charles and Ray Eames were able to produce appropriate prototypes, and in November 1942 received the Navy's first order for 5,000 molded plywood leg splints. Together with former colleagues, they set up a production company and research lab, the Plyformed Wood Company. Further commissions followed from the army, and Charles Eames became head of research in the Molded Plywood Division at the Evans Product Company, which, among other things, developed molded plywood parts for airplanes. He and his staff acquired valuable technological experience which proved useful when they began concentrating on civil projects after the war was over.

Their interest continued to focus on the development and production of inexpensive, fashionable furniture while taking into account the general scarcity of raw materials. The plywood technology met two criteria: it ensured frugal use of materials and offered comfort, for the furniture was molded to the human body.

The "DCW" (Dining Chair Wood) and the "LCW" were the first items to enjoy high popularity. The "Organic Armchair", from 1940–1, had already revealed the difficulties involved in forming a complete chair shell with complex curve radii from plywood. The Eameses treated the different functions of the shell independently, so that the convex forms did not have to be as strong. Furthermore, the modular character of the design yielded a number of possible combinations of the seat and backrest, with various foot rests available either in laminated wood or metal. These were initially attached with elastic rubber shock mounts that were firmly welded to the wood using a modified Chrysler process.

In the autumn of 1945, Molded Plywood Division produced a number of chairs and armchairs from a wide variety of woods, with fabric, imitation leather, leather, or hide coverings for the seat and backrest; Evans Products organized marketing and distribution. The prototypes were presented to the press in December 1945 at a preview showing at the Barclay Hotel in New York. In February 1946 they were displayed at an Architectural League exhibition and finally, in March 1946, in a solo MoMA exhibition entitled "New Furniture – Designed by Charles Eames" in New York.

While Evans Products delayed expanding its furniture branch, the new design director at the Herman Miller Furniture Company, George Nelson, came across the plywood furniture as a result of these publicity activities. The companies worked out a cooperation agreement in which the Molded Plywood Division guaranteed production and Herman Miller took over marketing. Serial production began in mid-1946. The unusually high degree of publicity which Herman Miller Furniture achieved with the Eames Plywood Collection induced the company to acquire the production rights in 1949. At that point, Charles Eames had already been working as a design consultant for Herman Miller for two years. *PD*

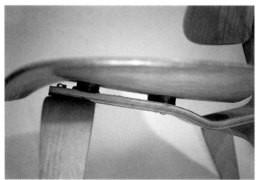

⌐ Detail with shock mounts
∧ Eames furniture in the exhibition "New Furniture – Designed by Charles Eames"
≪ C. and R. Eames: Chair shell from molded laminated wood pieces, 1946
< Test model for the "DCW"

58

Name: FSW (Folding Screen Wood)
Designer: Charles and Ray Eames
Design: 1946
Production: 1946-55

Manufacturer: Molded Plywood Division
of the Evans Products Company, Venice,
California
Size: 173 x 200 x 12.5 cms (opened),
173 x 25 x 15 cms (folded)
Material: molded plywood, canvas

■

One of the first experiments in molding plywood consisted simply of bending it around an axis, as is familiar in works by Thonet and Alvar Aalto. The trials carried out by Charles and Ray Eames yielded a series of U- or V-shaped profiles which, when laid side by side, suggested the idea of using them to form a room divider. The most difficult task was to create a suitably flexible hinge that would allow the screen to be folded up to save space. Based on the extensive experience that Eames and his staff members had acquired during the war, they solved the problem with a vinyl strip and a synthetic adhesive developed during that period. The strip was attached from outside on both sides on the longitudinal edge of two panels; however, it did

not prove to be sufficiently durable and broke after the screen had been folded a number of times. In a subsequent and final version, the individual elements were joined by a tough strip of canvas, which was glued into cut longitudinal slots. The eight identical sections were reciprocally connected. The wavy cross-section ensured stability irrespective of the angle formed by the individual elements when open. When opened asymmetrically, "FSW" reminds the observer of the natural folds in curtain fabric, a motif used by Alvar Aalto in 1938–9 for his "wavy wall" project which constituted part of the wall covering in the Finnish pavilion at the world's fair in New York. Unlike "FSW," this wall design is stiff, yet unusually dynamic, and

prompted the jury to award all three first competition prizes to Aalto's team.
The plywood folding screens were available in two heights of 173 and 86.5 cm, and later in three lengths of ten, eight or six elements. Production was initially handled by Evans Products and then by the Herman Miller Furniture Company. However, it was discontinued in 1955 because a large share of the work had to be done by hand, which drove up the price. Production was resumed in 1990 by Vitra AG in Basel, and by Herman Miller, Inc. in 1994. *PD*

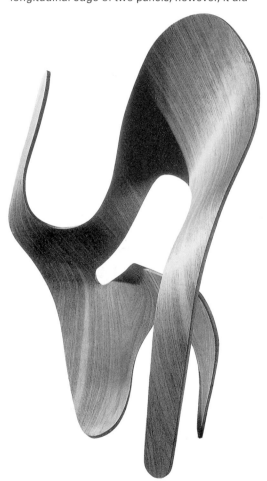

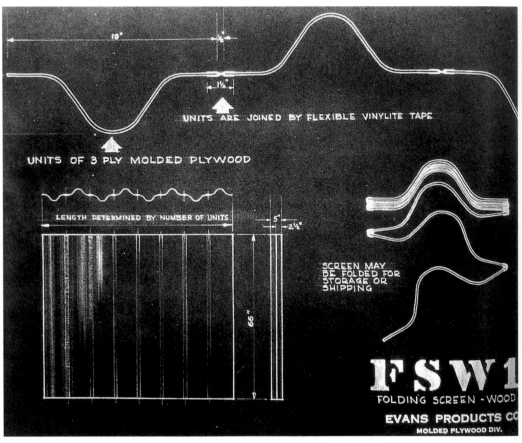

Γ C. & R. Eames: Sculpture made of molded laminated wood, 1943
∧ Don Albinson: Drawing for "Folding Screen Wood," 1946
< C. & R. Eames: Experiments with molded plywood, 1946

59

Name: Chess Table IN-61
Designer: Isamu Noguchi
Design: 1947-8
Production: 1948-9

Manufacturer: Herman Miller Furniture
Company, Zeeland, Michigan
Size: 49 x 67 x 67 cms (closed)
Material: black corroded plywood,
lacqered cast aluminum, plastic inlays

■

Isamu Noguchi was more a sculptor than a designer. Thus, it makes more sense to view the objects he designed as sculptures with practical value, "things for everyone's pleasure." His sculptural approach had a lasting impact on design in the fifties; his organic, biomorphic formal language has had a continued influence up to the present.

Noguchi's development was quite multifarious. As the son of a Japanese-American couple, both of whom were writers, he spent the first twenty-five years of his life in America, Japan, and Europe. At different times he wanted to be a cabinetmaker, artist, and doctor, until in the end – almost against his will – he became a sculptor. Noguchi's work has been influenced to some extent by the deindividualized sculptures of Constantin Brancusi, which he had admired on a 1926 visit to the Brummer Gallery in New York.

With the help of a scholarship from the New York Guggenheim Museum, he was able to work with Brancusi in Paris in 1927 and 1928. Brancusi must have been quite convinced of Noguchi's talent, for he was the only one of Brancusi's numerous pupils who was allowed to polish his mentor's sculptures.

The chess table combines two formal, sculptural principles of Noguchi's works. The wooden base is a reference to the folded, irregularly formed, mostly flat elements that Noguchi discovered during his collaboration with Alexander Calder. The base supports a trough-shaped shell made of lacquered cast aluminum. The shell is an analogy to the numerous small-format plaster or bronze models of relief square or garden designs he created for demonstration purposes.

The chess pieces also have a shell form, as they are sculptural elements of the table. Access can

be gained to the larger two of the four troughs by swiveling the table top, which is fixed to an axis. At the same time, the table top serves as the chess board, although this only becomes apparent after a second glance. Larger round inlays made of transparent plastic are used for the thirty-two white squares, while small embedded red pegs form the black. Together they yield the familiar grid on a dynamically curved surface. The alphanumeric coordinate system is missing. Because of this, and also because of the extremely unusual, expensive design, the table convinced only a few passionate chess players. As a result, production was discontinued relatively quickly, making the piece an extremely rare item found in few collections. *PD*

《 I. Noguchi: Loudspeaker "The Radio Nurse," 1937
< I. Noguchi: *Fish Face,* 1959
∨ I. Noguchi: *Contoured Playground,* 1941

60

Name: DAX (Dining Armchair with X-Base)
Designer: Charles and Ray Eames/
University of California, Los Angeles
Design: 1948
Production: 1950-89

Manufacturer: Herman Miller Furniture
Company, Zeeland, Michigan
Size: 75 x 63 x 62; seat height 43 cms
Material: fiberglass, round steel bars,
rubber

■

The "DAX" armchair was designed in 1948. It belongs to a group of shell chairs and armchairs with a variety of bases which Charles and Ray Eames entered for the international competition for "Low-Cost Furniture Design" at the New York MoMA. Although the Eameses also submitted a design for a chair made of fiberglass-reinforced plastic (see "La Chaise"), the actual intention was to make the chairs using varnished or Neoprene-coated steel or sheet aluminum. The couple worked closely with engineers at the University of California in Los Angeles, producing several aluminum prototypes, a task that proved to be unusually difficult because the provisional molded forms kept bursting.

In the eyes of the jury, which included Ludwig Mies van der Rohe, making seating furniture out of sheet metal held promise as a method of mass production, and had even proven useful in the automobile industry. Thus, the first prize went to a sheet metal chair by Don R. Knorr, and the shell chair series by Charles and Ray Eames placed

second. While drawings and plaster models were acceptable for the competition, the planned exhibition of the prize-winning pieces was to show realistic prototypes for mass production. As a result, the exhibition date was continually put back, until the show finally opened in March 1950. Meanwhile, Irv Green, Sol Fingerhut and Milt Brucker of Zenith Plastics presented their fiberglass process at the Eameses' studio. This technology had been developed during the war for radar housing (Radom) on the noses of airplanes. In cooperation with the Herman Miller Furniture Company, the first series of 2,000 armchair shells was manufactured by hand – still with a cord embedded around the edge for reinforcement – and displayed at the Chicago Showroom and the Museum of Modern Art in New York.

With a patent for welded-on shock mounts developed by Chrysler, it was possible to mount the shell-shaped seats dyed in different colors on different bases without having to alter the shell.

This enabled the hydraulically controlled positive/negative metal molds to be produced efficiently while retaining the greatest variation among the models.

With the "DAX" armchair, the formal ideas central to the "Organic Armchair" designed by Charles Eames and Eero Saarinen in 1940 (see above) were brought to bear in mass production via a detour into concepts for metal furniture that was never manufactured.

It is the first chair with an unlined fiberglass shell to be produced in large quantities by Herman Miller and Vitra AG. Production was discontinued in 1989. *PD*

From a Herman Miller catalogue, 1952

61

Name: La Chaise
Designer: Charles and Ray Eames
Design: 1948
Production: 1990 to the present

Manufacturer: Vitra AG, Basel
Size: 82.5 x 150 x 85; seat height 37 cms
Material: fiberglass, iron rods, wood

The priority given to arms production and the influx of numerous refugees at the end of the World War II created a dire housing shortage in the United States; at the same time, there was a very limited selection of low-priced, space-saving furniture available on the market.

The Museum of Modern Art in New York, and the Museum Design Project, Inc., a non-commercial association of furniture producers and retailers, announced an international competition entitled "Low-Cost Furniture Design" on January 5, 1948, as a means of coping with the emergency. The organizers expected that the high-profile nature of this project would serve to inspire designers and producers throughout the world. The hope was that the development of a new generation of fresh, novel furniture designs to be distributed on a broad basis would help to improve the housing situation.

The competition, which closed on October 31 of the same year, met with such an unexpectedly high international response that the judging of

entries and the creation of prototypes of prize-winning models for the planned exhibition had to be delayed. A total of 3,000 drafts were submitted from thirty-one countries; 2,500 of these came from the United States, 500 from Europe. Charles and Ray Eames won second prize with their designs for molded, nonupholstered seats made of sheet steel or aluminum (see the "DAX" chair). While "La Chaise" was not one of the prize-winning designs, its elegant form made it one of the most notable competition entries, and it accordingly appeared in the catalogue and the exhibition, both realized in 1950.

"La Chaise" consists of two very thin fiberglass shells that have been glued together and separated by a hard rubber disk; the resulting cavity is filled with styrene. Unlike Eero Saarinen's "Womb Chair," the Eameses' plastic shell is not upholstered. The base is created by five metal rods in a partly diagonal arrangement that has been set into a construction of intersecting pieces of wood. With the "Organic

Armchair," a joint Charles Eames and Eero Saarinen project dating from 1940, the gap between the back and the seat was technically necessary, as it allowed the laminated veneer layers to be shaped three-dimensionally. By contrast, this gap is a design element in "La Chaise," as molding plastic rendered it redundant. The lightness of the structure was underscored visually by perforating the part with the largest volume, a stylistic device also used by sculptors such as Henry Moore. Formal analogies to sculptural elements in Salvador Dalí's surrealist pictures are discernible (e.g., *Atavistic Ruins after the Rain*, 1934; and *Sleep*, 1937). Charles and Ray Eames imagined that a flowing sculpture by the influential French-American sculptor Gaston Lachaise (1882–1935) would blend in well with their chair, hence the name. *PD*

^ Eames furniture at "An Exhibition for Modern Living" of the Detroit Institute of Art, 1949
⌐ Salvador Dali: *Atavistic Ruins after the Rain*, 1934
≫ C. Eames and E. Saarinen: Drawing for the competition "Organic Design in Home Furnishings," 1940
> Gaston Lachaise: *Floating Figure*, 1927

Name: Arabesco
Designer: Carlo Mollino
Design: 1949
Production: 1950

Manufacturer: Apelli & Varesio, Turin, Italy
Size: 54 x 123 x 53 cms
Material: bent laminated maple wood,
safety glass, brass

His friends called him "Carlo il Bizarro." The son of an upper-class contractor, architect Carlo Mollino was always attempting to escape the monotony of the everyday working world. He engaged in numerous activities outside the profession he had learned. Photography was a special passion, in particular the works of Surrealist Man Ray and shots of the female body. He built and drove race cars, setting a lap record on the track at Le Mans which remained unbroken for two years. He worked as a fashion designer, creating wardrobes for beautiful women, and designed shops. He composed essays, designed company canteens, and apparently *en passant* designed or built office buildings, schools, factories, cemetery monuments, chapels, churches, and alpine cable car stations. Mollino acquired numerous patents for concrete honeycomb constructions, tubular steel joints, and molded plywood elements, inventing devices for creating perspective drawings, streamlined race car bodies, automatic drift correction instruments for airplanes, and improved chain and sprocket drives for bicycles. Mollino designed the first "Arabesco" table in 1949 for the living room of Casa Orenga in Turin. For the first time, Mollino saw pieces of furniture as autonomous objects rather than architectural elements; this insight explains the table's unique appearance. "Arabesco" is similar to the table which Mollino modified in 1950 for the Singer company canteen in Turin, in which the stand doubles as a magazine rack. The tabletop derives its shape from the rear-view perspective in *Reclining Nude*, a drawing by Léonor Fini, and is an affirmation of Mollino's predilection for incorporating erotic associations into his furniture designs. The perforated plywood table frame is a reference to Surrealist motifs in the paintings of Salvador Dalí or the reliefs by Jean Arp, in which the pattern of these amoebaelike forms obeys the law of chance. Further variations on the "Arabesco" exist, for example from Lisa and Gio Ponti's house. *PD*

^ The Apelli & Varesio workshops, Turin, 1950
⌐ C. Mollino: Skilift station at Lago Nero, 1946
⌐ Interior of Casa Timbrata, 1949
> Léonor Fini: *Reclining Nude* and the shape of the "Arabesco" tabletop

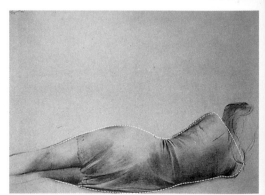

Name: Dinette Table IN-20/(Stool)
Designer: Isamu Noguchi
Design: 1949-50
Production: 1949-50

Manufacturer: Herman Miller Furniture Company, Zeeland, Michigan
Size: 66 x 130 x 91.5 cms/45 x 35.5 x 45; seat height 45 cms
Material: birch wood, steel rods/birch wood, steel rods, rubber

When sculptor Isamu Noguchi began his work in design, one of his focal points was the table. In 1939 he designed a one-of-a-kind model with a two-piece, sculptured base and a glass top for A. Conger Goodyear, then President of the MoMA in New York. In a modified version, Noguchi simplified the form of the base, which then consisted of two identical elements, one of which was inverted and glued to the other. Herman Miller, as well as a great many imitators, were able to sell this table in large numbers at a very low price because its simple structure made it easy to produce. Thus, "Coffee Table IN-50"

became Noguchi's best-known design, along with the "Akari" luminaires made of China paper. "Dinette Table IN-20" was only manufactured for a short time. Unlike "Coffee Table IN-50," it dispenses with the sculptural effect. This undoubtedly also has to do with the fact that the wooden tabletop tends to emphasize the table's function, while a glass top is optically less striking and does not interfere with the view of the sculptured base. Nevertheless, the table still exhibits formal analogies to Noguchi's sculptures, which are based on molded, flat elements, usually bent at right angles.

In certain sculptures, these elements evoke associations with fish shapes, while the wooden leg of "Dinette Table" is reminiscent of a fin. The steel rod table legs appear lightweight and reiterate the motif of an opening that characterizes the sculptures. The overall impression is of a "floating" balance struck between forms of different weights, as in the mobiles of Alexander Calder, whom Noguchi assisted between 1928-9. *PD*

^ I. Noguchi: "Coffee-Table IN-50," 1944
> From a Herman Miller brochure, 1949-50

65

**Name: Sedia per la Casa Cattaneo, Agra
(La Casa sull'Altopiano di Agra), "feminine"
Designer: Carlo Mollino
Design: 1953
Production: 1953**

**Manufacturer: Apelli & Varesio, Turin, Italy
Size: 92 x 40.5 x 50.5; seat height 44.5 cms
Material: bent plywood, brass**

■

Carlo Mollino designed a chair duo, "male" and "female," as part of the furniture for the house owned by L. Cattaneo on the high plateau of Agra in Luino, also built by Mollino between 1952-3. Mollino frequently made chairs using solid wood elements which he imbued with the style of Catalan designer Antoni Gaudí, whose work inspired them. The distinguishing feature of the matching chairs for Casa Cattaneo is that the

seat, back, and legs are all made of plywood. The back legs are a continuous extension of the backrest, and via a bow lead to the front legs, which in turn become the seat.
One is almost led to believe that the entire chair was built of a slit and bent rectangular plate (like Gerald Summer's plywood armchair), but appearances deceive. In processing the chair, parts of the seat, base, and backrest would

normally overlap. This visual sleight of hand requires costly individual production involving craftsmanship. Apparently, Mollino found the resulting fascination with how the structure managed to stand to be well worth the effort. *PD*

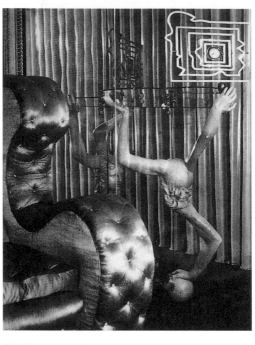

C. Mollino: Interior of Casa Devalle, 1939-40

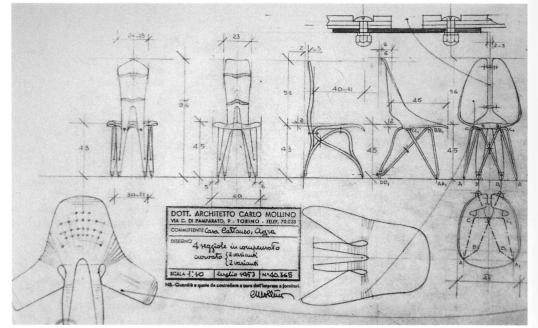

C. Mollino: Drawing of the chair for the Cattaneo house

66

Name: Butterfly
Designer: Sori Yanagi
Design: 1954
Production: since 1954

Manufacturer: Tendo Mokko Co., Ltd.,
Tokyo
Size: 41.5 x 47.5 x 34; seat height 35 cms
Material: bent plywood, brass

The postwar years in Japan were marked by the reconstruction effort. As Japan was under the supreme command of the Allied Forces, the Institute of Industrial Art was instructed to develop furniture and electrical appliances for houses for the occupation forces and to produce them throughout the entire country as quickly as possible. The scheme lasted until 1947, and, based on American models, led the Japanese to adopt Western technology. Americanisms permeated daily Japanese life; and the influence of Western style remains undiminished even today. In 1950, when the Korean War broke out, Japan profited immensely as a neighboring country and experienced a tremendous economic upswing.

This upswing was fueled further when the occupation of Japan ended in 1951. Renewed independence led to the founding of numerous companies, universities, and cultural establishments. In 1952 Sori Yanagi was among the founders of the Industrial Design Association (JIDA) and the Japan Design Committee, which

had set itself the task of fostering the influence of designers within company hierarchies, for they had previously been excluded from decision-making processes: their job consisted solely in lending existing products a new (in other words, Western) look. That same year, Yanagi opened his own design studio and won first prize for a turntable in the very first Japanese design competition.

Against this background, the "Butterfly" stool can be regarded as extraordinary for several reasons. Yanagi borrows no known Western forms. This is all the more astonishing given that he spent a great deal of time with Charlotte Perriand between 1940-2, and later as well. She went to Japan on the invitation of the Japanese Secretary of Commerce and Industry to give design a new orientation. Yanagi was at that time a French student, and accompanied Charlotte Perriand on her travels through Japan, thus becoming acquainted with the European classic Modernity. This was quite possibly the source of Yanagi's interest in seating furniture, which did

not exist in Japanese culture. Even today many urban households are quite content without any seating furniture whatsoever; traditionally, one sits on tatami mats on the floor.

Yanagi used the plywood molding technique made famous by the Eameses to mass-produce the stool at the Tendo Mokko Company. The stool features an unusually clever construction: two identical forms are attached together symmetrically around the axis using two screws underneath the seat and a threaded brass rod. This yields a shape which on the one hand is reminiscent of the torii (portals) of Shinto shrines and is thus Asian in expression; on the other hand, it resembles the wings of a butterfly, from which it derives its name. In 1957 the stool was awarded a gold medal at the Milan Triennial. *PD*

∧ Torii of the Itsukushima shrine on Miya-jima, Japan
Γ Japanese character for sky

67
Name: Tulip Chair, No. 151
Designer: Eero Saarinen
Design: 1956
Production: 1956 to the present

Manufacturer: Knoll Associates, Inc.,
New York
Size: 80,5 x 49,5 x 54; seat height 48 cms
Material: varnished fiberglass-reinforced
polyester, varnished cast aluminum,
foam rubber, textile

The "Tulip Chair" is one of a series of chairs, armchairs, stools, tables, and side tables developed by Eero Saarinen within a five-year period. The characteristic feature of the series is that the supporting structure has been pared to a central supporting stem "like a wineglass" in order to emphasize the uniformity of table and chair. "The bases of tables and chairs in a typical furniture arrangement create an ugly, confusing, and restless world. I wanted to design a chair as an integrated whole once again. All important furniture of the past always had a holistic structure, from King Tut's chair to that of Thomas Chippendale. Today, we are parting ways with this holism with our predilection for plastic and laminated wood shells. In current production methods, pedestal furniture is half plastic and half metal. I am looking forward to the point when the plastics industry will be capable of manufacturing the chair using just one material, the way I have designed it." [16] The "Tulip Chair" is still produced today in its original form. *PD*

⌐ Biedermeier chair, Vienna, 1820-30
⩘ E. Saarinen: Studies for the "Tulip Chair," 1956
⌃ From a 1962 Knoll catalogue
⟩ E. Saarinen: TWA terminal at the John F. Kennedy Airport, 1962

68

Name: Panton-Chair
Designer: Verner Panton
Design: 1959-60
Production: 1968 to the present

Manufacturer: Herman Miller AG/
Vitra AG, Basel
Size: 88.5 x 50 x 74; seat height 43 cms
Material: varnished high-resistance foam
(Baydur)

Danish designer Verner Panton is one of the group of designers who broke with the Scandinavian tradition of producing handcrafted teak wood furniture. He shares this distinction with Poul Kjaerholm and Arne Jacobsen, in whose architecture studio he worked from 1950-2.

As early as 1949-50, Panton began drafting chairs with no rear legs during his studies at the Royal Academy of Art in Copenhagen. In 1955 a chair emerged that was made of molded laminated wood and featured one unbroken S-curve; it was part of an entire furniture line. However, Panton was fascinated by the opportunities opened up by the new plastics, which, due to their lack of structure, do not limit the designer to any particular forms, and engender inexpensive products. This new formal freedom caused him to reconsider the theme "chair," and he again returned to the S-chair and modified it. The crucial feature was the curved lower part, which rendered the base of the S-chair superfluous and afforded the desired leg room.

At the end of the fifties, together with Dansk Acrylic Teknik, he developed the prototype for the "Panton-Chair" in plastic and exhibited it at the Mobilia-Club on Eriksholm, near Helsingör, in the hope of finding a suitable manufacturer with

whom he could realize his idea. He found none and the cantilever-base plastic chair initially remained a dream. Panton returned again to working with laminated wood.

In 1962-3 he paid a visit to Vitra. Only after making contact with the owners Willi and Rolf Fehlbaum, who manufactured Herman Miller products under license, did years of experimentation finally yield the first fiberglass-reinforced polyester prototypes in 1967. However, the desire to make the "Panton-Chair" stackable once again delayed production, as the thickness of the material had to be reduced without forfeiting stability.

The final version went into serial production in 1968 at Vitra under the label of the Herman Miller Furniture Co. It was made of Baydur, an HR polyurethane foam produced by the Bayer Leverkusen company, and was varnished in seven colors. The "Panton-Chair" was thus the first product developed jointly by Vitra and Bayer Leverkusen to be included in the Herman Miller collection. It quickly won fame and became a Pop Art icon.

In 1970 Vitra replaced the costly production technology, which required thirty minutes to produce one piece, with Thermoplast injection molding. Using a dyed granulate Luran-S

made by BASF, the edge profiles had to be strengthened and reinforcing ribs placed underneath the seat.

In the long run, however, the material did not adequately withstand dynamic stress; Vitra discontinued production in 1979 and the license was returned to Verner Panton. Starting in 1983, Horn GmbH & Co. KG in Rudersberg began making the chair using HR foam again, and sold it until the end of the eighties through the WK association. Since 1990 Vitra has been producing the "Panton-Chair" using HR foam.

The colorful history of the first serially produced cantilever-base chair made of one single piece of plastic includes numerous quarrels as to the true designer. Because Panton had unsuccessfully sought a manufacturer for quite some time, he had already made his ideas available to a limited audience despite the fact that mass production did not seem imminent. When the "Panton-Chair" finally went into serial production, many other designers claimed they had also pursued this idea, although without taking steps to publicize it, have it serially produced, or obtain a patent. *PD*

⌐ V. Panton: "Muremail" wall design, c. 1975
∧ V. Panton: Developmental model of the "Panton-Chair," c. 1960
⌐ V. Panton: "S-Chair," 1955
< Production of the "Panton-Chair"

69
Name: 3-benet Skalstol
Designer: Hans J. Wegner
Design: 1963
Production: 1963-89

Manufacturer: Johannes Hansen,
Copenhagen
Size: 73.5 x 90 x 82.5; seat height 35 cms
Material: varnished bent plywood, bent and
varnished laminated birch wood

Hans J. Wegner is considered to be an important innovator in traditional furniture design as well as a pioneer in Danish Modernism. He earned fame with his exclusive, perfectly crafted chairs, which often drew on traditional models and were made by hand.

After participating in "Low-Cost Furniture Design," the 1948 competition held by the MoMA in New York, he began working with the relatively new process of forming laminated wood, although only on a two-dimensional level. A preliminary "Skalstol" prototype from 1949, with its three separate shells, was probably a forerunner of the Eames's "Lounge Chair" from 1956.

It already features the intelligent, highly stable leg construction which consists of just two pieces of laminated wood and thus saves material inputs. In 1963 Wegner manufactured another "Skalstol" prototype, this time with a distinctive form that could almost be called classic.

The latter chair only has three legs, and the rear leg doubles as the mounting for the backrest. Wegner tested several leg configurations with 1:5 scale models and ultimately opted for the solution which had already proven successful in 1949. He highlighted the curvature of both pieces of laminated wood visually by having the front legs extend sideways rather than forward. The

distinctly raised ends of the plywood shell in combination with an extremely low center of gravity lend the chair a representative form that evokes chairs used by African rulers. Japanese tradition was the source of Wegner's idea of coating the surface with red varnish, and it often played an important role in other works, too. Wegner always saw himself as a craftsman whose foremost task was to create comfortable chairs. As the "Skalstol" demonstrates, a traditional notion of one's role can also yield great originality and elegance. *MK*

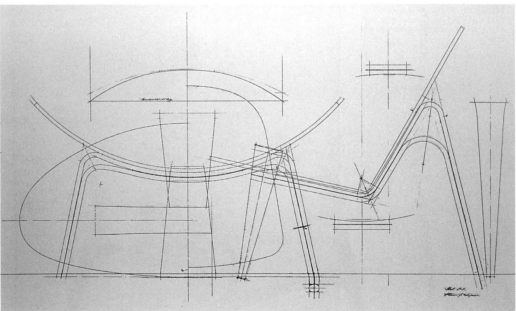

⎸ H. Wegner: "Skalstol," 1949
⎿ Stool from the Sudan
≪ H. Wegner: Various models for the "3-benet Skalstol," 1963
⌃ H. Wegner: Drawing for the "3-benet Skalstol," 1963

Name: No. 577
Designer: Pierre Paulin
Design: 1966
Production: since 1967

Manufacturer: Artifort, Maastricht
Size: 61 x 89 x 95; seat height 31cms
Material: Tubular steel frame, rubber belts,
foam rubber, nylon-jersey covering

■

As a designer, Pierre Paulin was quite versatile. He worked as an interior designer in the automobile industry (Citroën) in addition to creating various electrical appliances (for Ericsson and Calor), packaging (Dior), and logos for the Musée d'Orsay in Paris. Since the late fifties, he has been involved in furniture design, initially with upholstered chairs made of laminated wood on chrome-plated metal legs for the Dutch producer Artifort. In 1966, he designed one of his most famous works, the stackable "No. 577" chair, again for Artifort.

The extremely low seat height indicates a changing outlook on life at the end of the sixties. Sitting was suddenly no longer seen as an erect, static posture, but as relaxed reclining into a variety of positions. A few years later, traditional chairs were replaced by deep-set furniture. This development was definitely furthered by the production of inexpensive polyurethane foam materials, which could be produced in slabs or as machined parts. Elastic nylon-jersey materials could be used to cover complex three-dimensional volumes, wrinkle-free and without costly tucks. The shapes of the chairs were no longer restricted by the qualities of the material. The upholstering process was drastically simplified, resulting in lower production costs.

The completely novel form of "No. 577" vividly reflects the production technology. Moreover, the thick material and the wavy design serve to create a stackable chair. The cover can be removed thanks to a zipper on the underside, thus living up to the most modern expectations.

In 1969 Mobilier National, the state authority responsible for stimulating the furniture industry, rewarded Paulin's efforts by commissioning him to furnish the private quarters of the Elysée Palace. In 1970 Paulin designed the furniture for the French pavilion at the world's fair in Osaka and included "No. 577," which is where it received its nickname "Osaka." It is also called "Langue" (tongue) because of its appearance when viewed from the front. *PD*

^ From an Artifort brochure
< Olivier Mourgue: "Bouloum," 1968

71/72

Name: Zocker/Sitzgerät Colani
Designer: Luigi Colani
Design: 1971/1972
Production: 1972-82/1973-82

Manufacturer: Top System Burkhard Lübke, Gütersloh, Germany
Size: 50 x 32 x 57; seat height 29.5 cms/ 65.5 x 54 x 66; seat height 38 cms
Material: Polyethylene (rotation sintering procedure)

■

The "Zocker" for children and the "Sitzgerät Colani" (Colani seating tool) strikingly reflect changes in living conditions and ways of life at the end of the sixties and the beginning of the seventies. The general acceptance of the new plastics also meant that new shapes were finding their way into apartments, often in the Pop and "shock" colors typical of the period.

Luigi Colani, who was facetiously referred to as the "Leonardo of the Plastics," had for quite some time been taking advantage of the ease with which plastic could be formed into almost any shape to realize his novel drafts.

In designing the "Zocker" chair for children, Colani completely broke with tradition by refusing to create a scaled-down version of an adult's chair. Typologically speaking, the "Zocker" consists of an integrated seat and desk. It offers several sitting positions – including straddling – and thus permits the child to move freely while playing.

The rounded edges and the smooth transitions between the seat, backrest, and desk reduce the risk of injury and ensure that the furniture is stable and stackable. In addition, the plastic is easy to clean and is shock- and scratch-resistant. Its light weight makes it mobile and even buoyant.

The numerous advantages of the child's version inspired Colani to create the "Sitzgerät Colani," a chair for adults; here, the monolithic "Zocker" design was replaced by a sleeker, more differen-tiated form. Its sculptural qualities render it a "*fine art object*."[17] What both models share is their multifunctionality, which led Colani to consider orthopedic aspects: "A person sitting in a relaxed position, leaning forward slightly, will support the shoulders above the elbows in such a way as to relieve pressure on the spine. I created a mold of the cavities formed by the human body in this position and stylistically turned them into a seating machine."[18] Characteristic of Colani's works are their highly functional properties, although they feature an organic, dynamic, biomorphic formal language that promotes ergonomic aspects. The latest design trends appear to use Colani's idiom. *PD*

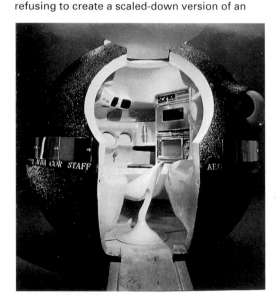

≪ L. Colani: "Kugelküche" (spherical kitchen), 1968-70
^ Advertising photograph of Top System, 1972
> L. Colani on "Sitzgerät Colani," from a Top System advertising poster, 1973

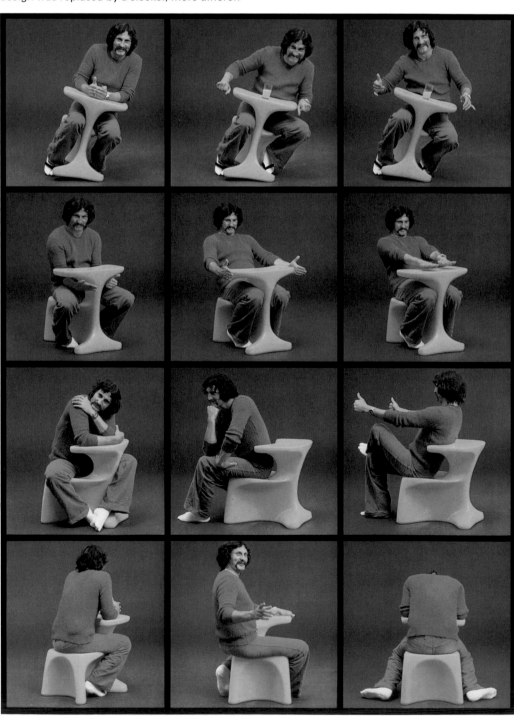

73

Name: MN-01 LC1, Lockheed Lounge
Designer: Marc Newson
Design: 1985-6
Production: since 1986

Manufacturer: Idée, Tokyo
Size: 86 x 166 x 57 cms
Material: fiberglass, riveted sheet aluminum

Australian Marc Newson is one of the youngest designers to attract attention in the design world. Born in 1963, he has been held in international regard since 1985.

There is often a causal relationship between his home town of Sydney, his hobby of surfing, and his work. The omnipresence of the sea in a city of over a million inhabitants, where there are more than 200 swimming coves, practically dictates such an outlook. His designs are therefore often compared with surfboards. What is usually not considered in light of this background is his education at the Sydney College of Arts, from which he graduated in 1984.

Sculpturally speaking, Marc Newson's works are highly distinctive. The bolide forms have their roots in the international streamline style of the thirties and fifties as well as international developments in the field of sculpture that were influenced by this movement. If one seeks analogies, the forms of his new works are similar in particular to Jean Arp's torso motifs from 1930 and 1931, Alexander Archipenko's *Torso in Space* sculpture from 1935, or Karl Hartung's *Reclining Person* from 1938. Thus, his high-gloss aluminum armchairs and lounge chairs, among them "Orgone" or "Alufelt," are actually more anthropomorphous seating sculptures that please our sense of touch than functional furniture.

The body of the "Lockheed Lounge," named after the American aircraft manufacturer, is made of fiberglass reinforced plastic, which can be processed easily and without costly technology. The legs smoothly descend from the natural curves and are covered with rubber, a stylistic principle to be found in many of Newson's works. The entire surface is covered with thin-walled aluminum sheets attached with blind rivetings. These sheets do not overlap but are joined together almost seamlessly, giving the impression of an airplane fuselage.

The "Lockheed Lounge" belongs to a series of sculptural furniture consisting of hard, technical materials. Form dominates comfort, and any sense of coziness is replaced by the aesthetics of the material.

Philippe Starck developed a sudden fascination for the "Lockheed Lounge" and integrated it into the New York Paramount Hotel which he remodeled in 1990. Designer Ron Arad, who also works with sheet metal, procured a commission for Marc Newson in London. *PD*

⌐ Alexander Archipenko: *Torso in Space,* 1935
∧ M. Newson working on the "Lockheed Lounge," c. 1986
⌐ M. Newson: The "Orgone" lounge chair and chair,
   the "Event Horizon" table, and the "Alufelt" chair, 1994

74

Name: W.W. Stool
Designer: Philippe Starck
Design: 1990
Production: 1992 to the present

Manufacturer: Vitra AG, Basel
Size: 97 x 56 x 53 cms
Material: varnished sand-cast aluminum

Philippe Starck describes himself as an autodidact who, at the age of nineteen, had already founded his first company for inflatable furniture. In the media he is regarded as a star. He came to fame in the late seventies and early eighties with his interiors for nightclubs and cafes in Paris, especially Café Costes (1984), which became famous for the three-legged chair sold worldwide that bore its name.

In 1982 Starck came to prominence, when the then-president of France, François Mitterrand, commissioned the newcomer to furnish his private chambers in the Elysée Palace.

Since the beginning of the eighties, Starck has successfully created designs for industrial production in various sectors. Among his preferences are aluminum and more or less long, streamlined "horns." This is no doubt a legacy of his father who, as an aircraft mechanic and inventor, worked with this material and these forms. However, Starck does not attempt to imitate aerodynamic profiles but instead reinterprets them biomechanically. His ingenuity appears inexhaustible, his repertoire of forms infinite. He christens his creations with names from science fiction novels, for example the "Ubik" series by the Italian manufacturer Driade, from the novel of the same name by American author Philip K. Dick.

The stool, or more accurately the standing aid "W.W. Stool," is part of an imaginative office ensemble which Starck sketched for film director Wim Wenders in 1990. A sculptural look dominates the surrealist appearance of this object. On the one hand, a "stool" is defined as a piece of seating furniture; on the other, it is defined as a sprout, which implies the possible source of inspiration. Thus, the sculptural surface of the seat and back has the effect of a germinating rhizome, with three roots growing into the floor, while the shoot winds its way upward. The branching of the front "root" serves as footrest. The biomechanical element in Starck's design style can be compared to that of Luigi Colani and his "bio-design"; both designers are also active in a wide range of design fields. *PD*

⌐ "Lady's Walking-Stick-Chair No. 3" by Thonet, c. 1890
∧ P. Starck: "Juicy Salif" lemon press, 1989-90
⌐ P. Starck: Staircase in the Asahi brewery, Tokyo, 1990
< Backrest from Zaire, 1900s

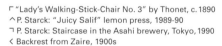

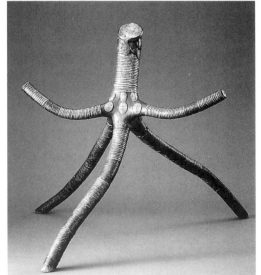

Decoration

A certain material or detail in the construction of furniture can function just as decoratively as an application or a pattern on the surface. It is also often difficult to separate decorative aspects clearly from areas such as materials or construction. Therefore, in the history of furniture design the main attempt has been to create a harmony between the two. At the turn of the century, concepts were devised in response to the eclectic use of decoration in the nineteenth century, concepts that placed the fine and the applied arts in a binding formal canon. With the avant-garde at the beginning of the twentieth century, decor became completely discredited. Modernity condemned ornament as a "crime" and came up with mottoes such as "form follows function" and "less is more." Even when, in the fifties, designers such as Charlotte Perriand and George Nelson quite manifestly used decorative elements, decoration remained taboo. The idealization of objectivity and efficiency was by then outdated, however, and by the sixties was being openly criticized. Since that time, imaginative or trivial forms of expression have existed as equals alongside classical styles. Particularly Postmodernism, which plays with all these forms as bearers of different meanings, reaffirmed the role of decoration. *MSC*

75

Name: Rocking Sofa No. 7500
Designer: Gebrüder Thonet, probably
August Thonet
Design: 1880-1883
Production: since 1883

Manufacturer: Gebrüder Thonet, Vienna
Size: 77.5 x 69.5 x 174 cms
Material: bent beech wood, canework

The "Rocking Sofa" is presumably a design made by August Thonet, who was in charge of construction and technology in the Thonet family company. The technically and artistically gifted son of the company's founder was the source of many novel furniture models as well as improved production techniques.

At the end of the nineteenth century, chairs with adjustable backs were already well-known, such as those designed by William Morris. Thonet, however, combined the idea with an elegantly bent supporting surface for the legs to create a form adjusted more to the human body. The idea of an adjustable chaise longue with a surface which is curved twice was evidently still felt to be innovative some fifty years later and given

a new lease on life in designs such as chaise longue "B 306" by Le Corbusier, Perriand, and Jeanneret, as well as "Siesta Medizinal" by the Luckhardt brothers.

Moreover, "Rocking Sofa" is an outstanding example of how the utility value of a piece of furniture can be translated into a decorative language. The transparent construction of the elegantly curved bentwood already conveys a sense of hovering, softly swinging movement in use. While the back forms an unbroken line with the armrests and the front curves of the runners, the reach of the leg supports is taken up by the scrolls under the back. Here, the crossed-over curved runners seem to consist of one long rod of bentwood. In actual fact, two pieces are

involved, which are butt-joint together prior to the intersection of the cross. Variants of the design are to be found in the Gebrüder Thonet sales catalogues, offered like the "Rocking Sofa" at a comparatively dear price and presumably sold only in small numbers: one is not a rocker but a chaise longue positioned on four large volutes; another is a so-called "Garten-Fahrsofa" (garden mobile sofa) with an adjustable back and wheels in the rear axle, enabling the bulky item to be pulled across a lawn.

Jakob & Josef Kohn, a company that copied numerous Thonet designs at the time, also offered a rocking chaise longue, but it was by no means as elegant. *MSC*

< From a Russian Thonet catalogue, 1902
∟ "Garten-Fahrsofa" by Thonet, 1883-4
∨ "Reclining Couch No. 2 with adjustable head" by Thonet, 1883-4

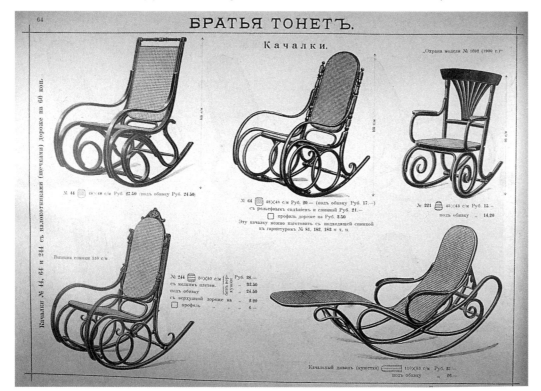

76

Name: No. 371
Designer: Josef Hoffmann
Design: 1905-6
Production: c.1906-1910

Manufacturer: Jakob & Josef Kohn, Vienna
Size: 109.5 x 44 x 50.5; seat height 47 cms
Material: bent and turned beech wood,
formed plywood

Like his "Sitzmaschine," this chair was designed by Josef Hoffmann for a country house, exhibited at the Vienna Art Show in 1908.
The chair stands out above all for its bold back, reminiscent of an upright spine. It emerges from the sturdy back legs which taper as they move upward and form two slender high arches connected by seven balls in the central axle. The chair was frequently called the "Seven Ball Chair" as a consequence.
The balls are repeated in the angles between seat and chair legs. Here they have not only

a decorative but also a constructive function, as they stabilize the joints. The saddle-shaped plywood seat offers a pleasant supporting surface and its rounded form with an upward thrust blends visually with the sturdy base.
The motif of the balls framed in the bentwood struts was probably first used as a decorative wall frieze, when in 1901-2 Jacob & Josef Kohn presented some of the company's interior designs at the Winter Exhibition of the Austrian Museum for Art and Industry. Evidently, this

prefigured the coming schism and the turn away from the symbolist trend of the Viennese Secession, moving instead toward a geometric idiom borrowed from architecture. With the craftsmanship orientation of the "Wiener Werkstätten," which Hoffmann with the architect Koloman Moser and the banker Fritz Wärndorfer founded in 1903, any allusions to the floral Art Nouveau disappeared from his work. *MSC*

^ J. & J. Kohn installation, Winter Exhibition of the Austrian Museum for Art and Industry, Vienna, 1901-2
Γ From a J. & J. Kohn catalogue, 1909

77
Name: Peacock Chair (Imperial Hotel)
Designer: Frank Lloyd Wright
Design: 1921-2
Production: unknown

Manufacturer: unknown Japanese company
Size: 96 x 38 x 50; seat height 44 cms
Material: oak, oil cloth covering, metal

The interior design of a house, and the fitted or movable furniture in it, up to and including lamps and even musical instruments, had a fixed place in the architecture of Frank Lloyd Wright. He regarded this as the ornamental extension of his buildings, just as he believed the buildings were abstractions and organic extensions of their environment.

A Constructivist aesthetics was in the foreground of his work, whereby an internal harmony of freedom and calmness was meant to pervade the outer form. To his mind, the unity of a city, a house, or an item of furniture depended on the integration of its parts, and each form had at the same time to reflect its origin. Wright believed that ornamentation was an essential expression of creative imagination, which produces "natural patterns to structure itself." [19]

He designed the "Peacock Chair," with its complicated and concentrated ornamentation for the Imperial Hotel in Tokyo, which was built between 1915 and 1922 – in terms of ground plan, elevation, and decoration the building is considered one of his most complex works.

The hexagons in the back and on the sides of the chair's base are also encountered in numerous places in the building: in the ceilings, on walls, and even in a coffee set designed by Wright. Since the chairs were quite fragile, they were changed at least three times in the life of the hotel, which was torn down in 1968. The presumably earliest models had wicker seat, sides, and back and a loose upholstered cushion. *MSC*

^ Aerial view of the Imperial Hotel, Tokyo
> F. L. Wright: "Peacock Room" of the Imperial Hotel in Tokyo

78

Name: Bibliothèque pour la maison de la Tunisie
Designer: Charlotte Perriand
Design: 1952
Production: 1953

Manufacturer: Les Ateliers Jean Prouvé, Maxéville, France
Size: 159.5 x 352.5 x 53 cms
Material: varnished wood, varnished sheet aluminum

At the beginning of the fifties, André Bloc, at that time publisher of the magazine *L'Architecture d'Aujourd'hui*, launched the group Espace. Its goal was to forge links between artists from the fields of painting, architecture, sculpture, and industry. The design for a student dormitory built by Jean Sebag for Tunisian university students in Paris was the first challenge the group faced. Bloc commissioned the designer Charlotte Perriand to handle the interior of forty rooms. Her spectacular shelves, which strongly influenced the overall impression of the rooms, were created in collaboration with artist Sonia Delaunay, who chose the colors, and Jean Prouvé's studio, which produced Perriand's

design. The idea was based on a simple shelf of blocks placed on top of each other and shelves made of wood, a plan Perriand had formerly realized together with Pierre Jeanneret.
In the case of shelves for the dormitory, metal tension rods hold the wood floors together. Colored aluminum panels can be pushed back and forth in front of the compartments made of bent sheet metal, rhythmically ordered to generate different color compositions. The shelf proper is positioned eccentrically on a long bench which forms a visual counterpoint to the dynamic of the colors. The overall construction rests on two elliptical feet made of wood. Below the bench, the shelf was supported in addition by

a wall mounting and functioned as the central eye-catcher in the rooms, which also featured colored furniture.
The shelf brings the "ESU" shelf series to mind, designed by Charles and Ray Eames shortly before. However, Charlotte Perriand's design stands out for its independent expressiveness, which furthers the purpose for which it was created: French art, industry, and craftsmanship are represented here in meaningful harmony. In addition to a further model for the rooms of the Mexican dormitory, other variants also exist. *MSC*

< C. Perriand: Room in the dormitory for Tunisian students, Cité Universitaire, Paris, 1953
└ Sonia Delaunay: *Rythme coloré,* 1953

79

Name: Marshmallow
Designer: George Nelson
Design: 1956
Production: 1956 - c. 1965

Manufacturer: Herman Miller Furniture
Company, Zeeland, Michigan
Size: 77 x 131.5 x 80; seat height 42 cms
Material: varnished steel tubing, aluminum,
vinyl cushions

George Nelson is one of the most influential personalities in U.S. design after 1945. As of 1946 he was for many years head of the Design Department at the Herman Miller company, on whose behalf he engaged designers hardly known at the time, such as Charles Eames, Isamu Noguchi, and Alexander Girard. And he was also inspired by other areas of culture: along with his work as an architect, he concerned himself with ongoing sociological and artistic themes.

Nelson's "Marshmallow" sofa must be considered one of the earliest Pop Art furniture designs: the transformation of a traditional sofa into a three-dimensional structure made of soft, colored cushioning. The seat and back are supported by a steel construction and the unit has the shape of an axially symmetrical folded-out waffle. Unlike traditional upholstered sofas, it was possible to make it available in numerous colors and sizes thanks to what was at the time a

completely novel, additive construction system. However, production required costly labor inputs; additionally, the unorthodox sofa hardly seemed to fit in contemporary interiors. Production at Herman Miller was therefore discontinued around 1965.
From 1988 to 1994, Vitra produced the "Marshmallow" sofa again. *MSC*

Andy Warhol: *100 Soup Cans*, 1969

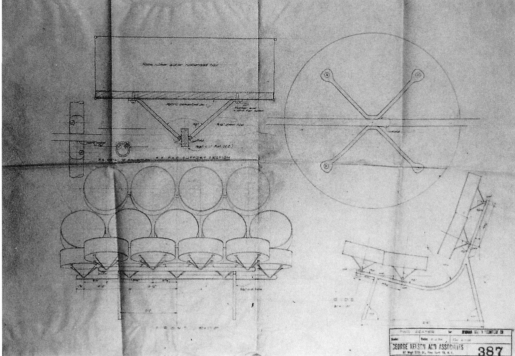

George Nelson Associates: Drawing for "Marshmallow," 1956

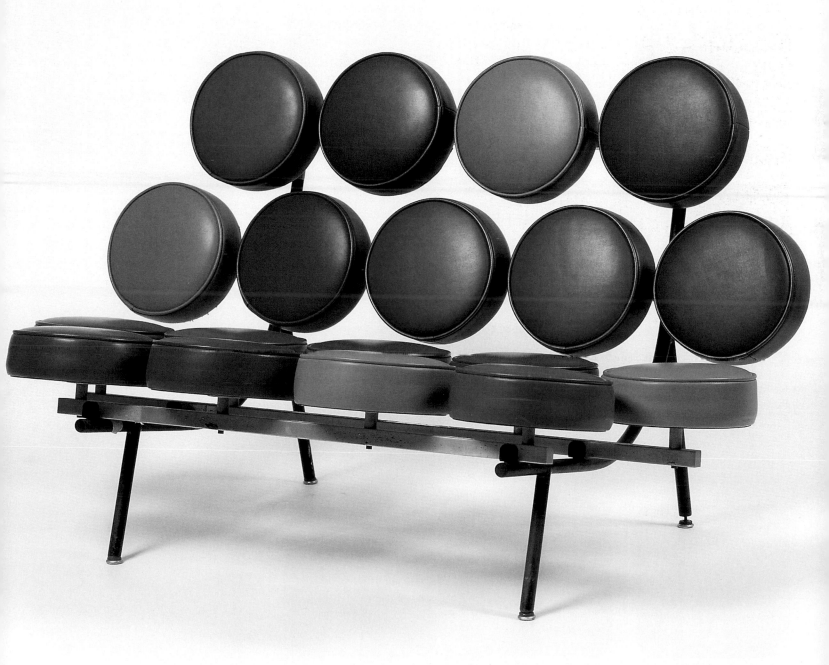

80

Name: M400
Designer: Roger Tallon
Design: 1964
Production: 1966-75

Manufacturer: Éditions Lacloche, Paris
Size: 86 x 38 x 45; seat height 44 cms
Material: polished cast aluminum,
polyester foam

Roger Tallon has made a name for himself as an industrial designer and, among other projects, worked on the design of the French high-speed train, the TGV.

In 1964 he created a series of chairs, stools and tables each with a floorspace of 400 x 400 mm (hence the name "Module 400"), measurements which corresponded to the size of the metal floor panels in the Parisian discotheque for which the furniture was intended. The resulting system was flexible yet could be firmly fixed in place; the uniqueness of the upholstery was further accentuated by the fact that the chairs blended in with the floor. The series was also marketed in furniture stores.

The elegant columnar base consisting of two cones is reminiscent of the "Tulip Chair" designed in 1956 by Eero Saarinen. However, instead of repeating the roundness of the column in the base and seat, Tallon creates a contrast using rectangular forms that are covered with untreated, gray pyramid-shaped pieces of foam. The nippled side of this packing material is turned outward and, despite its bizarre, cold effect, in fact affords some degree of comfort. The contrast between the carefully designed aluminum base column and the industrial *objet trouvé* (both high-tech products) engenders a hybrid and somewhat Surrealist piece of furniture.

The sound-absorbing effect of the foam, which is used in recording studios, was also a factor in furnishing the discotheque. This effect is enhanced if a large number of chairs are unoc-cupied, and creates similar acoustic conditions to those of a crowded discotheque, in which the customers themselves dampen the sound. *MK*

^From a 1966 Éditions Lacloche brochure
< Series "M400," from a 1966 Éditions Lacloche brochure

81

Name: Poltrona di Proust
Designer: Alessandro Mendini
Design: 1978
Production: since 1978

Manufacturer: Studio Alchimia, Milan
Size: 107 x 105 x 94; seat height 35 cms
Material: painted wood, painted upholstery

The "Proust" chair is the most famous design by Italian designer Alessandro Mendini, a highly influential champion of design in the eighties. As designer, journalist, and teacher, he has traced the cultural and substantive issues in the field of design, often working closely with related disciplines such as art, architecture, philosophy, and literature. Two of his basic ideas are essential for an understanding of his work: on the one hand, design today must be aware of its position within a nexus of existing ideas and images; on the other, according to Mendini, it can only be expressed externally and on the surface of things, if it is to convey its messages to a trivial, fast-moving world.

In 1978, with the "Proust" chair, Mendini programmatically began a furniture series of so-called "redesigns" in which he reinterpreted the shape and ornamentation of existing designs that were typical of their day. Two years previously, he had begun work on a fabric pattern for Cassina which was to be a reflection on French author Marcel Proust. While researching the upper-middle-class environment associated with Proust, Mendini came across a copy of a chair in the Neo-Baroque style of eighteenth-century France. Inspired by this discovery, he expanded the fabric project to yield a furniture design. He covered the chair completely with a colorful, handpainted swarm of dots which reproduced an enlarged section of a Pointillist painting by Paul Signac. Impressionism, which attempted to recreate the atmospheric appearance of nature through painting, was highly valued by Proust, and its presence here is a reference to the author and his time. However, by equally painting all parts of the chair, irrespective of their structure and purpose, Mendini succeeds in citing not only Impressionism but also the Baroque, using the infinite as a central motif. Impressionist painting and the Baroque are imitated and trivialized in the pattern of the "Poltrona di Proust," turning the chair into a flickering vision imbued with meaning. Classic design qualities such as originality, a functional construction, or cost-saving production are thereby fundamentally called into question. The armchair was originally conceived as the only one of its kind, but variations were later manufactured by Mendini's studio as individual pieces or in limited editions. *MSC*

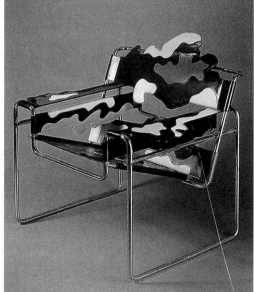

⌐ Paul Signac: *Balise rouge,* 1895
∧ A. Mendini: Staircase in the Museum of Groningen, 1994
⌐ A. Mendini: Redesign of the "Wassily" by Marcel Breuer, 1979
∨ A. Mendini: Swatch clock "Lots of dots," 1992

82

Name: Wink
Designer: Toshiyuki Kita
Design: 1980
Production: 1980 to the present

Manufacturer: Cassina s.p.a., Milan
Size: 100 x 81 x 85; seat height 40 cms
Material: steel tubing, polyurethane foam,
polyester cushioning, fabric, plastic

Mulitfunctional furniture was a major trend in the eighties. The "Wink" chair was the first of a new generation of furniture aiming to provide such versatility. By unfolding the footrest, the chair can be transformed into a recliner, and additional covers in various colors for the seat, back, and footrest are easy to change. Japanese designer Toshiyuki Kita was no doubt inspired by the function and shape of automobile bucket seats. Like the latter, the angle of the "Wink" backrest can be smoothly adjusted by turning the knob on the side. Both parts of the headrest can be tilted completely backward if desired, thus allowing to use them as armrests when sitting sideways in the chair. Kita devoted a great deal of attention to how the individual materials could be used optimally in a design. He concluded that using recyclable materials was not enough: rather, each object had to be given the longest possible service life, something determined by material wear-and-tear as well as visual obsolescence. He thus included the extra covers to protect the places subject to the greatest wear; it can be removed and washed when dirty. If the material wears out after longer periods of use, another cover can be ordered, eliminating the need to have the chair professionally reupholstered at high cost.

The flexible construction corresponds to the interchangeable colors: these two features ensure the chair will never bore its owner. "Wink" has a cheerful appearance, in particular due to the headrests which look like Mickey Mouse ears; it thus is a favorite among children as well. *PD*

From a 1980 Cassina pamphlet

83

Name: Carlton
Designer: Ettore Sottsass Jr.
Design: 1981
Production: 1981 to the present

Manufacturer: Memphis s.r.l., Pregnana
Milanese, near Milan
Size: 195.5 x 190 x 40 cms
Material: wood, laminated plastic

When the Milan design group Memphis gave the first public presentation of their work in September 1981, the Ettore Sottsass room divider "Carlton" was among the most noted pieces. "Carlton" symbolizes essential traits of the style which as a consequence of Memphis became known almost overnight as New Design. Mundane and depthless laminated materials are trademarks of Memphis. Their aseptic, bold superficiality makes them the ideal medium for a new, decorative aesthetic. The iconography of the patterns is the result of blending graphic or geometric structures, imitation marble or wood, African symbols, comic strips, and loud colors. (The base of "Carlton," for example, shows the first ornamentation designed by Sottsass, the

"Bacterio" patterns from 1978). As in the world of telecommunications, the viewer no longer perceives an object in itself, but rather a medium that catches the eye by virtue of its surface and structure, and which triggers sensory perceptions.

Despite their provocative nature, Sottsass designs are always based on precise relationships between individual parts. Thus, the colors of "Carlton" are carefully matched, and the structure is based on the imaginary form of a rhombus. Ornamentation and construction create a unity conveying the "software," or the object's expressive contents. Traditional wall shelving, with its horizontal and vertical structure, is turned into a multipurpose, dynamic, encom-

passing object that, like a sculpture, claims the right to stand unrestricted in its own space. "Carlton" can be completely dismantled, which is a considerable advantage given its consider-able weight.

The anthropomorphic image on the green shelf unit reminds one of a juggler or a totem figure and lends a cultish feel to the furniture. This combination of meaningful symbolism and rampant consumerism is typical for Sottsass, who derives great inspiration from Indian culture.

Sottsass left Memphis in 1985, after the group had evolved from an experiment into a commercially successful venture. *MK*

E. Sottsass: Cupboard shelf, 1964

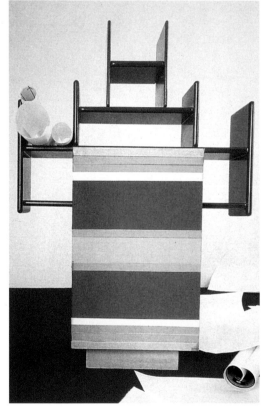

E. Sottsass: "Il Harakiri dell'architetto," 1966

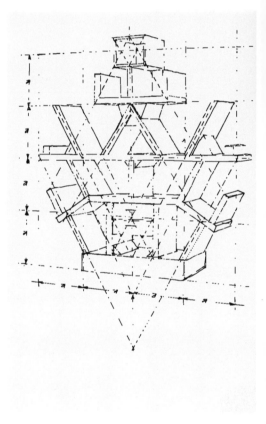

Axel Müller-Schöll: Scale study of "Carlton"

84

Name: Queen Anne
Designer: Robert Venturi
Design: 1979-84
Production: 1984 to the present

Manufacturer: Knoll International, Inc.,
New York
Size: 98 x 68 x 61; seat height 49 cms
Material: molded multiplex, laminated
plastic, imitation leather cushions

Since the publication of his influential 1966 essay *Complexity and Contradiction in Architecture*, American architect Robert Venturi has been considered one of the founders of Postmodernism. He vividly described the principle underlying this style as "both – and" instead of "either – or," and brilliantly countered Mies van der Rohe's tenet of classic Modernity that "less is more" with "less is a bore."[20] Venturi's most famous furniture design consists of a series of nine chairs, which he designed for Knoll International between 1979 and 1984. By means of clichéd simplification, his chairs cite models from United States' and European furniture history, ranging from the eighteenth-century Queen Anne chair to Art Deco of the thirties. Venturi was interested in the image, the representative side, of these models. Thus, his two-piece structure for "Queen Anne" is based on sawed-out and bent laminated wood panels for the back, legs, and seat which presents the chair as a silhouette copy, a backdrop. The "Queen Anne" chair shown here was presumably inspired by a Giles Grendey design dating from 1730 on display in the New York Metropolitan Museum. When seen from the side, the chair brings to mind the plywood furniture of Alvar Aalto or Marcel Breuer from the thirties; at the same time, the surfaces have been printed on both sides, revealing just how solid they are. The so-called "Grandmother" pattern on the surface, which Venturi also used to upholster one of his sofas, is similar to the laminates designed by the Milan Memphis group around the same time. In fact, the pattern consists of two motifs superimposed upon each other: a favorite tablecloth of the grandmother of colleague Robert Schwartz, and diagonal stripes, a quotation from paintings by artist Jasper Johns.

The numerous possibilities for the shapes and patterns in which the furniture is available result in complex, thoroughly contradictory statements. They are both an ironic commentary as well as an affirmation of the desire on the part of the consumer society to be linked into in a historic continuity. *MSC*

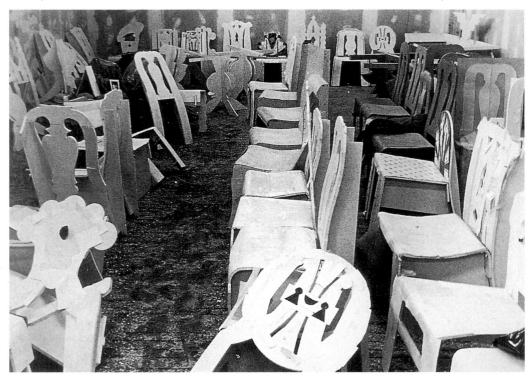

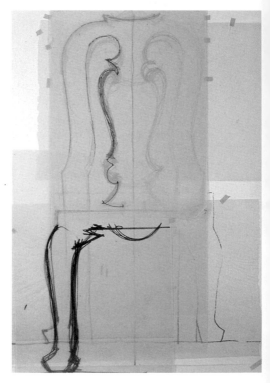

∧ Studies of Venturi's furniture series for Knoll
⌐ R. Venturi: Study for "Queen Anne," c. 1981
> R. Venturi: Candlesticks for Swid Powell, 1986

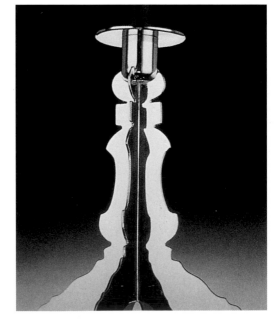

85

Name: How High The Moon
Designer: Shiro Kuramata
Design: 1986
Production: 1987 to the present

Manufacturer: Vitra AG, Basel
Size: 73 x 95 x 82; seat height 36 cms
Material: nickel-plated rib mesh

Shiro Kuramata, one of Japan's most prominent designers, explored the possibilities for furniture design presented by unusual new materials such as Plexiglas and rib mesh. He traced the expressive capacity of these materials, and, by tapping the psychological effect they could have, created objects that straddled the borderline between function and suggestion. In the chair entitled "How High The Moon," named after a jazz piece by Duke Ellington, the gleaming, dematerialized surface evokes pale moonlight and weightlessness. Kuramata has reduced the back, armrests, and seat to simple, cube-shaped forms and soldered them together to form a surprisingly lightweight chair. The generous proportions and the elasticity of the rib mesh guarantee the necessary sitting comfort. A weighty symbol of bourgeois life was translated into the idiom of Postmodern industrial aesthetics, and transposed from the living-room into the universe. *MK*

∧ S. Kuramata: Issey Miyake boutique, Tokyo, 1987
⅂ S. Kuramata: "Homage to Josef Hofmann," 1986
〉 S. Kuramata: Sketch of "How High The Moon"

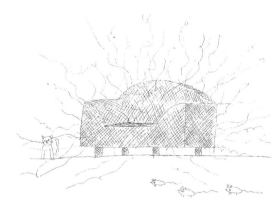

86

Name: Toledo
Designer: Jorge Pensi
Design: 1986-8
Production: 1989 to the present

Manufacturer: Amat s.a., Martorell, Barcelona
Size: 77 x 56 x 56.5; seat height 44.5 cms
Material: epoxy-coated cast aluminum and aluminum tubing

Jorge Pensi originally designed the stackable "Toledo" chair for the terraces of Spanish street cafés. Today, however, the chair is available in four different versions, and its uses range from gardens via cafés to conference rooms. Lightness and stability characterize both the material chosen, namely cast aluminum, as well as the construction itself. The obvious stability of the chair may have given it its name (during the Middle Ages the Toledo fort was considered impregnable). The slits, inspired by the slits in Japanese Samurai armor, enable the chair to be used outdoors, as they provide both ventilation and rainwater drainage. In combination with an artistic, carefully worked out design for the backrest and seat, the "Toledo" slits form a symbolic unity which leaves a lasting impression. The armrests are not an extension of the aluminum tube that forms the front and rear legs, but were instead manufactured using the more expensive casting process. This attests to the effort to give ergonomics and aesthetics precedence over cheaper methods of production. The natural curves of the interconnections of the individual parts and the perforated elements bring to mind the formal idiom of architect Antoni Gaudí, a prominent figure in Barcelona. Designers such as Jorge Pensi, who with his "Toledo" chair has succeeded in creating a synthesis of local heritage and highly developed industrial design, have helped Barcelona become one of the centers of design in Europe. *MK*

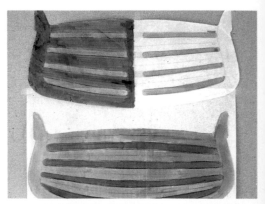

≪ J. Pensi: Colour study for "Toledo," 1986
∧ Antoni Gaudí: Chairs from the Calvet house, 1898-1904
< From an Amat pamphlet

87
Name: Miss Blanche
Designer: Shiro Kuramata
Design: 1988
Production: 1989 to the present

Manufacturer: Kuramata Design Office, Tokyo
Size: 90.5 x 62.5 x 60; seat height 45.5 cms
Material: acrylic resin, plastic, epoxy-coated aluminum tubes

The "Miss Blanche" armchair is named after the central figure in the Tennessee Williams drama *A Streetcar Named Desire*. Kuramata's Plexiglas roses refer to the dreamlike world of illusion in which Blanche lives. The use of nature as an ornament is reinterpreted by means of a technological process. In keeping with our world of perfected illusions, ornamentation is no longer merely superficial. Rather, it is nature preserved in a dreamlike state of suspense between presence and inaccessability. The contrast between the ultra-modern materials and the reduced design of the armchair underscores the archetypal symbolism of the rose.
The imitation roses are poured by hand into a mold with liquid acrylic resin, which can be processed at room temperature. The mixture then dries slowly. The air bubbles that develop around the roses have to be suctioned off, a costly procedure. In the end, the acrylic glass is the reason why the chair is so immensely heavy, weighing in at seventy kilos, a sharp contrast to its dematerialized appearance.
By handling his materials in a poetic way, Kuramata creates objects that appear to have transcended the laws of gravity and function. *MK*

S. Kuramata: 'bAP' bar, 1989

Manifesto

There are items of furniture which serve as especially good representative examples of the fundamental ideas of a group of designers or of the character of a cultural movement. Their importance has less to do with their direct use and more to do with the radical way in which they present a critique of existing notions and a new vision of a culture of living. They are not always based on a manifesto laid down in writing. Rather, their message stems from their expressive impact, in which the borderline between applied and the fine arts disappears.

The ideas of the De Stijl group and of the Bauhaus, formulated at the beginning of the century, had a long-lasting influence on the culture of the home. As society and consumer behavior have become ever more differentiated, the number of concepts has increased, so that their respective significance has dwindled: a development parallel to that in the fine arts, in architecture, and in music. The Pop Art of the sixties was perhaps the last programmatic movement that seized hold of all these disciplines and decisively shaped the outward appearance of international furniture design. *MSC*

88

Name: Roodblauwe stoel
Designer: Gerrit Thomas Rietveld
Design: 1918
Production: since 1918

Manufacturer: Gerard van de Groenekan, Utrecht
Size: 86 x 66 x 82.5; seat height 32 cms
Material: varnished wood

■

Gerrit Rietveld conceived of each piece of furniture as an ideal, abstract composition of surfaces and lines in space. The rigor with which he put this into practice makes "Roodblauwe stoel" a key object in modern furniture design. The form of abstraction Rietveld adopts here bears comparison to painter Piet Mondrian. Mondrian, and later Rietveld, were among the artists and architects who grouped around Theo van Doesburg and his journal *De Stijl*, and whose radical concepts had a lasting impact on twentieth-century art. Both Mondrian and Rietveld reduced given realities to their linear and surface characteristics: where Mondrian took landscapes as his model, Rietveld focused on the concept of a traditional, massive armchair, which he transformed into a geometric entity. In doing so, as Rietveld himself explains, he was concerned with joining "the components without crippling them, so that to the greatest degree possible the one is not dominated or made dependent on the other; most importantly, the work in its entirety must be able to stand freely and brightly on its own two feet, and the form must triumph over the material."[21]

The followers of "De Stijl" adopted the "Roodblauwe stoel," at that point still in its first, unpainted version, as their manifesto. It was the initial object which served to illustrate the principles of the group to the public at large, and provided Theo van Doesburg with an outstanding example of furniture as "abstract, realistic sculptures for our future interiors."[22] However, Rietveld's own remarks raise doubts as to whether he, like van Doesburg, actually claimed to be pursuing the social utopia of universal harmony. He apparently did not believe that his furniture could contribute to causing universal social change, and built it primarily for himself and his private acquaintances. As a result, there is no specific prototype of the chair, only a number of variations which have relatively little in common. As Reyer Kras, curator of the Stedelijk Museum in Amsterdam, writes, Rietveld was evidently conscious of the fact "that formal order has nothing to do with precalculated, strictly repeated sizes and proportions, but rather is exclusively the domain of a good eye."[23] However, Rietveld felt it should in principle be possible to produce his chair on an industrial

scale. The elements used were excellently suited both for self-assembly furniture and for mass production, as they could be manufactured with the simplest mechanical means and were already available as standardized wood lengths. The first version of the "Roodblauwe stoel," still unpainted and somewhat larger than the later model, as well as having side panels under the armrests, was built by Rietveld around 1918, in other words shortly before he joined De Stijl. The well-known version – from which the design took its final name – with its red back, blue seat, and yellow front on black struts, first appeared alongside different-colored variations around 1923, when Rietveld already belonged to the inner circle of the group. The differentiation of the colors on the surfaces further underscores the contrast between the abstract form and the material quality of the furniture. The Italian company Cassina has been manufacturing this version of the chair since 1973. *MSC*

⌃ G. Rietveld: Color study for the Schröder house, 1924
⌐ G. Rietveld sitting in front of his workshop, second from left: G. Groenekan, 1918
≫ G. Rietveld: Interior of the Schröder house
⟩ G. Rietveld: Original version of the "Roodblauwe stoel," 1918

89

Name: B 3, Wassily
Designer: Marcel Breuer
Design: 1925
Production: 1926-7

Manufacturer: Standard Möbel
Lengyel & Co., Berlin
Size: 72.5 x 76.5 x 69.5; seat height 43 cms
Material: cold bent, nickel-plated tubular
steel; polished-yarn fabric

■

Steel tubing was first used for hospital furniture as of about 1890, for car seats by Czech manufacturer Tatra starting in 1919, and for airplane seats in the Fokker plants as of 1924. It was first introduced to home furnishings with Breuer's steel club armchair, which marked an aesthetic turning point in furniture production as well as the start of an important branch of industry. Although the chair was not a direct product of the Bauhaus workshops, its history is a perfect example of the spirit underlying this influential institution. For Bauhaus followers, industrial production was " the most modern means of design,"[24] as Walter Gropius, the founder of Bauhaus, wrote in 1923 – and thus its economic and aesthetic model. The choice of material and construction clearly place "B 3" in an industrial context that Breuer expected would lend living a more functional aspect: "This metal furniture is to be nothing more than a necessary device for modern-day living."[25]

Breuer's enthusiasm with the stability of his newly procured Adler bicycle gave him the idea of using tubular steel to make furniture. At that time, he was the director of the Bauhaus wood workshop in Dessau. He first turned to the bicycle manufacturer in 1925 in the hope of realizing his idea. However, Adler was not interested in furniture production. He then commissioned Mannesmann, the company which had developed the seamless cold-draw process for tubular steel in 1885–6, to bend the necessary components into the proper shape. Subsequently, he employed the services of a plumber and collaborated with him in building the first prototypes. In the same year – perhaps a historical coincidence – Le Corbusier presented a staircase made of tubular steel in the Pavillon de l'Esprit Nouveau in Paris, a staircase that was built "like a bicycle frame."[26]

The most important innovation of Breuer's design lay in reducing the basic design of a heavy club armchair to a light frame made of welded steel tubes. The "B 3" also reveals the influence that Gerrit Rietveld's furniture had on Marcel Breuer's Bauhaus designs, as the position of the seat and backrest clearly evokes Rietveld's

"Roodblauwe stoel." To a far greater extent than with wood structures, the reflective nickel-plated surfaces of the steel tubes rendered the construction transparent, an effect further enhanced by reducing the surfaces to thin lengths of fabric. Breuer's ideal, which he formulated in a film from 1926, was to make sitters think they were sitting on "springy columns of air."[27] The taut material prevents the user from coming in contact with the cold steel parts of the complex frame, and, in addition, forms an appealing contrast to the metal. In deciding upon the upholstery, which was to mirror the shine of the tubular steel, Breuer first considered a horsehair weave, which proved to be too expensive and too complicated to work with. Furthermore, he discovered that it was unstable, as the loops around the steel tubes broke easily. Finally, so-called "Eisengarn" was developed in keeping with Breuer's concept. This material was used in many subsequent designs, such as the "B 35." In what is presumably the first version, known only from a photograph, the welded frame of the tubular steel chair had four separate legs and the backrest was shaped like an upright U. The next version was sold as the "B 3" by Standard Möbel, a company founded by Breuer, Kálmán Lengyel, and Anton Lorenz in 1926 to market Breuer's designs. The first "B 3" consisted of nine separate welded parts. The seat and back were separate units in a frame consisting of an endless loop of tubular steel, in which both pairs of legs were joined together to form parallel runners that served as the base. Breuer had most likely discovered this motif in the nearby Junker airplane factory, where the runners of the worktables enabled them to be pushed aside more easily. Standard Möbel then made additional changes to the design: to start, the components of the construction were no longer welded, but instead were held together with screws, nuts, and slot-in connectors. The back was no longer made of a U-shaped tube, but was now constructed of two separate L-shaped side pieces attached to the seat with screws. When taken apart, more than fifty chairs can be stored in a crate measuring just one cubic meter,

even more than Thonet's legendary model "No. 14." In a later stage of development, the back was stabilized by bringing together the side pieces to form an arch at the top. In 1929 Standard Möbel was bought by Thonet, which kept "B 3" in its program for only two years, but during that time made even further changes: both runners were braced with a straight cross-strut, and instead of the connector located in front of the seat, which interfered with the sitter's legs, a bent cross strut that ran under the upholstery was used to strengthen the seat frame. In 1962 production was relaunched by the Italian company Gavina, which was later acquired by Knoll. In honor of Bauhaus master Wassily Kandinsky, who from early on had called attention to the revolutionary aesthetics of the chair, Gavina dubbed it "Wassily," as it is popularly known today.

Initially "B 3" only caught the admiring attention of architects, designers, artists, and visitors at the Bauhaus in Dessau, where it stood in a number of homes in the master's settlement. At Breuer's 1926 solo exhibition at the Kunsthalle in Dresden, the chair was already being acclaimed as a masterpiece. Breuer's fascination for space-saving collapsible furniture also led him to design a folding version of the "B 3" in 1926, and he obtained the German patent for both models in 1927. Along with the tubular steel furniture that had meanwhile been produced by Mart Stam, Mies van der Rohe, and others, Breuer presented his chair at the prestigious exhibit "Die Wohnung" (the apartment) in Stuttgart. For the first time, industry and the public at large were able to feast their eyes on the "B 3." People quickly learned to appreciate tubular steel furniture due to its lightness, hygienic qualities, and resistance to wear-and-tear. In the thirties, it even became a fashion in its own right, and today is the epitome of the spirit of Modernity in the first half of the twentieth-century. *MSC*

1929 flyer from Thonet Frères, Paris

First version of the "B 3," 1925

90

Name: MR 90, Barcelona Chair
Designer: Ludwig Mies van der Rohe
Design: 1929
Production: 1929-30

Manufacturer: Berliner Metallgewerbe
Josef Müller, Berlin
Size: 75 x 76 x 77; seat height 43 cms
Material: chrome-plated steel strip,
leather belts, leather cushions

■

Mies van der Rohe designed the German pavilion and corresponding furniture for the 1929 world's fair in Barcelona. Among other things, his pavilion served as the setting for the inaugural ceremony led by the Spanish royal couple, Alfonso XIII and Victoria Eugenia.
While Mies van der Rohe implemented his ideas of avant-garde steel and glass architecture for the building design, he drew his inspiration for the furniture from historic models.
Mies van der Rohe took as his starting point the ancient, scissors-shaped collapsible folding chair, already a symbol of power among Egyptian rulers. In ancient Greece, this chair represented the throne used by gods and mortal rulers alike, and in the Roman empire served as a magistrate's chair, *sella curulis* (curule chair). It had been manufactured in various cultures – in particular on the Iberian peninsula – through to modern times, although it has lost its previous importance. It owed this popularity to its clever folding mechanism, variations of which gave rise to the deck chairs found on large oceanliners at the beginning of the century.
In keeping with the occasion, Mies van der Rohe adopts the representative qualities of the scissors chair, although he does without the

folding function and interprets it afresh.
In order to match the overall impression of luxury in the pavilion, evoked by wall panels made of onyx and marble, as well as delicate, chrome-plated steel supports and stained glass of various colors, Mies van der Rohe chose not to use wood like the historic models, but instead employed chrome-plated steel strip and white leather upholstery with button stitching. Despite the use of different materials, various features in the construction of the first series bring to mind the model made of wood.
While the gently curved pieces of strip steel that form the sides were generously welded at the intersections, the right and left sides were joined with steel transverse braces of equal diameter. These were mounted with screws, using the "square corner halving process" employed in wood-frame construction.
Subsequently, this form of assembly was shifted from the corners to the interior of the frame, as the screws could be hidden there behind the leather straps. A number of variations on the joints from this early production phase are known, all of which were extremely costly. In 1948 they were finally replaced by a frame that was welded throughout. At the same time,

the volume of the welded points of intersection on the sides was reduced, lowering the need for regrinding and polishing of the welds. Finally, as of 1964, the chrome-plated steel strip was replaced with polished high-grade steel.
A feature common to all variations is the weave of the leather upholstery, which evokes the alternating cross pattern of the slats used in the wood chairs.
Interior photographs of the Tugendhat house in Brno, Czechoslovakia, built a year after the Barcelona pavilion, already show variations on the frame with different numbers of straps, for example the version with square corner halving shown here. This feature classifies it as belonging to the first batch produced by Berliner Metallgewerbe Josef Müller in Berlin.
The pavilion was torn down after the fair. However, along with the furniture, it was retrospectively acknowledged as a showcase for the International Style that had taken hold throughout the world.
The Barcelona pavilion was reconstructed and rebuilt in 1986. *PD*

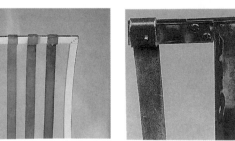
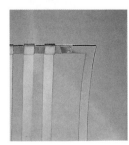
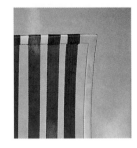

⌐ Folding chair, anonymous, 1927-8
⌃ German pavilion at the Barcelona world's fair, 1929
‹ Variations on the frame for the "Barcelona" chair in chronological order

91

Name: Mezzadro
Designer: Achille and Pier Giacomo Castiglioni
Design: 1954-7
Production: 1970 to the present

Manufacturer: Zanotta s.p.a., Nova Milanese, near Milan
Size: 52 x 49 x 53,5; seat height 52 cms
Material: chromed steel, beech wood, lacquered sheet steel

■

The first model of the "Mezzadro" (sharecropper) was presented at the X. Milan Triennial in 1954. It was part of the theme "Art and Production," and belonged conceptually to the section "Industrial Design" which was mainly devised by the Castiglioni brothers. Within the scope of the exhibition, they presented around 150 design objects from all over the world, organizing these according to formal and typological aspects. Drawings, photos and especially informative semifinished products were displayed as explanations for the objects. At the dawn of the era of the rejuvenation of the Italian economy, people in Italy were not merely concerned with satisfying primary functional needs but in infusing everyday culture with some kind of aesthetics. Thus, it was not enough for form to follow function – the main tenet of Functionalism. Instead, the functions were analyzed so as to determine their optimal visual form. In order to do this, Achille and Pier Giacomo Castiglioni drew on well-known forms which they felt left no room for improvement, and related them to one another in new contexts. This procedure for *objets trouvés* or ready-mades brings to mind works by Marcel Duchamp (e.g., *Bicycle Wheel*, 1913) or, to a limited extent, those of Pablo Picasso (*Assemblage: Tête de taureau*, 1943). The Castiglionis used a typical tractor seat for their springy metal seat, and attached it with a bicycle wing nut to a swinging strip steel bow, which in a tractor absorbs the jolts that result from driving on uneven ground. They stabilized the reduced cantilever-base chair (see Mies van der Rohe's preference for strip steel) with a crossbrace which resembles the rungs of a wooden ladder. Each of these parts clearly embodies its individual task within the overall functional interplay.

The Castiglioni brothers consider an object to be successful when all superfluous elements have been removed, and the object has been reduced to its essentials, yet lent optimal formal expression.

In 1957, they presented the "Mezzadro" in its present-day form at the exhibition entitled "Colori e forme nella casa d'oggi" at Villa Olmo in Como, which contained pieces chosen according to these very criteria, including a Thonet bentwood chair, "No.18," and the "Sella," a telephone seat.

"Mezzadro" first went into production in 1970, at which time it received its present name. Together with the Castiglionis' design for a stool entitled "Primate," it was the only piece from the extensive Zanotta collection on exhibit at the 1970 Milan furniture fair. *PD*

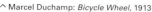

^ Marcel Duchamp: *Bicycle Wheel*, 1913
⌐ A. and P. G. Castiglioni: Installation "Colori e forme nella casa d'oggi," Villa Olmo, Como, 1957
> A. and P. G. Castiglioni: Prototype of the "Mezzadro," 1954
» A. and P. G. Castiglioni: "Sgabello per telefono," "Mezzadro," and "Sedile per mungitore"

92

Name: Pratone
Designer: Gruppo Strum
Design: 1966
Production: 1971 to the present

Manufacturer: Gufram s.r.l., Balangero, Italy
Size: 95 x 140 x 140 cms
Material: cold-foamed polyurethane,
green varnish

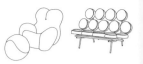

■

"Pratone" (lawn) is an allegory of a longing for nature which came to the fore during the second half of the sixties as part of the hippie protest against a glutted consumer society. Television commercials, Pop Art, and psychedelic experiences were featured via enlargement, graphic processing, and "softening." Thus, "Pratone" confronts us as an artificial, mutant, and trivialized piece of nature, sparking feelings of curiosity and conflict in the observer. The passivity of sitting is portrayed as behavior typical of consumerism and juxtaposed to sensual, archaic aspects. Users first have to create a seat from the sculptural, cold impression given by this chair. Natural landscape has become a garden landscape, and, ultimately, an interior landscape, a domesticated playground. The fact that this playground can be enlarged as one wishes by joining together a number of "Pratone" elements corresponds to the concept of community and "happenings." However, the material (green, varnished polyurethane foam) takes the yearning for nature to the point of absurdity. It is not clear whether sitting "on the lawn" is intended as a lost idyll or should be seen ironically as an outdated utopia. This is left up to the user.

At the end of the sixties, the introduction of polyurethane foam was sensational in furniture design, although there are few pieces in which the features and effects of the materials were employed as consciously and overtly as in "Pratone." The early pieces that survived until today are no longer suitable for use, as the material becomes brittle and cracked with age. Since 1986, when it was decided to limit the edition to 200 pieces, Gufram has produced sixteen "Pratone" chairs, selling them mainly to museums and galleries. At present, Gufram has manufactured a total of approximately sixty "Pratones." *MK*

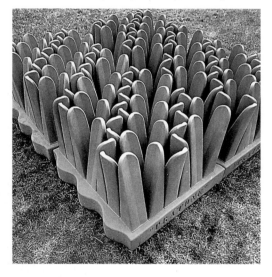

Several "Pratone" elements as a "playground"

From a Gufram pamphlet, c. 1972

Objects from limited editions by Gufram, 1986

93
Name: Pantower
Designer: Verner Panton
Design: 1968-9
Production: since 1969

Manufacturer: Herman Miller AG, Basel
Size: 200 x 200 x 67 cms
Material: wood, foam rubber, fabric

■

With his visionary, colorful home furnishings, Verner Panton sought comprehensive ways to fashion a stylistically uniform, imaginative interior. In the early sixties, he had already helped establish a color spectrum that dominated design until the mid-seventies. In the middle of the housing shortage, he promoted the principle of the high-rise and attempted to structure living space vertically.

His first design based on this concept, the "Living Tower" dating from 1965, resembles a miniature high-rise with two floors and a clearly visible metal rod construction on the outside. By contrast, his 1969 "Pantower" is a tribute to the spirit of experiment and adventure which characterized the late sixties. The furniture is divided into four seats of varying height, and opens up a multitude of new sitting and reclining possibilities. The top and bottom of the wood frame can be removed, and it has been lavishly upholstered and covered with a fluffy synthetic fabric. Thus, "Pantower" is a cuboid shape with an interior featuring natural curves that can be "mastered" either squatting, climbing, crouching, or lying down. Here, Panton supports new forms of communal living with a novel furniture concept. Epithets such as "living room wall," "living room cave," "seating tower," "living room honeycomb," "seating cave," etc., which the press used in an attempt to characterize the "Pantower," attest to the wealth of associations it inspires.

"Pantower" was manufactured for short time by Herman Miller AG, and Fritz Hansen took over production in 1970. However, only a few pieces were made as costs were too high, and production was discontinued permanently in 1975. *MK*

V. Panton: "Living Tower," 1965

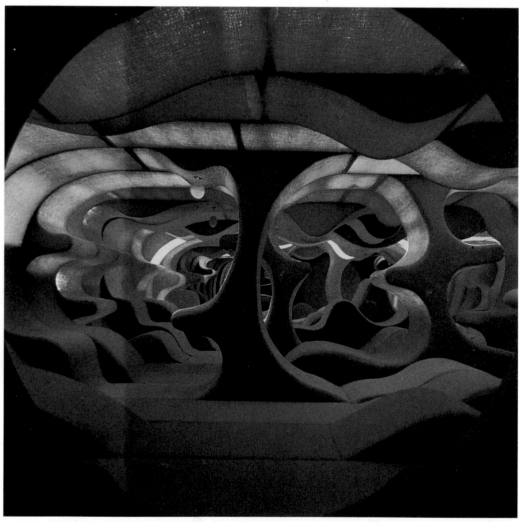

V. Panton: Interior landscape at "Visiona II" of Bayer AG at the 1970 Cologne furniture fair

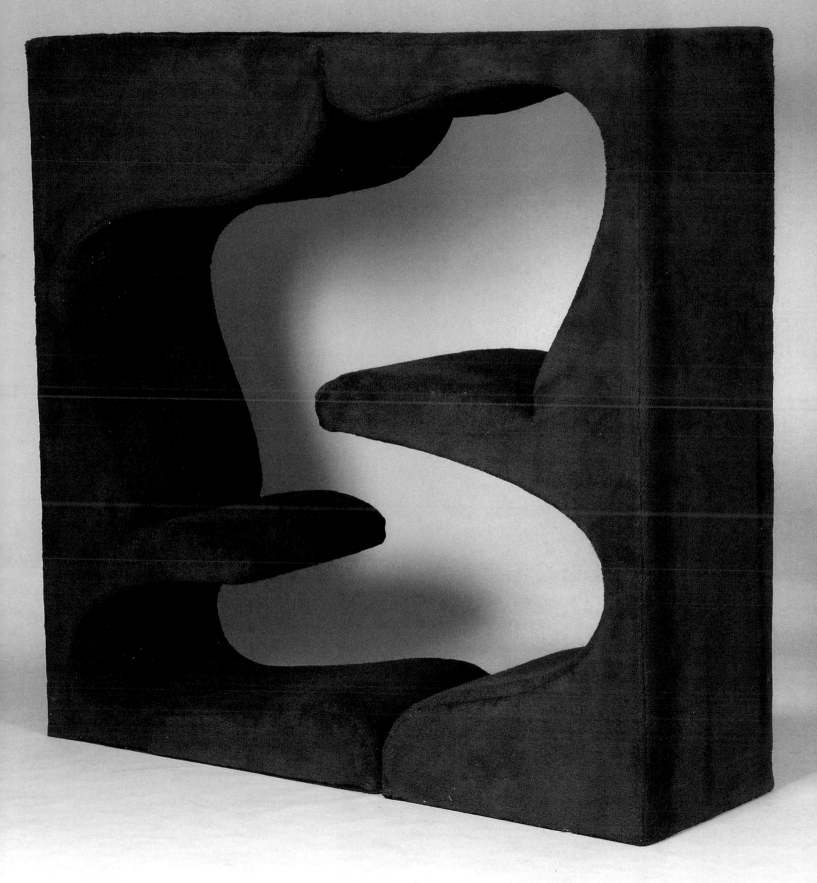

94

Name: Mies
Designer: Archizoom Associati
Design: 1969
Production: since 1969

Manufacturer: Poltronova s.r.l.,
Agliana, near Pistoia, Italy
Size: 76 x 74 x 128.5; 30 x 104.5 x 20 cms
Material: chrome-plated steel, rubber,
hide cushions, light bulb, cable with plug

■

Nineteen sixty-nine was an unusually fruitful year for formulating new ways of looking at things within the discourse on architecture and design. These can be seen as a reaction to retrospective – in other words conservative – trends in culture and society. This retrospective approach found expression in the so-called wave of nostalgia and the remake of classic Modern furniture. (Starting in 1962, Gavina began production of the "B 3" club chair by Marcel Breuer with the popular name "Wassily," taken over by Knoll in 1969; in 1964 Cassina acquired the rights to Le Corbusier's tubular steel furniture, which went into series production starting in 1965; between 1960 and 1970, Knoll considerably expanded the Mies van der Rohe Collection.) Dedicated designers saw this as an almost existential threat to the development of contemporary design, not to mention their own possibilities as designers; and they attacked unrestrained growth as a

product of misdirected consumerism. In 1966 the Archizoom Associati group in Florence not only acted as a provocative antipode to the dazzling design metropolis of Milan, but also became a seedbed of Radical Design.

The "Mies" chair reflects the ambivalent currents of this period (i.e., resuming production of tubular steel furniture despite mounting criticism of the Bauhaus and Functionalism).

Ludwig Mies van der Rohe, the last Bauhaus director, was one of the most prominent personalities of classic Modernity. (He died on August 17, 1969.) His love for detail yielded wonderfully elegant buildings and furniture which even today retain all their fascination.

In this regard, the name of the chair can superficially be understood as a kind of tribute. On the other hand, the "Mies" chair refutes the widely cited formula of Functionalism, namely that "form follows function": The seat, made of

tightly spanned latex rubber, gives the chair a wedgelike appearance when it is not in use, and thus makes it seem unfit for sitting. However, it gives elastically to the weight of the user and therefore even offers a certain degree of seating comfort, which is enhanced by the footstool. The sharp edges of the design form a deliberate contrast to the idyllic playfulness of the indirectly illuminated footstool. The hide-covered upholstery is a reference to Le Corbusier's preference for hide as a furniture covering; a later version sports a neck-roll similar to the one made famous by his "B 306" chaise longue.

The members of Archizoom Associati went their separate ways in 1974, and their individual designs have also been successful. *PD*

"Mies," loaded

Ludwig Mies van der Rohe: Project for an office building in Berlin, 1919

Joseph Beuys: *Fettstuhl*, 1963

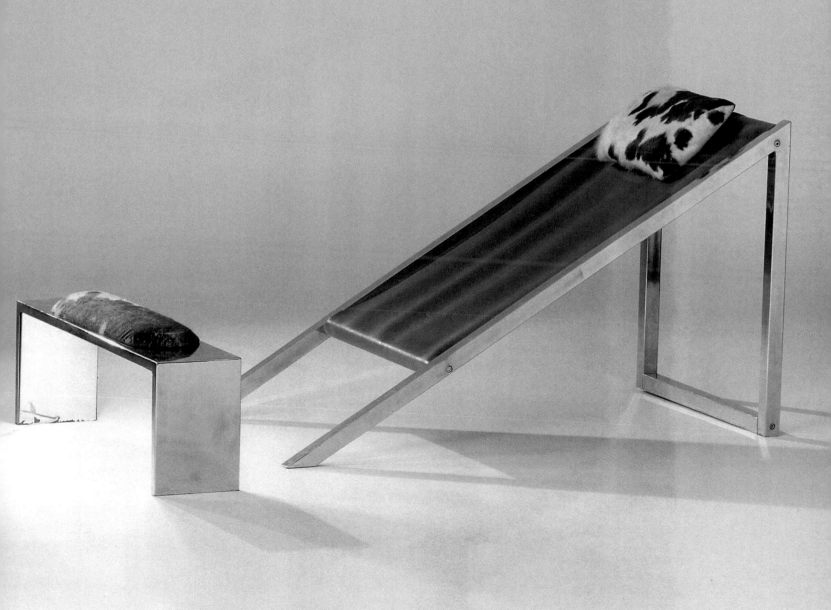

95

Name: Lassù
Designer: Alessandro Mendini
Design: 1974
Production: 1974

Manufacturer: Alessandro Mendini, Milan
Size: 136 x 85 x 85 cms
Material: semi-burned colored wood

■

Since the seventies, journalist, artist, architect, and designer Alessandro Mendini has been propagating a visual idiom that is a collage of the trivial, the fantastic, the traditional, and the artistic.

In 1974 he set two identical chairs on fire in front of the offices of *Casabella*, the magazine of which he was then editor, for the cover of issue no. 391. Each chair bore the name "Lassù" (up there). One of them was burned almost completely, and today its remains can be found in the archives of the University of Parma. The second is the piece

shown here, part of the Vitra Design Museum collection.

Typically of his *œuvre* as a whole, with "Lassù" Mendini eliminated the boundary between art and design. Burning the chairs was akin to a ritual and served to create an impressive image along the lines of Arte Povera. The visible traces left on the object by the act symbolically place the idealized chair within the context of life and death, and lend it a profound, human dimension. During a second demonstration organized the same year, Mendini set fire to a "Lassù" that had

been furnished with steps – for a photographic image of the "Bracciodiferro" (iron arm) product line by Italian furniture producer Cassina, a series of objects intended to underscore the contradiction between designers and industry. Alessandro Mendini's first designs were included in this product line. In a reduced version, "Lassù" is one of Mendini's series of "mini-monuments for spiritual use." *MSC*

^ Giulio Paolini: *Senza titolo,* 1962-3
> The burning of "Lassù," 1974

96

Name: First
Designer: Michele De Lucchi
Design: 1983
Production: 1983 to the present

Manufacturer: Memphis s.r.l.,
Pregnana Milanese, near Milan
Size: 90 x 66 x 46 cms; seat height 45,5 cms
Material: varnished tubular steel, varnished
wood, rubber

■

Michele De Lucchi was one of the cofounders of the Milan designer group Memphis, which emerged at the end of 1980 around the central figure of Ettore Sottsass. The group's very first exhibition unleashed a frenzy of enthusiasm. Since then, the shrill, sensual, and playful designs produced by Memphis have exploded all academic convention and substantially influenced the world of design.

G. S. Sowden, also a cofounder of Memphis, writes: "The ornamental style belongs to the world of electronics, just as functionalism is part of the world of machines and machine aesthetics."[28] The prevalent criterion for design was no longer the ability to solve technical problems, but rather the object's capacity for communication. It was necessary to confront the multiplicity of Postmodern styles in order to capture the *Zeitgeist* in a fast-paced, experimental design idiom. "First" by Michele de Lucchi was one of the few designs intended for the broad public, and quickly became a bestseller. The back and armrest construction is a true eye-catcher. It consists of a steel tube, bent to form a circle,

which supports a flexible backrest comprising a round wooden disk on rubber bearings and two wooden spheres as armrests. The tube is welded to the front legs of the simple stool, which forms the seat frame, almost completely engulfing the sitter. Although the construction is extremely stable, the reduced elements radiate a strong impression of lightness. The restrained use of decorative elements gives "First" an almost classic air among the Memphis objects, making it suitable for furnishing conventional interiors. *MK*

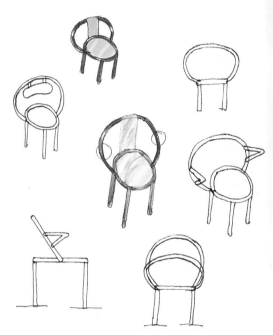

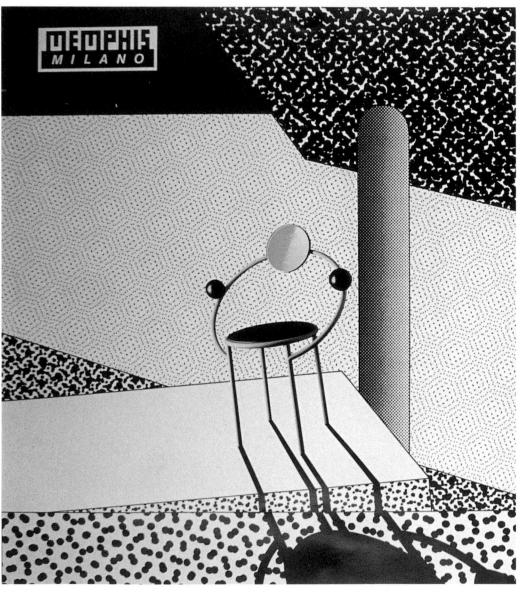

^ Memphis advertising poster, 1983
˥ M. De Lucchi: Sketches for "First," 1983

97

Name: Consumer's Rest
Designer: Stiletto
Design: 1983
Production: since 1984

Manufacturer: Stiletto Studios, Berlin
Size: 94 x 73.5 x 76; seat height 45 cms
Material: varnished steel, plastic

■

Like Marcel Duchamp's ready-mades, "Consumer's Rest" is an everyday object chosen from among vast numbers of manufactured goods, reinterpreted, and invested with a new function. Stiletto, who refers to himself as a practitioner of design and has been involved in experimental graphic design and other forms of art since 1981, says of his furniture designs: "They are to have a lucid structure, fulfill their intended function in terms of length by width by height, be industrially sound, stable, and solid, serially produced. I can meet these conditions most easily when I use containers taken from the everyday

consumer cycle as my starting material.... Redesign here has less to do with recycling and more with rebirth. The design is about soul and character, not 'packaging design'."[29] Stiletto is not concerned with improving a product; instead, he simply makes use of what is available and has stood the test of time. Department stores and supermarkets but also junk yards provide plenty of ideas and material. The point of departure here is a supermarket shopping cart, a standard, ubiquitous everyday object, which hardly appears to have "design value." Stiletto takes the shopping cart apart, reshapes

it, and sprays each half with different color tones. The transparent covers are made of the thick, soft foil normally used only for industrial purposes, for example in swinging doors in warehouses. They alone ensure that the seat, armrests, and back afford a minimum of comfort, and make clear that what we are looking at is indeed for sitting.
"Consumer's Rest" and a smaller children's version, "Short Rest," have been manufactured by Brüder Siegel in Leipheim, Germany since 1990. *PR*

^ Stiletto: "Consumer's Rest" sofa and table, c. 1983
> Duane Hanson: *Supermarket Shopper,* 1970

98

Name: Verspanntes Regal
Designer: Wolfgang Laubersheimer
Design: 1984
Production: since 1984

Manufacturer: Pentagon, Cologne
Size: 250 x 42 x 31; base 31 x 31cms
Material: 3 mm-thick sheet steel,
steel cable, tensioner

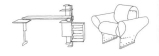

■

The eighties are characterized by the awakening of a general interest in design. At no other time in the history of designing the everyday world was the focus on objects in our immediate surroundings so widespread and so animated. Of course, the acceptance of the provocative, or what did not correspond to the ideal or the dictates of "good form," can be attributed to economic preconditions and the need of individuals to be able to shape their own private sphere. The New Design of the eighties was not based on industrial mass production, but was often home-grown, in that design, manufacture, and sale were all carried out by the designer himself.

One-of-a-kind objects and miniseries displayed in the galleries at first earned smiles at best from the established manufacturers of high-quality, accepted design products; however, the concept of industrial design was soon called into question. Creating a longlife product, or a design for serial production, was no longer accepted as the decisive criteria for a successful design. Instead, design was able to concentrate on objects manufactured in varying quantities. The draft, be

it sketch, model, one-of-a-kind object, or series, could all be considered different forms of creative expression. The previously meaningful classification of craftsmanship versus (industrial) design was replaced with new ideas that bridged the gap between the two: "art which makes itself useful" or applied art. Industry began tapping creative potential. Designer furniture or limited editions no longer attempted to meet everyone's needs, but rather catered to those of a limited market segment. The pluralism of the styles corresponds to the insignificance of previous dictates of fashion. One of the icons of New Design is the "Verspanntes Regal" (taut shelf) by Wolfgang Laubersheimer. He is a cofounder of Pentagon, a group of designers who joined forces in Cologne in 1985 and set up their own gallery there. The name of the group is a reference to the number of its members. In 1987 Pentagon exhibited their works at the "documenta 8" art show in Kassel, and furnished the high-profile Café Casino there. Today, the shelf is no longer part of the Pentagon collection (the gallery had to close in 1990). Laubersheimer took over production himself, enhancing the collec-

tion of the Nils Holger Moormann design agency in Aschau, Germany. The shelf is still equated with Pentagon and is without a doubt the group's most famous and widely sold product.

On one hand, it can be understood as a playfully ironic attack on the aesthetics of the right angle, an integral part of Functionalism. On the other, it poses a novel, convincingly constructive solution to an ongoing problem. Any shelf made of thin sheet steel, which in terms of the ratio of surface area to thickness is unusually fine, would be highly unstable. This instability can only be compensated with a brace which traditionally runs along the diagonal, as in a half-timbered house. Laubersheimer devised a way to brace the longitudinal axis. He countered the springy properties of the steel lateral surfaces with the tensile strength steel cable affixed to the sides, which generated a stable equilibrium between the forces. The black steel plate was left untreated, a sign of the new material aesthetics which took up the Italian art trend of Arte Povera, a style quickly adopted by many commercial suppliers in "anonymous design". *PD*

< Pentagon: Café Casino at the "documenta 8," Kassel, 1987
∨ W. Laubersheimer: Draft for "Verspanntes Regal," 1984

Name: Animali Domestici
Designer: Andrea Branzi
Design: 1985
Production: since 1985

Manufacturer: Zabro s.r.l., Milan
Size: 95 x 60 x 65; seat height 45 cms
Material: varnished wood,
birch wood

■

"Animali Domestici" (pets) is a series of furniture and garments designed by Andrea Branzi and his wife, Nicoletta, in order to nurture the domestic sphere anew in keeping with future demands. According to Branzi, a large part of our life and work will take place at home. As the germ cell of social and urban life, the home is taking on ever greater importance, and new developments in telecommunications will help shape our notion of the world from within the home. Various individual and social cultures are thus drafting a new language which is multifaceted and ephemeral, yet common to us all, similar to the idiom that already exists in pop music.

Branzi terms the objects he has designed for the new culture of the private sphere "Animali Domestici" – for they are to be understood as pets, living beings from a foreign yet related world. As hybrids of archetypal materials and anonymous industrial goods, a combination of Arte Povera and precision design, they lend their very own expression to the search for possible ways to combine technical feasibility and respect for nature. *MSC*

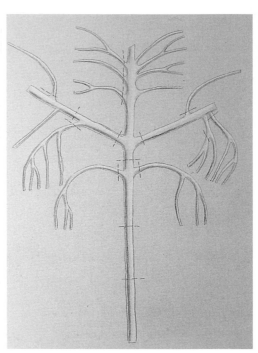

A. Branzi: Study for "Animali Domestici," 1985

From an 1857 Hutchinson and Wickersham catalogue, in *Animali Domestici* by A. Branzi, 1987

100
Name: Vodöl
Designer: Coop Himmelblau
Design: 1989
Production: 1989-93

Manufacturer: Vitra AG, Basel
Size: 78.5 x 200 x 90; seat height 42 cms
Material: varnished steel, brushed high-grade steel, leather upholstery

■

'Coop Himmelblau' is a group of Austrian architects who are considered to be Deconstructivists. This stylistic trend attempts to break away from Functionalism by pursuing ways of fragmenting a building and reorganizing its components into unusual structures. With "Vodöl," Coop Himmelblau for the first time takes on the classic forms of Modernity at the level of furniture design.
The starting point for their design was the "Fauteuil grand confort," designed in 1928 by

Le Corbusier, Pierre Jeanneret, and Charlotte Perriand. There, a symmetrical tubular steel frame surrounds rectangular, stacked cushions in a perfect fit, whereas in the "Vodöl" the entire volume of the furniture seems to have come unhinged and been lifted into a slant by a steel double-T support – a quotation from the architecture of Mies van der Rohe. The cushions appear to be beveled, and the surrounding steel tube resembles a bent-open paper clip.
It is difficult to tell whether one can sit comfort-

ably upright in the chair. However, steel springs have been installed under the seat, letting it swing easily, and providing an unexpected degree of comfort.
With the name of the chair – the French word *fauteuil* written in Viennese dialect, and thus a reference to the model which inspired it – and the color chosen for the leather covering, Coop Himmelblau has given the piece their unmistakably subversive stamp. *MSC*

Le Corbusier, Pierre Jeanneret, Charlotte Perriand: "Fauteuil grand confort, petit modèle," 1928

Coop Himmelblau: Loft extension for a law office in Vienna, 1983-9

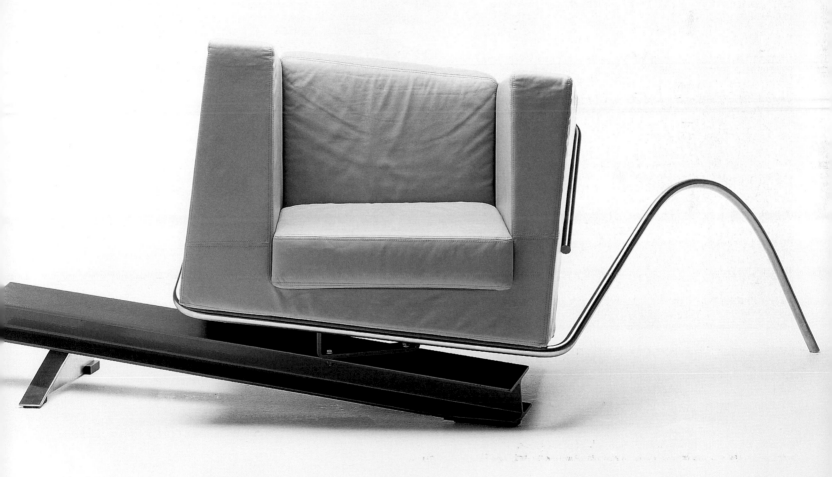

Notes

1
Adolf G. Schneck, Der Stuhl (Stuttgart, 1928), 6f.

2
Gaetano Pesce, "Progetti n. 34, 44. Serie di imbottiti 'UP'," in Mario Mastropietro. Un' Industria per il Design (Milan, 1982), 212.

3
Frank O.Gehry, quoted in Marilyn Hoffmann, "Liberated Design," The Christian Science Monitor, Boston, April 19, 1972.

4
Frank O.Gehry, quoted in Frank Gehry and his Architecture, exhibition catalogue (Walker Art Center, 1989), 64.

5
Alberto Meda, Statement, 1987, Vitra Design Museum Archive.

6
Jean Prouvé, quoted in Benedikt Huber, ed., Jean Prouvé – Architektur aus der Fabrik (Zurich: Artemis, 1971), 142.

7
Gerrit T. Rietveld, "We zijn er nog niet …," Goed Wonen, XVI (1963) 12: p.12; quoted in Peter Vöge: The Complete Rietveld Furniture (Rotterdam: 010 Publishers, 1993), 38.

8
Harry Bertoia, quoted in Karl Mang, Geschichte des Modernen Möbels, (Stuttgart: Hatje, 1978), 143.

9
Harry Bertoia, Interview by Richard S. Wurman, 1977, Vitra Design Museum Archive.

10
Sergius Rugenberg (staff member under Mies van der Rohe), 1985; quoted in Der Kragstuhl (Beverungen, Stuhlmuseum Burg Beverungen, 1986), 50.

11
Wassili Luckhardt, "Vom Entwerfen," in: Stadtbaukunst alter und neuer Zeit, no.11, (1921), quoted in Brüder Luckhardt und Alfons Anker (vol. 21 of the Schriftenreihe der Akademie der Künste (Berlin, 1990), 122.

12
Hans Luckhardt, "Moderne Stahlmöbel," Innendekoration (January 1931), quoted in Brüder Luckhardt und Alfons Anker (vol. 21 of the Schriftenreihe der Akademie der Künste (Berlin, 1990), 306.

13
Gio Ponti, "Senza aggetivi," Domus 268 (Milan, March 1952), 1.

14
Alvar Aalto "Zu meinen Möbeln" (1957), quoted in Werner Blaser, Alvar Aalto als Designer (Stuttgart, 1982), 92.

15
Organic Design in Home Furnishings, ed. Eliot F. Noyes, exhibition catalogue (New York: Museum of Modern Art, 1941), inside flap.

16
Eero Saarinen, "Furniture Design 1947 to 1958," quoted in Aline B. Saarinen, Eero Saarinen on His Work (New Haven, 1962), 66.

17
Der Spiegel, 35 (Hamburg, 1973), 111.

18
Schöner Wohnen (Hamburg, January 1974), 114f.

19
Frank Lloyd Wright, quoted in David A. Hanks, The Decorative Designs of Frank Lloyd Wright (New York: Dutton, 1979), 7.

20
Robert Venturi: Complexity and Contradiction in Architecture, exhibition catalogue (New York: Museum of Modern Art, 1966), in Michael Collins and Andrea Papadakis, Post-Modern Design (New York: Rizzoli, 1989), 103.

21
Gerrit T. Rietveld, quoted in Jan van Geest and Otakar Mácel, Stühle aus Stahl (Cologne, 1980), 16f.

22
Gerrit T. Rietveld, quoted from Reyer Kras, "Gerrit Thomas Rietveld 1888–1964 – Furniture Maker and Architect," in Gerrit Rietveld: A Centenary Exhibition (New York: Barry Friedman, Ltd. 1988), 13.

23
Reyer Kras "Gerrit Thomas Rietveld 1888-1964 – Furniture Maker and Architect," in Gerrit Rietveld: A Centenary Exhibition (New York: Barry Friedman, Ltd., 1988), 15.

24
Walter Gropius, Ideen und Aufbau des staatlichen Bauhaus Weimar (Munich: Bauhausverlag, 1923).

25
Marcel Breuer, "metallmöbel und moderne räumlichkeit," (footnote 23), quoted in Werner Möller and Otakar Mácel, Ein Stuhl macht Geschichte (Munich: Prestel, 1992), 44.

26
Le Corbusier, Almanach d'Architecture Moderne (Paris, 1925), 145, quoted in Werner Möller and Otakar Mácel, Ein Stuhl macht Geschichte (Munich: Prestel, 1992), 14.

27
Marcel Breuer, quoted in Christopher Wilk, Marcel Breuer – Furniture and Interiors, exhibition catalogue (New York: Museum of Modern Art, 1981), 41.

28
George P. Sowden, quoted in Barbara Radice, Memphis Design (Munich: Bangert, 1988), 88.

29
Stiletto, Prototypen (Uitgeverij, Rotterdam: 010 Publishers, 1986).

Concise Biographies

Hugo Alvar Henrik Aalto
born 1898 Kuortane, Finland
died 1976 Helsinki, Finland

1916–21: studied architecture at
the Helsinki Polytechnic;
1923–7: architectural studio in
Jyväskylä, Finland; 1927–33:
architectural studio in Turku,
Finland; 1928: member of Congrès
Internationaux d'Architecture
Moderne (CIAM); 1928–30: designed the office building for the
Turun Sanomat newspaper in
Turku; 1929: worked with Otto
Korhonen in an experimental
workshop for laminated wood in
Turku; 1929–33: built and furnished
the tuberculosis sanitarium in
Paimio; 1933–76: architectural
studio in Helsinki; 1935: set up the
Artek furniture company; patented
the first self-supporting wooden
chair frame; 1937: built the Finnish
pavilion at the world's fair in Paris;
1938: solo exhibition at the MoMA
in New York; 1939: designed the
Finnish pavilion for the New York
world's fair; 1946–8: professor at
Massachusetts Institute of
Technology, Cambridge,
Massachusetts; 1947–9: built the
MIT dormitory; 1953: designed
the main building of the Helsinki
Technical University;
1957: received a Royal Institute of
British Architects gold medal;
until 1976: extensive activity as
architect.
Alvar Aalto's major architectural
endeavors range from regional
planning, to churches and
public buildings, to single-family
houses. He was a pioneer in
research on forming laminated
wood in architecture and furniture
construction.
Figs. 54, 55

Jacques André
born 1904 Nancy, France
died 1985

Studied architecture; founded an
architectural studio together with
his brother Michel André; 1934:
member of the Union des Artistes
Modernes (UAM); starting in 1945:
urban planning for the reconstruction of Saint-Dié, France; contact
with Le Corbusier; industrial
and public building projects;
1966: designed the Steel Museum
in Jarville, France; 1972: built the
Centre Tripostal, Nancy.
Architect Jacques André was
concerned primarily with public
buildings and industrial plants.
Fig. 6

Ron Arad
born 1951 Tel Aviv, Israel

1971–3: studied at the Art Academy
in Jerusalem; 1973: moved to
London; 1974–9: studied at the
Architectural Association, London;
1979–81: worked in a London
architectural studio; 1981: together
with Caroline Thorman opened his
own design studio, One Off Ltd.
in London; first successful furniture
designs; 1983: opened 'One Off'
showroom in London;
1984: solo exhibition at Galerie
Zeus, Milan; 1986: participated in
the exhibition "Wohnen von
Sinnen" at the Dusseldorf Museum
of Art; 1989: established the
design and architectural studio
Ron Arad Associates, Ltd.; furniture
designs for Vitra and Poltronova;
1990: together with Alison Brooks
designs interior of the Tel Aviv
opera house; participated in
various exhibition, e.g., at Centre
Georges Pompidou, Paris, and the
Victoria and Albert Museum,
London; designed the "Soft
Volumes" furniture series for
Moroso; solo exhibition "Sticks and
Stones" at the Vitra Design
Museum, which also tours Tel Aviv,
Darmstadt, and Warsaw;
1993: teaching activities at the
College of Applied Art in Vienna;
numerous designs for furniture
companies; interior furnishings;
1994: established Ron Arad
Associates branch office in Italy;
exhibition "L'Esprit du Nomade" at
the Fondation Cartier, Paris;
designed a furniture series using
laminated wood for Driade;
1995: solo exhibition at the
Museum of Applied Art, Helsinki.
Ron Arad manufactures
one-of-a-kind furniture pieces in
his welding workshop. He also
designs furniture for serial
production and works as an interior
designer.
Fig. 52

**Archizoom Associati
(Andrea Branzi,
Gilberto Coretti,
Paolo Deganello,
Massimo Morozzi;
and as of 1968:
Dario Bartolini, Lucia Bartolini)**

1966: foundation of the architecture
and design group Archizoom
Associati; designed the exhibition
"Superarchitettura" in Pistoia, and
1967 in Modena, Italy; 1968: created
the Center of Eclectic Conspiracy
for the Milan Triennial; 1969–71:
project "Non-Stop City"; 1972:
participated in the exhibition "Italy
– The New Domestic Landscape";
1973: together with other architects
the group established the Global
Tools group.
Archizoom Associati drew on
influences of Pop Art to formulate
provocative, avant-garde ideas for
reorganizing living space.
Fig. 94

**Grupo Austral
(Antoni Bonet, Jorge Ferrari-Hardoy, Juan Kurchan)**

1937: Jorge Ferrari-Hardoy received a degree in architecture from the University of Buenos Aires; subsequently traveled to Europe and worked in Le Corbusier's studio; 1939: established the architectural studio Grupo Austral in Buenos Aires; active in urban development and public building construction; 1944: developmental planning for San Juan, a city destroyed by an earthquake.
Fig. 44

Helmut Bätzner
born 1928 Stuttgart, Germany

Prior to 1960: received training in carpentry; studied architecture at the Stuttgart Technical College; 1962–3: study-related stay at Villa Massimo, Rome; 1963–6: lecturer at the Vocational Art College in Krefeld, Germany; as of 1964: freelance architect in Karlsruhe; design for the Baden State Theater in Karlsruhe, the Karlsruhe Psychiatric Clinic, and the Aachen Technical College administration building.
Fig. 13

Mario Bellini
born 1935 Milan, Italy

Prior to 1959: received a doctorate in architecture from the Milan Polytechnic;
1961–3: head of design at the La Rinascente department store chain; 1962: wins the Milan Triennial Compasso d'oro, the first of seven such distinctions;
1962–5: professor at the College of Industrial Design, Venice;
1963: established an architectural studio together with Marco Romano; 1963: design consultant for Olivetti; developed a series of important typewriters and calculators for Olivetti; set up the environmental research group Environmedia; 1973: opened the design and architectural studio Studio Bellini in Milan; 1978: research and design consultant at Renault; as of 1979: member of the scholarly advisory council of the Milan Triennial;
1981: launched the magazine *Album*;
1982–3: taught at the Applied Art College in Vienna; 1983–5: taught at the Domus Academy in Milan; as of 1986: editor-in-chief of the magazine *Domus*; numerous architectural projects worldwide; 1987: solo exhibition at the New York MoMA.
Mario Bellini is renowned worldwide as an architect, industrial designer, furniture designer, journalist, and lecturer.
Fig. 38

Harry Bertoia
born 1915 San Lorenzo, Italy
died 1978 Bally, Pennsylvania

1930: emigrated to the United States; until 1936: studied at the Cass Technical College in Detroit; active in jewelry design and painting; 1937–43: received a scholarship to the Cranbrook Academy of Art, Michigan, where he founded and directed the metal workshop; 1943: moved to California along with Charles and Ray Eames; assisted with their experiments in molding laminated wood for leg splints and aircraft components; designed acoustic sculptures made of wire; 1950: returned to Pennsylvania on invitation from Knoll; designed a series of wire chairs for Knoll; wire sculptures for the Massachusetts Institute of Technology chapel;
1953: consultant for Knoll, otherwise active only as a sculptor; 1956: received the American Institute of Architects' Craftsmanship Medal; further distinctions and lecturing positions.
Harry Bertoia saw himself first and foremost as a sculptor, although he brought his metalworking expertise to bear on areas of the applied arts.
Fig. 31

André Bloc
born 1896 Algiers, Algeria
died 1966 New Delhi, India

1898: emigrated to France; until
1920: trained as an engineer; in
1920: worked in a motor factory,
subsequently in a turbine factory;
1921: met Le Corbusier; 1922:
organizational head of the magazine *Science et Industrie*; 1923:
organizational head of *Revue de
l'Ingénieur* journal; 1924: established the *Revue Générale du
Caoutchouc* journal; 1930: founded
the magazine *L'Architecture
d'Aujourd'hui*; as of 1940: first
sculpture projects; 1949 and 1956:
large-scale sculptures in Paris;
early fifties: established the group
Espaces; 1952: designed the
Bellevue house in Meudon; until
1966: worked predominantly
as a sculptor and interior designer;
various projects in Tehran, Nice,
Jacksonville, Dakar.
Fig. 46

Andrea Branzi
born 1938 Florence, Italy

Prior to 1966: studied architecture
in Florence; 1966: cofounder
of the group Archizoom;
1969–71: involved in the Archizoom
"Non-Stop City" project; 1971–3:
several articles for the magazine
Casabella; 1973: dissolution of
Archizoom; worked as an exhibit
designer for the Milan Triennial
and as a freelance designer; 1977:
cofounded the Studio Alchimia
design group; 1980: anthology of
his theoretical writings appears
entitled *Moderno, postmoderno,
millenario*; 1982: worked together
with the Memphis group;
director of the Domus Academy;
1983–4: instructor at the University
of Palermo; 1983–7: publisher
of the magazine *Modo*;
1984: published *La Casa Calda*;
as of 1984: guest lecturer at
universities in France, the United
States, Japan, Argentina, Brazil,
Canada; 1986: published *Animali
Domestici*; 1987: received the
Compasso d'oro speciale prize
for his *œuvre*; as of 1991: director
of the Domus Design Agency in
Tokyo; 1991–3: participated
in the "Citizen Office" project for
the Vitra Design Museum;
1992: published *Luoghi*, an anthology of his most important
projects from 1966–91.
Andrea Branzi is one of the
leading Italian design theorists.
Figs. 37, 94, 99

Marcel Breuer
born 1902 Pécs, Hungary
died 1981 New York, New York

1920–4: studied at the Vienna
Academy of the Arts, and at the
Bauhaus in Weimar; 1924: worked
in an architectural studio in Paris;
1925: head of the Bauhaus furniture
workshop; designed the "B 3"
tubular steel club chair; 1925:
numerous additional tubular steel
furniture designs; 1926: together
with Kalman Lengyel set up the
Standard Möbel company; 1927:
furnished the Piscator residence in
Berlin; 1928: opened his own
architectural studio in Berlin
together with Walter Gropius; 1930:
participated in the exhibition
"Société des Artistes Décorateurs"
in Paris; 1932–4: spent time in
Switzerland and Budapest; 1932:
collaborated with the Swiss
company Embru; 1934: designed
the Doldertal houses in Zurich for
Sigfried Giedion; 1935: emigrated
to England; opened his own
architectural studio in London
together with architect F.R.S.Yorke;
developed laminated wood
furniture for Isokon; 1937: moved to
the United States; taught at Harvard
University; 1937–41: launched an
architectural studio in Cambridge,
Massachusetts, with Walter
Gropius; 1941: started his own
architectural studio; 1946: transferred his office to New York; built
numerous private houses; 1947:
built his own residence in New
Canaan, Connecticut; 1948: solo
exhibition at the MoMA, New York;
1956: head of Marcel Breuer &
Associates; took part in designing
the UNESCO buildings in Paris.
Along with Mies van der Rohe,
Marcel Breuer was the most influential Bauhaus furniture designer
and left behind an important legacy
of architectural work.
Figs. 4, 5, 25, 89

Achille Castiglioni
born 1918 Milan, Italy

Prior to 1944: architectural degree
from Milan Polytechnic;
1944: together with his brothers
Livio and Pier Giacomo opened an
architectural studio; worked with
Livio until 1952, and with Pier
Giacomo until 1968; focused mainly
on urban planning, construction
projects, and industrial design;
1952: worked with Pier Giacomo
Castiglioni as an interior and
exhibition designer;
1956: cofounder of Associazione
per il Disegno Industriale (ADI);
designed the exhibition "Colori e
forme nella casa d'oggi" in Villa
Olmo, Como; 1962: designed the
Gavina branch office in Milan;
1963: designed the exhibition
"Vie d'acqua da Milano al mare"
in the Palazzo Reale, Milan;
1969: received a doctoral degree;
1969–77: taught architecture at the
Turin Polytechnic;
1977–80: professor of interior
design at Turin Polytechnic;
1981: professor of interior design
at Milan Polytechnic; 1984: traveling exhibition "Achille Castiglioni"
in Vienna, Berlin, and Milan;
1986: honorary member of the
association of industrial designers
at the Royal Academy of Art,
London; recipient of seven
Compasso d'oro awards.
Achille Castiglioni is a pioneer in
innovative industrial design
in Italy.
Fig. 91

Pier Giacomo Castiglioni
born 1913 Milan, Italy
died 1968 Milan, Italy

Prior to 1938: completed studies in architecture at Milan Polytechnic; 1938: designed the "Phonola" radio; specialized in lighting systems as well as furniture design and technical instruments; 1944: together with Achille and Livio Castiglioni opened an architectural studio; 1952: Livio Castiglioni left the group; until 1968: cooperated with Achille Castiglioni in design interiors and exhibitions.
Fig. 91

Pierre Chareau
born 1883 Bordeaux, France
died 1950 East Hampton, New York

1899–1914: was trained and employed as a technical draftsman at Waring & Gillow in Paris; 1919: opened his own studio for interior design in Paris; his first furniture exhibition at the Paris autumn salon; 1922: first exhibition in the Salon of the Société des Artistes Décorateurs; 1924: opened La Boutique interior furnishings studio, Paris; worked together with blacksmith Louis Dalbet; 1926: his first architectural commission, the clubhouse for Emile Bernheim in Beauvallon; 1928: furnished the Grand Hotel, in Tours; designed the Maison de verre; 1929: cofounded 'Union des Artistes Modernes' (UAM); 1931: completed 'Maison de verre'; member of the advisory committee at *L'Architecture d'Aujourd'hui*, a journal founded by André Bloc; 1936: exhibition of school furniture that could be dismantled at the Paris autumn salon; 1940: emigrated to the United States via Morocco; built a residence for painter Robert Motherwell.

As a furniture designer, interior designer, and architect, Pierre Chareau created works that combined Art Deco with Classic Modernism.
Fig. 22

Luigi (Lutz) Colani
born 1928 Berlin, Germany

1946: studied painting and sculpture at the Berlin College of Visual Arts; 1948: studied aerodynamics in Paris; carried out futuristic studies for car and motorcycle magazines; 1952–3: "high-speed" and material research for the Douglas aircraft company in California; 1954: returned to Europe; received the Goldene Rose award for a Fiat car-body; worked for Alfa-Romeo, Lancia, VW, and BMW; 1972: experimental design for Thyssen, Boeing, Rosenthal, Rockwell (NASA), Villeroy & Boch; 1973: established a Colani Design Center in Japan; 1983: moved to Japan; 1988: professor emeritus at the University of Bremen; 1990: architectural projects in Japan and Thailand; 1992: first extensive Colani retrospective in Dortmund, Germany; previous exhibitions in Japan and Switzerland; 1993: designed computer hardware for VOBIS; 1995: opened a Colani Design Center in Lünen, Germany. Colani's designs, which ranged from airplanes to furnishings and tableware, have helped popularize organic design.
Figs. 71, 72

Coop Himmelblau:
Wolf D. Prix
born 1942 Vienna, Austria
Helmut Swiczinsky
born 1944 Poznán, Poland

1968: established the architectural studio Coop Himmelblau; 1981: designed the bar Roter Engel in Vienna; 1982: received the Berliner Förderpreis für Baukunst award; 1988: designed the interior for a loft at a law firm in Vienna; won the Architekturpreis der Stadt Wien award; opened a second office in Los Angeles; took part in the exhibition "Deconstructive Architecture" at the MoMA in New York; Wolf D. Prix taught at the Southern California Institute of Architecture; 1988–9: first large industrial commission to design the Funder chipboard plant in Carinthia; 1989–90: received the Progressive Architecture Award; 1990: solo exhibition "Architects Art" at the Gallery of Functional Art in Los Angeles; Wolf D. Prix became professor of the master class for architecture at the University of Applied Art in Vienna; 1991: Frank Stepper became the group's third partner; 1992: planning for the German Museum of Hygiene in Dresden and the Munich Academy of the Visual Arts; 1993-4: took part in designing the Groninger Museum; 1995: participated in the Venice Biennial. In architectural circles, the Coop Himmelblau group is considered to be one of the key representatives of Deconstructionism.
Fig. 100

Hans Coray
born 1906 Wald near Zurich,
Switzerland
died 1991

Prior to 1929: studied Romance
languages; 1931: middle-school
teacher in Aarau and Zuoz;
first furniture designs; 1932–8:
continued education in graphology,
astrology, religious philosophy,
and design; began work in metal
design; 1941: participated in a
course on metalworking in Zurich;
as of 1945: active as a designer,
artist, and art dealer; 1983: solo
exhibition at the Strauhof building
in Zurich.
Fig. 7

Paolo Deganello
born 1940 Este, Italy

Prior to 1966: studied architecture
in Florence; 1966: cofounder of the
Archizoom group in Florence;
1963–74: cooperated in the urban
planning of Calentano, Florence;
1971–4: taught at the Architectural
Association in London; 1972:
dissolution of Archizoom; worked
as a journalist for *Domus, Casabella, Modo*, and IN; 1977: set up
the Collettivi Technici Progettisti
group; 1978: participated in the
Venice Biennial; 1981: opened his
own design studio; 1983: designed
a showroom for Schöner Wohnen
in Zurich; 1985–6: teaching position
at the Institute for Industrial Design
in Rome; took part in "documenta
8" in Kassel.
Paolo Deganello works as an
architect, interior designer, furniture designer, and journalist.
Fig. 37

Sonia Delaunay
born 1885 Gradzihsk, Ukraine
died 1979 Paris, France

1903–4: studied at the Karlsruhe Art
Academy; 1905: studied at the
Académie de la Palette, Paris; 1913:
first fabric designs; later initial
designs for theater costumes; 1923:
created designs for fabrics for a
manufacturer in Lyon; soon
afterwards ran a business selling
the materials; 1930: left the
business world to become a
painter. Painters Sonia and Robert
Delaunay were proponents of
'Orphism', the colorful, geometrically abstract artistic style.
Fig. 78

Michele De Lucchi
born 1951 Ferrara, Italy

1969–75: studied architecture in
Ferrara and at the Florence Art
College; 1973: established the
Cavart group; 1976–7: assistant in
the Department of Architecture at
the University of Florence; 1976: set
up the Architetture e altri Piaceri
studio in Florence; 1977: moved to
Milan; 1979: design consultant for
Olivetti; 1980: participated in the
group Studio Alchimia; 1981:
cofounder of Memphis; 1983:
presented a prefabricated house
at the Milan Triennial; 1986: established Solid, a group of young
designers in Milan; along with
Giancarlo Fassina designed the
"Tolomeo" lamp; 1986: instructor
at the Domus Academy in Milan;
designed office and apartment
buildings; 1987: taught at the
Cranbrook Academy of Art, Michigan; 1991: won the competition to
redesign the Deutsche Bank branch
offices; 1991–3: participated in
the "Citizen Office" project for the
Vitra Design Museum.
Until the eighties, Michele De Lucchi
was involved in experiments in the
area of 'New Design'; today, he is
one of Italy's most successful
architects, theorists, and industrial
designers.
Fig. 96

Jonathan De Pas
Donato D'Urbino
Carla Scolari
Paolo Lomazzi

1966: opened an office for architecture, urban development, and industrial design; 1967: designed inflatable and modular furniture; 1970: took part in designing the Italian pavilion at the Osaka world's fair; 1972: participated in "Italy, the New Domestic Landscape," an exhibition sponsored by the MoMA in New York; 1979: awarded the Milan Triennial Compasso d'oro prize for the "Scangai" clothes rack; 1980: designed the exhibition "Italian Furniture Design 1950–1980" at the Cologne Municipal Museum; 1987: exhibition of the group's work in Kyoto; designs for Acerbis, Artemide, Cassina, Poltronova, Zanotta.
Fig. 14

Charles Eames
born 1907 Saint Louis, Missouri
died 1978 Saint Louis, Missouri

1925–8: studied architecture at Washington University; 1928–30: worked in various architectural studios; 1930: opened his own architecture studio together with Charles M. Gray, and later with Walter E. Pauley; 1935: established a new architectural studio with Robert T. Walsh; planning for the St. Mary Church in Helena, Arkansas; 1937: first contact with Eero Saarinen; 1938: received a scholarship to the Cranbrook Academy of Art in Michigan through Eliel Saarinen; 1939: taught design at the Cranbrook Academy of Art; 1940: together with Eero Saarinen won first prize in the MoMA "Organic Design in Home Furnishings" competition; head of the Department of Industrial Design at the Cranbrook Academy of Art; 1941: married Ray Kaiser.

Ray Eames, née Kaiser
born 1912 Sacramento, California
died 1988 Saint Louis, Missouri

Prior to 1933: studied painting at the May Friend Bennet School in Millbrook, New York; until 1937: took courses in portrait painting at the Hofman School; 1937: participated in the first exhibition of American abstract artists at the Riverside Museum in New York; 1940: matriculated at the Cranbrook Academy of Art; 1941: married Charles Eames.

Charles and Ray Eames

1941–3: designed stretchers and leg splints from molded laminated wood which they produced with the help of the Evans company in Los Angeles; 1946: exhibition of experiments in molded laminated wood at the Museum of Modern Art in New York; Eames furniture designs were manufactured by Herman Miller; 1948: participated in "Low-Cost Furniture Design," a MoMA competition; 1949: built the Case Study House No. 8; starting around 1955: extensive activities as photographers and filmmakers; 1964: honorary degrees from the Pratt Institute in New York; 1964–5: IBM pavilion at the New York world's fair; 1969: participated in the exhibition at the Musée des Arts Décoratifs in Paris, "Qu'est-ce que le design?"; 1970–1: Eliot Norton Chair of Poetry at Harvard University; 1973: exhibition at the Museum of Modern Art in New York, "Furniture by Charles Eames." Charles and Ray Eames worked primarily in the fields of architecture, furniture design, photography, film, exhibition design, and graphic design, and were trendsetters in international design as of 1945.
Figs. 8, 10, 11, 30, 33, 56, 57, 58, 60, 61

Piero Gatti
born 1940 Turin, Italy
Cesare Paolini
born 1937, Genoa, Italy
Franco Teodoro
born 1939 Turin, Italy

Starting in 1965: cooperated on projects in the areas of architecture, urban development, product development, photography and graphic design in Turin; 1979: received the Compasso d'oro prize for their "Sacco" chair; 1983: dissolution of the group.
Fig. 50

Frank Owen Gehry
born 1929 Toronto, Canada

1947: moved from Toronto to Los Angeles; prior to 1954: studied architecture at the University of Southern California in Los Angeles; 1956–7: studied urban planning at the Harvard Graduate School of Design; subsequently worked in the architectural studios of Viktor Gruen and Pereira & Luckman in Los Angeles, and at André Remondet in Paris; 1962: set up the Frank O. Gehry & Associates architectural studio in Los Angeles; 1969–72: designed the block furniture series "Easy Edges"; 1974: taught at Yale University; was elected member of the American Institute of Architects; 1976: designed the Jung Institute in Los Angeles; 1978: built his own house in Santa Monica, California, as well as several other single-family residences; 1982–4: designed the Californian Aerospace Museum, Los Angeles; taught at Harvard University; 1983: received the Arnold W. Brunner Award from the American Academy of Arts and Letters; 1984: designed the Norton apartment house in Venice, California; 1987: exhibition entitled "The Architecture of Frank O. Gehry" at the Walker Art Center in Minneapolis; 1989: built the Vitra Design Museum in Weil am Rhein as well as the Schnabel residence in Los Angeles; received the Pritzker architecture prize from the Hyatt Foundation; 1992: won the Japanese Praemium Imperiale from the Japanese Art Association; 1993: designed the American Center in Paris; 1994: built the Birsfelden Vitra Center near Basel, Switzerland.
Frank O. Gehry is one of the most important contemporary American architects.
Fig. 16

Eileen Gray
born 1878 Enniscorthy, Ireland
died 1976 Paris, France

1898–1902: studied painting at the Slade School of Fine of Art in London and at the Académie Colarossi and the Académie Julian in Paris; began learning Japanese varnishing techniques with Sugawara; 1914–18: spent time in London; 1918: returned to Paris; until 1919: worked exclusively as a furniture designer; 1922: established her own studio for interior and furniture design; 1923: exhibition at the Salon des Artistes Décorateurs in Paris; 1925: first tubular steel furniture; 1927–9: designed the E 1027 house in Roquebrune, France; created a wide range of tubular steel furniture to furnish the house; additional architectural projects; 1937: together with Le Corbusier exhibited a number of projects at the Pavillon des Temps Nouveaux at the Paris world's fair; 1972: first retrospective in London.
Eileen Gray was a self-taught architect who designed elegant, avant-garde tubular steel furniture and interiors.
Fig. 21

Willy Guhl
born 1915 Stein am Rhein, Switzerland

1930–33: trained in cabinetmaking in Schaffhausen; 1939: opened his own workshop; 1946–7: began working with reclining chairs; designed the first plastic-shell chair in Europe; 1948: participated in the MoMA competition "Low-Cost Furniture Design"; 1951–80: head of interior design at the Vocational Arts College in Zurich; 1954: designed a garden chair and other products for the Eternit AG company; 1965–80: head of product design at the Vocational Arts College in Zurich.
Trained as a craftsman, Willy Guhl became one of the most influential industrial designers in Switzerland.
Fig. 48

René Herbst
born 1891, Paris, France
died 1982, Paris, France

1908–14: studied architecture in Paris and took various vocational courses in London and Frankfurt; 1921: first exhibition at the Salon of the Société des Artistes Décorateurs; 1925: Member of the jury for Société des Artistes Décorateurs; 1930: cofounder of Union des Artistes Modernes (UAM); 1935: along with Le Corbusier, Fernand Léger, and others participated in the Exposition International de Bruxelles; 1946, 1949, and 1955: president of the Union des Artistes Modernes; 1950–69: president of the Form Utiles group; 1951: published a text about Jean Puiforcat; 1954: published a text about Pierre Chareau; 1954, 1957, and 1960: architect for the Xth, XIth and XIIth Milan Triennials.
René Herbst worked as an architect, interior designer, exhibition designer, and furniture designer.
Fig. 40

Josef Hoffmann
born 1870 Pirnitz, Moravia
died 1956 Vienna, Austria

Prior to 1892: studied architecture at the State Academy of Arts and Crafts in Brno; 1892–5: continued studies at the Academy of Visual Arts in Vienna, as well as in Munich; 1895: established the Siebener Club, whose members also included Josef Maria Olbrich and Koloman Moser; study-related travels to Southern Italy; 1896–9: staff member in the Otto Wagner architectural studio; 1897: joined the Viennese Secession; 1899–36: professor of architecture, interior design, and enamel painting at the Viennese Academy of Applied Art; 1900: designed the hall for the Viennese Secession at the Paris world's fair; 1902: traveled to England with Koloman Moser; was introduced to Charles Rennie Mackintosh; 1903: established the Wiener Werkstätte; 1905: built and furnished a sanitarium in Purkersdorf near Vienna as well as Palais Stoclet in Brussels; 1908: cofounder of the Österreichischer Werkbund; 1920: chief architect for the city of Vienna; 1925: designed the Austrian pavilion at the Exposition des Arts Décoratifs, Paris; 1932: created terrace houses at the International Werkbund Settlement.
Josef Hoffmann's work as an architect, furniture designer, and craftsman underwent numerous trends and styles and influenced both Classic Modernism and Postmodernism.
Figs. 20, 76

Arne Jacobsen
born 1902 Copenhagen, Denmark
died 1971 Copenhagen, Denmark

Trained in masonry; 1924: completed studies at the Copenhagen Technical College; 1925: won a silver medal at the Paris world's fair for a chair design; until 1927: studied architecture at the Royal Art Academy in Copenhagen; 1927–30: worked in the Paul Holsoe architectural studio; 1929: presented the circular house of the future in an exhibition at the Royal Art Academy in Copenhagen; 1930–71: runs his own architectural studio; extensive work as an architect; 1930–5: designed an apartment complex in Bellevue, the Copenhagen beach district; 1937–42: designed the City Hall in Arhus; 1945–7: emigrated to Sweden; 1956–65: professor at the Royal Art Academy in Copenhagen; 1958–60: designed and furnished the Royal Hotel in Copenhagen; 1957: received a silver medal at the Milan Triennial; 1962: member of the American Institute of Architects; 1966: honorary doctorate from Oxford University; 1967: designed the "Cylinda Line" product series for the Danish company Stelton; 1971: received a gold medal from the Frankfurt Architecture Academy; 1961–71: designed the Danish National Bank, Copenhagen (completed in 1978).
Arne Jacobsen was one of the most important Scandinavian architects and industrial designers.
Fig. 47

Pierre Jeanneret
born 1896 Geneva, Switzerland
died 1967

1913–15 and 1918–21: studied architecture at the École des Beaux Arts, Geneva; 1921–3: worked with the Perret brothers in their studio; 1923–40: worked together with his cousin Le Corbusier, and with Charlotte Perriand as of 1927; 1926–7: with Le Corbusier won first prize for the competition to design the League of Nations Palace in Geneva; 1945: occasionally worked with Jean Prouvé; 1951–65: director of the Architecture School of Chandigarh in India. (Pierre Jeanneret on the right, with Charlotte Perriand, and Le Corbusier)
Figs. 23, 24

Toshiyuki Kita
born 1942 Osaka, Japan

Prior to 1964: studied industrial design at Namiwa College in Osaka; opened his own studio for industrial and furniture design; 1969: moved to Italy; worked in the studios of Mario Bellini and Silvio Coppola, as well as at Bernini and Cassina; 1977 and 1979: solo exhibitions in Tokyo and Osaka; 1981: received the Kitaro Kunii Industrial Design Award; 1987: participated in the exhibition "Les avant-gardes de la fin du XXème siècle" at the Centre Georges Pompidou; 1989: designed a multi-purpose hall for the Sony Center in Tokyo. Toshiyuki Kita is active in industrial and furniture design. He is considered one of Japan's "most European" designers.
Fig. 82

Poul Kjaerholm
born 1929 Oster Vra, Denmark
died 1980 Copenhagen

Prior to 1949: trained as a carpenter; 1949–52: graduated from the Copenhagen Vocational Arts College; 1952–6: assistant at the Copenhagen Vocational Arts College; 1955–76: taught at the Royal Art Academy in Copenhagen; worked together with E. Kold Christensen; 1957: recieved the Milan Triennial Compasso d'oro; 1958: Lunning Prize; 1960; Compasso d'oro; 1972 and 1977: Annual prize of the Association of Danish Furniture Producers; 1976–80: director of the Royal Art Academy in Copenhagen. Kjaerholm, who was greatly influenced by the International Style, made a significant contribution to Scandinavian design.
Fig. 36

Shiro Kuramata
born 1934 Tokyo
died 1991 Tokyo

Prior to 1953: studied architecture at the Tokyo Technical College; 1956: trained as a cabinetmaker at the Kuwasawa Institute for Design in Tokyo; 1954: worked for the furniture producer Teikoku; 1957–64: member of the advertising department at San-Ai; 1965: set up the Kuramata Design Studio in Tokyo; 1969: furnished the Judd Club in Tokyo; 1981: received the Japanese Cultural Prize for design; 1981–4: designs for Memphis in Milan; 1987: furnished the Issey Miyake boutiques in New York, Paris, and Tokyo as well as other boutiques and clubs.
With his poetic, minimalist concepts, furniture and interior designer Shiro Kuramata played a decisive role in spotlighting Japanese design.
Figs. 85, 87

Wolfgang Laubersheimer
born 1955 Bad Kreuznach, Germany

Prior to 1989: trained as an industrial manager at Siemens; apprenticeship at a publishing company in Cologne; studied sculpture at the Cologne Technical College of Art and Design; 1982: established the group Unikate together with Reinhard Müller; 1985: cofounder of the group and gallery Pentagon; as of 1991: professor of production technology at the Cologne Technical College of Art and Design.
Fig. 98

Le Corbusier
(Charles-Édouard Jeanneret-Gris)
born 1887 La Chaux-de-Fonds, Switzerland
died 1965 Cap Martin, France

1900: trained as an engraver at the La Chaux-de-Fonds Vocational Arts College; 1905: designed Villa Fallet (his first building project); 1908: worked in Auguste Perret's architectural studio in Paris; 1910–11: lived in Germany; apprentice of Peter Behrens; 1912–14: taught architecture at the La Chaux-de-Fonds Vocational Arts College; 1914: designed the Domino house; 1917: resettled in Paris; also active as a painter; 1918: together with painter A. Ozenfant published the programmatic treatise *Après le Cubisme*; 1920: launched the journal *L'Esprit nouveau*; took on the pseudonym "Le Corbusier"; 1922: built the Ozenfant residence; 1923: published *Vers une nouvelle architecture*; 1925: designed the Pavillon de l'Esprit Nouveau at the Exposition des Arts Décoratifs, Paris; designed a housing estate in Bordeaux-Pessac; 1927: designed experimental houses for the Weissenhof Settlement in Stuttgart; 1928: cofounder of the Congrès Internationaux d'Architecture Moderne (CIAM); 1929: cooperated with Charlotte Perriand and Pierre Jeanneret on furniture designs; 1942–4: developed the Modulor system of proportions; 1944: published *Charta of Athens*; 1950–4: built the church Notre-Dame-du-Haut in Ronchamp; until 1969: numerous architectural projects and publications.
As an architect and theorist, Le Corbusier was responsible for promoting a reduced form of Modernist architecture and is considered one of the most influential twentieth-century architects.
Figs. 23, 24

Hans Luckhardt
born 1890 Berlin
died 1954 Bad Wiessee, Germany

Wassili Luckhardt
born 1889 Berlin
died 1972 Berlin

Hans Luckhardt studied at the
Technical University in Karlsruhe,
Wassili Luckhardt at the Technical
University in Dresden and in
Berlin-Charlottenburg; 1921: the
Luckhardt brothers start working
together; 1922–3: first building
project: residence in Berlin's West
End; 1924: began working with
Alfons Anker; 1927: first experiments with chairs containing
moving parts; first tubular steel
furniture; 1928: several building
projects; model home at the "Heim
und Technik" exhibition in Munich;
1930: published *Zur neuen
Wohnform*; 1952: Hans Luckhardt
s made professor at the Berlin
College for Visual Arts; 1956:
Wassili Luckhardt becomes a
member of the Berlin Academy of
the Arts; *Lichtarchitektur* published
by Wassili Luckhardt and Walter
Köhler; 1957: Bavarian State Public
Utilities Building in Munich designed by Wassili Luckhardt; received
the Art Prize of the City of Berlin.
The creative work of Hans and
Wassili Luckhardt had a great influence on architecture in postwar
Germany.
Figs. 28, 41

Alberto Meda
born 1945 Lenno Tremezzina, Italy

Prior to 1969: studied mechanical
engineering at Milan Polytechnic;
1973: technical director at Kartell;
starting in 1979: consultant
engineer and designer at Alias,
Brevetti, Kartell, CSI, Colomo
Design, and Swatch Italia; 1981–5:
project director at Alfa Romeo;
1983–7: professor of production
technology at the Domus Academy,
Milan; 1989: received Compasso
d'oro prize for the "Lola" lamp
made of carbon fibers; 1990: solo
exhibition in Tokyo; 1994: professor
at the Domus Academy.
Industrial designer Alberto Meda
approaches engineering from a
design perspective.
Fig. 17

Alessandro Mendini
born 1931 Milan

Studied architecture at Milan
Polytechnic; prior to 1970: worked
in the Nizzoli Associati architectural
studio; 1970: member of the
scholarly advisory council at the
Domus Academy; 1970–6; chief
editor of the magazine *Casabella*;
1973: cofounder of the group
Global Tools; 1977: cofounder of
the Alchimia group; 1977–81:
founder and chief editor of the
magazine *Modo*; 1978: published
Paesaggio Casalingo; received the
Milan Triennial Compasso d'oro;
first "redesigns"; 1980: exhibition
"L'oggetto banal banale" with
Alchimia at the Venice Biennial;
1980–5: chief editor of *Domus*
magazine; 1981: published
Architettura Addio; 1983: taught
design at the Academy of Applied
Art, Vienna; published *Il progetto
infelice*; 1983: created designs for
Alessi; 1983–8: together with
Achille Castiglioni and Aldo Rossi
built the Casa della Felicità for
Alessi; 1988–94: built and furnished
the Groninger Museum; 1993: solo
exhibition at Artiscope, Brussels;
1994: designed numerous Swatch
branch offices.
With his theoretical and practical
work, and in particular his reinter-
pretations of designs by others,
Alessandro Mendini has since the
seventies made an important
contribution to the Postmodern
design discussion.
Figs. 81, 95

Ludwig Mies van der Rohe
born 1886 Aachen, Germany
died 1969 Chicago, Illinois

1897–1900: attended the Dombau-
schule in Aachen, subsequently
drafted stucco ornamentation for
an interior decorator in Aachen;
1901–7: studied with Bruno Paul
and at the Berlin Vocational Arts
College; 1907: first building
designs; 1908–11: worked together
with architect Peter Behrens and
Walter Gropius; subsequently as a
freelance architect in Berlin; 1920:
designed villas as well as exhibition
architecture; 1926–32: vice-pres-
ident of the Deutscher Werkbund;
1927: designed and patented the
first cantilever-base tubular steel
chair; general director of the
Weissenhof Settlement, Stuttgart;
1929: designed the German
pavilion for the Barcelona world's
fair; designed metal furniture
for both buildings; 1930: Villa
Tugendhat in Brno, Czechoslovakia;
replaced Hannes Meyer as Bauhaus
director; 1931: signed a contract
with Thonet for the exclusive
marketing of fifteen chair designs;
1938: emigrated to the United
States; professor in the Department
of Architecture at the Armour
Institute (later the Illinois Institute
of Technology), Chicago; at the
same time ran his own studio in
Chicago; 1940: designed a number
of the buildings at the Armour
Institute; 1958: designed the
Seagram Building, New York;
1962–7: designed the New National
Gallery in Berlin.
Ludwig Mies van der Rohe's
prominent work in architecture and
furniture characterized the
International Style, an elegant
variety of Classic Modernism.
Figs. 39, 90

Carlo Mollino
born 1905 Turin, Italy
died 1973 Turin

1929: studied art history at the
University of Ghent; 1930: architectural studies in the Aosta valley,
Italy; 1931: architectural degree
from the University of Turin;
worked in his father's engineering
firm (Eugenio Mollino) in Turin;
1934: first building project in
Cuneo, Italy; first photographic
works and first literary publications;
1937: designed the building for
Società Ippica Torinese; worked as
an interior designer; 1943: project
proposal for an "elevated house,"
published in the magazine *Stile*;
1947–55: built Maison du soleil,
Cervinia, Italy; 1949: gave his first
lectures on architecture at Turin
Polytechnic; 1950: furnished the
RAI auditorium in Turin; published
Il messaggio dalla camera oscura;
1952–53: designed a house for
L. Cattaneo in Luino, Italy; 1954:
designed the cars "Osca 110" and
"Bisiluro"; 1956: professor of
architecture at Turin Polytechnic;
1957: exhibited his own furniture
designs at the Milan Triennial; after
1964: designed the Chamber of
Commerce building and the Teatro
Regio, both in Turin.
Carlo Mollino left behind a legacy
of original, innovative work in the
fields of architecture, interior design, photography, design, machine
construction, and literature.
Figs. 62, 65

Jasper Morrison
born 1959 London

1979–82: attended the Kingston
School of Art; 1982–5: graduated
from the Royal College of Art,
London; 1984: received a scholarship to the Berlin Academy of Arts;
1986: opened his own design
studio; 1987: designed the installation for Reuter's News Center at
"documenta 8," Kassel; 1988:
installation "Some New Items for
the House I" in Berlin; 1989:
installation "Some New Items for
the House II" for Vitra GmbH in
Milan; 1992: published *A World
Without Words*; received the
german Bundespreis für Produkt-
design award for a series of door
handles created for Franz Schneider
Brakel GmbH; 1993: installation for
the Museum of Applied Art, Vienna;
1995: solo exhibition in the architectural center Arc en rêve,
Bordeaux; numerous teaching
positions and workshops.
Jasper Morrison's industrial and
furniture designs have helped
define the term "new simplicity."
Fig. 53

George Nelson
born 1908 Hartford, Connecticut
died 1986 New York, New York

1931: degree in architecture from
Yale University; 1932–4: studied at
the American Academy, Rome;
1936–41: together with William
Hanby opened an architectural
studio in New York; 1935–44: chief
editor of the magazine *Architectural
Forum*; 1945: published *Tomorrow's House*; 1946: established his
own studio for architecture and
industrial design; designed the
"Basic Storage Components" shelf
system; 1946–66: director of design
at Herman Miller Furniture
Company, where he succeeded
Gilbert Rohde; 1953: published
Chairs; 1957: published *Problems
of Design*; 1958: designed the
"Comprehensive Storage System"
for Herman Miller Furniture
Company; 1964: designed several
pavilions at the New York world's
fair; 1968: designed the "Editor"
typewriter for Olivetti; 1968–75:
member of the Conseil supérieur de
la création industrielle, Paris; 1977:
published *How to See*; 1983:
designed the exhibition "Design
since 1945" at the Philadelphia
Museum of Art.
In his theoretical and practical
work, in particular as an architect
and furniture designer, and in his
numerous lectures, he incorporated
fundamental social and cultural
questions into his approach to
design and gave them an international slant.
Figs. 32, 34, 35, 79

Marc Newson
born 1963 Sydney, Australia

Prior to 1984: studied sculpture and
jewelry design at the Sydney
College of Art; 1986: set up the POD
design studio; clock designs; first
furniture exhibition at the Roslyn
Oxley Gallery, Sydney; 1987:
worked in Tokyo; produced various
chair and lamp designs for the Idée
company in Tokyo; 1988: solo
exhibition in Tokyo; 1989: exhibition at the gallery Il Milione, Milan;
1991: exhibition at the gallery VIA
in Paris; 1992: furnished boutiques
in Frankfurt and Berlin; 1993:
received the Créateur de l'année
distinction from the Paris Furniture
Salon; 1995: participated in the
exhibition "13 nach Mem-phis"
at the Frankfurt Museum of Arts
and Crafts; commissioned to
design an interactive installation for
Fondation Cartier, Paris; as well
as for the Swatch watch tower at
the 1996 Olympic Games in Atlanta;
interior furnishings in London
and Tokyo.
Marc Newson designs furniture,
lamps, and clocks, and also works
as an interior designer.
Fig. 73

Isamu Noguchi
born 1904 Los Angeles, California
died 1988 New York, New York

1906: moved to Tokyo; 1918:
returned to the United States from
Japan; 1922: worked as a sculptor;
1923–5: attended medical school at
Columbia University; 1924: began
studies in sculpture at the Da Vinci
Art School, New York; opened his
own studio; 1927–8: studied
sculpture with Constantin Brancusi
in Paris on a Guggenheim scholarship; 1928: first exhibition in New
York; 1930–1: studied Chinese
painting with a master artist in
Beijing; worked with a ceramics
artist in Japan; 1935–6: sculpted
monuments in downtown Mexico
City; 1937: returned to New York;
1941–2: spent six months in a
resettlement camp; 1946: participated in the exhibition "Fourteen
Americans" at the MoMA, New
York; 1949–50: scholarship from the
Bollingen Foundation; world tour;
1951–2: designed the gardens at
Keio University, Tokyo; built two
bridges in Hiroshima; 1956–8:
gardens for the UNESCO buildings
in Paris; 1960–5: designed a
sculpture garden for the National
Museum in Jerusalem; 1968:
retrospective in the Whitney
Museum, New York; 1974: participated in the exhibition "Masters of
Modern Sculpture" at the Guggenheim Museum, New York; 1977:
designed a fountain for the Chicago
Art Institute; numerous other
works.
Isamu Noguchi was an internationally acclaimed sculptor who also
designed gardens, stage sets, and
furniture.
Figs. 59, 63, 64

Verner Panton
born 1926 Gamtofte, Denmark

1947–51: studied architecture at the
Royal Art Academy in Copenhagen;
1950–2: worked in Arne Jacobsen's
architectural studio; 1953–5: studied in various European countries;
1955: opened his own architecture
and design studio; 1957: designed a
cardboard house; 1963: moved to
Switzerland; 1966: won the Rosenthal-Studio-Preis; 1968: exhibited
his interior "Visiona" on the Bayer
ship at the Cologne furniture fair;
1969: interior for the Spiegel
publishing company, Hamburg;
participated in the exhibition
"Qu'est-ce que le design" at
Centre Georges Pompidou, Paris;
1974: interior for the Gruner & Jahr
publishing company, Hamburg;
1984: visiting professor at the
Offenbach College of Design; 1987
and 1988: retrospectives at the
furniture fairs in Brussels and
Copenhagen; 1994: several chair
designs for the German company
Polythema.
Verner Panton played a large part in
defining the predominant color
schemes used in the sixties and
seventies. He has worked as a
designer in the areas of furniture,
lamps, fabrics, interiors, and
exhibitions.
Figs. 68, 93

Pierre Paulin
born 1927 Paris

Studied sculpture at École
Camondo, Paris; 1954: first seating
furniture for Gebrüder Thonet;
1968: took part in designing new
furnishings for the Louvre; 1969:
American Industrial Design Award;
1970: furniture designs for the
French pavilion at the Osaka
world's fair; 1971: furnished the
private chambers of the French
president in the Elysée Palace;
1975: set up ASDA & Partners for
Industrial Design company; has
since been active in industrial
design; 1983: furniture designs for
the French president's study in the
Elysée Palace; 1987: Grand Prix
National de la Création Industrielle.
Pierre Paulin works as a furniture,
industrial, and interior designer.
Fig. 70

Jorge Pensi
born 1946 Buenos Aires, Argentina

Began his career as a designer in
Argentina; 1977: emigrated to
Spain; acquired Spanish citizenship; cofounder of Grupo Berenguer
in Barcelona; specialized in
furniture design, lighting, and
exhibition design; worked for
Perobell and other companies in
Italy, Germany, Finland, the United
States, South America, and
Singapore; lecturer; 1988: received
an award for the "Toledo" chair
from Salón Internacionál de Diseño
para el Habitát, Barcelona; Silver
Delta medal from Assoziazione del
Disegno Industriale; 1994: designed
the exhibition "Salón Internacionál
de Diseño para el Habitát".
Jorge Pensi works as an industrial
and furniture designer.
Fig. 86

Charlotte Perriand
born 1903 Paris

Prior to 1925: studied interior design at École des Arts Décoratifs, Paris; 1926: presented metal furniture at an exhibition of the "Société des Artistes Décorateurs;" 1927–37: worked with Le Corbusier and Pierre Jeanneret; 1929: presented her "L'équipement d'une habitation" at the Paris autumn salon; left Société des Artistes Décorateurs; joined Union des Artistes Modernes(UAM); 1930: together with Le Corbusier and Pierre Jeanneret participated in the first UAM exhibition; 1930 and 1933: traveled to the Soviet Union; 1940: together with Jean Prouvé set up an office for coordinating aspects of construction; 1940–2: lived in Japan; until 1946: lived in Indochina; 1950: cofounder of the Formes Utiles group; active as an interior designer; 1958: with Jean Prouvé presented "La maison du Sahara" at Salon des Arts Ména-gers; 1962–8: traveled to South America; 1969: furnished the residence of the Japanese ambassador in Paris; 1993: presented a teahouse as part of the UNESCO event "Dialogue of the Cultures" in Paris.

Until today, Charlotte Perriand worked in Europe, Japan, and Brazil as an interior and furniture designer.
Figs. 23, 24, 78

Gaetano Pesce
born 1939 La Spezia, Italy

1959–65: studied architecture and industrial design at the University of Venice; 1959: established Grupo N in Padua; worked with similar groups of artists in Milan, Paris, and Germany; 1961: opened a studio with designer Milena Vettore; research in the area of serial and kinetic art; starting in 1962: active as an interior designer; 1969: designed a self-inflating furniture series for Cassina & Busnelli, Italy; 1971: established the company Bracciodiferro in order to manufacture experimental objects; 1972: participated in the exhibition "Italy – the New Domestic Landscape" at the MoMA, New York; starting in 1975: professor at the Institute for Architecture and Urban Planning in Strasbourg; 1978: project for a skyscraper in Manhattan; 1983: moved to New York; 1985–7: professor at the Cooper Union School of Architecture and Art; 1987: Pluralist Tower project in Sao Paulo; 1989: designed mineral water bottles for Vittel, France; 1993: designed the offices of the Chiat Day advertising agency in New York; until 1995: extensive activity as an architect as well as a designer of interiors, furniture, and products; numerous additional teaching activities.

Gaetano Pesce has been a leading proponent of experimental design since the seventies.
Fig. 15

Giancarlo Piretti
born 1940 Bologna, Italy

Degree in art education from the Bologna Art Academy; subsequently taught interior design at the same institution for seven years while simultaneously working as a furniture designer for Castelli; 1971: received the SMAU prize for the "Plia" chair; 1973: Gute Form award by the German Design Council, Darmstadt; 1975: advisory member of the ISIA Design College, Florence; 1980: National Industrial Design Award, United States; 1984–6: worked for Castilia, a subsidiary of Castelli; 1988: presented the "Piretti Collection," a seating system manufactured in the United States, Italy, Japan, Korea, Israel, Singapore, Venezuela, and Argentina; 1991: received the Compasso d'oro; 1994: Roscoe Award (U.S.) and G Mark (Japan) for the "Xylon" chair series. Giancarlo Piretti works as furniture and industrial designer.
Fig. 51

Gio (Giovanni) Ponti
born 1891 Milan
died 1979 Milan

Prior to 1921: studied architecture at the Milan Polytechnic; worked in the architectural studio of Mino Fiocchi and Emilio Lancia; 1923–30: designs for the ceramic manufacturer Ricardo Ginori, in Doccia and Sesto Fiorentino; 1925–79: directed the Monza Biennial; 1927: opened his own architectural studio in Milan together with Emilio Lancia; 1928: launched the magazine *Domus*, of which he was publisher until 1979; 1933: established the studio Ponti-Fornaroli-Soncini; received an Art Prize from the Italian Academy; 1936–61: taught at Milan Polytechnic; 1941: initiated the magazine *Stile*; 1954: solo exhibition at the Institute of Contemporary Art, Boston; 1956: built the Pirelli Tower in Milan; Compasso d'oro; 1958: designed an administration building in Bagdad, Iraq; 1964: built the San Francesco church, Milan; 1968: honorary doctorate from the Royal College of Art, London; gold medal from the French Academy for Architecture; 1969: solo exhibition in the UCLA gallery, Los Angeles; 1970: built the Montedoria building in Milan; until 1976: comprehensive architectural activities; gave lectures on architecture worldwide.

As an architect, furniture designer, industrial designer, publisher, and professor, Gio Ponti was one of those men and women whose work led to the international fame of Italian design in the postwar era.
Fig. 49

Jean Prouvé
born 1901 Paris, France
died 1984 Nancy, France

1916–21: apprenticed to two metal craftsmen in Paris, and studied at the École Supérieure, Nancy; 1923: opened his own smithy in Nancy; 1923–6: first furniture made of thin sheet steel; 1929: cofounder of Union des Artistes Modernes (UAM); 1930–1: established the stock corporation Société des Ateliers Jean Prouvé; 1944: became mayor of Nancy following the end of German occupation; starting in 1947: opened Les Ateliers Jean Prouvé, a metal and aluminum processing plant in Maxéville (near Nancy) which manufactured steel girder constructions; 1957: the plant is acquired by Compagnie Industrielle de Matériel de Transport; professor at the CNAM in Paris; freelance architect in Paris; 1971: headed the jury for the design of the Centre Georges Pompidou, Paris.
Jean Prouvé emphasized visible metal constructions both in architecture and furniture design, and was thus an important forerunner of high-tech.
Figs. 26, 27

Gerrit Thomas Rietveld
born 1888 Utrecht
died 1964 Utrecht

1899: trained as a carpenter in his father's workshop in Utrecht; 1904–11: draftsman at a goldsmith's shop; attended evening classes at the Utrecht Museum of Arts and Crafts; 1906: pupil of the architect P.J.C. Klaarhamer; 1917: worked as a freelance cabinetmaker in Utrecht; 1918: became acquainted with Theo van Doesburg; joined the De Stijl group; 1919: opened his own architectural studio in Utrecht; first exhibitions with De Stijl; 1925: built the Schröder residence in Utrecht; 1927: began experimenting with new materials such as tubular steel, particle board, sheet aluminum, and laminated wood; 1928: cofounder of Congrès Internationaux d'Architecture Moderne (CIAM); 1947–51: taught at the College of Art and Science, Rotterdam; 1950–4: taught at the Art Academy of the Hague; 1951: major De Stijl retrospective in Amsterdam; numerous commissions; 1954: built the Dutch pavilion at the Venice Biennial; 1954–8: built the Institute of Applied Art, Amsterdam; 1958–63: built the Arnheim Academy of Visual Arts; 1961: opened an architectural studio together with J. van Dillen and J. van Tricht; 1964: received an honorary doctorate from the Delft Polytechnic.
Furniture designer and architect Gerrit Rietveld was a major figure in rational Modernism and opened new doors in furniture construction through his experiments.
Figs. 29, 43, 88

Eero Saarinen
born 1910 Kirkkonummi, Finland
died 1961 Ann Arbor, Michigan

1923: the Saarinen family emigrated to the United States; 1929–30: Eero Saarinen studied sculpture at the Académie de la Grande Chaumière, Paris; 1930–4: studied architecture at Yale University, New Haven, Connecticut; 1934–6: traveled throughout Europe; 1936: worked in his father's architectural studio and assisted him in his activities as a professor at the Cranbrook Academy of Art; 1940: began working with Charles Eames; together they won first prize for their "Organic Armchair" in the MoMA competition "Organic Design in Home Furnishings;" 1941: designs for Knoll International; 1948: won the Jefferson Memorial Competition; 1950: opened his own architectural studio; 1953–5: built the chapel and auditorium for the Massachusetts Institute of Technology, Cambridge; 1957: built the Milwaukee War Memorial, Wisconsin; 1960: member of the American Academy of Arts and Letters; 1962: designed the TWA terminal at the John F. Kennedy Airport, New York.
In addition to his decisive impact on the world of architecture, Eero Saarinen also had a significant influence on American furniture design, not least of all through his close working relationship with Charles Eames.
Figs. 9, 56, 67

Richard Sapper
born 1932 Munich

1956–8: employed in the design department at Daimler-Benz after completing studies in mechanical engineering; 1958: worked in Gio Ponti's architectural studio in Milan; 1958–77: worked with Marco Zanuso; 1970: designed the successful "Tizia" table lamp; 1970–6: consultant at Fiat and Pirelli for test vehicles and car accessories; 1980 consultant at IBM; designed office furniture.
Fig. 12

Karl Friedrich Schinkel
born 1781 Neuruppin, Germany
died 1841 Berlin

1798: studied architecture with Berlin master builder David Gilly; 1802–3: various building commissions in Potsdam and in Brandenburg; also furniture designs and theoretical studies at the Berlin Academy of Architecture; 1803–5: first trip to Italy; 1805–10: predominantly active as a painter; 1810: secret chief building inspector at the Technical Buildings Inspectorate, Berlin; commissions from the royal family and the ministries; furnished the State Chancellery in Hardenberg; 1815: designed and furnished several buildings for members of the Prussian royal family; 1816–8: built the Neue Wache in Berlin; 1818–21: designed the Berlin Playhouse; 1820: professor of architecture in Berlin; member of the Academy of the Arts; starting in 1830: planned and built several churches and castles.
Karl Friedrich Schinkel was one of the most important and progressive Classicist architects.
Fig. 1

Ettore Sottsass Jr.
born 1917 Innsbruck, Austria

1935–9: studied architecture at Turin Polytechnic; until 1945: prisoner-of-war in Sarajevo; until 1949: involved with painting and sculpture; 1949–52: worked on different projects in Sardinia and Turin; 1950–5: Fourteen architectural projects to rebuild demolished cities in northern Italy for an insurance company; 1956: worked with George Nelson in New York; 1958–92: chief consultant for product design at Olivetti; cooperation on the design for the first electronic computer, the "Elea 9003"; 1959: Compasso d'oro for "Elea 9003"; 1960: opened his own office in Milan; 1961: extended trip to Asia; 1964–5: designed the "Valentine" typewriter for Olivetti; 1966–7: furniture designs for Poltronova; first use of laminated materials; also manufactured ceramics; 1969: Delta di oro prize for the "Valentine" typewriter; 1970: gave a series of lectures in Great Britain and Japan; honorary doctorate from the College of Art, London; 1972: designs for Alessi; participated in the exhibition "Italy, the New Domestic Landscape" at the MoMA, New York; 1973: cofounder of the Global Tools group; 1976: established Studio Alchimia; large retrospective of Sottsass' works in Berlin, Paris, Jerusalem, and Sydney; 1980: established Sottsass Associati; 1981: set up the Memphis group; 1985: quit 'Memphis'; as of 1986: Sottsass Associati handles industrial design, interior design, and visual communication projects as well as numerous architectural projects worldwide. For decades, Ettore Sottsass has been one of the most influential personalities on the international design front. In his extensive *œuvre,* he has reinterpreted shapes and colors as expressive elements in architecture and design.
Fig. 83

Philippe Starck
born 1949 Paris

1966–8: studied at the École Centrale des Arts Décoratifs, Paris; 1968: established the Quasar company to produce inflatable objects; 1971–2: artistic director at Pierre Cardin studio; 1979: furnished the Paris nightclub Les Bains-Douches; opened his own design studio in Monfort l'Amaury; 1980: launched his own production company, Starck Products; 1982: designed the private chambers of the president of France in the Elysée Palace; 1984: designed Café Costes in Paris; 1986: taught at the Domus Academy in Milan and at the École des Arts Décoratifs; 1988: Grand Prix National de la Création Industrielle; 1989: first architectural project implemented: administration buildings for the Asahi Brewery in Tokyo; designed the multifunctional building Nani Nani in Tokyo; 1990: designed the Teatriz restaurant in Paris and Green Baron office building in Tokyo; planned the Red Baron; 1992: Honor Award from the American Institute of Architects for the Paramount Hotel, New York; 1993: designed the prefabricated house Starckinette for the company Les 3 Suisses.
Philippe Starck works in nearly all areas of design and has also been active for a number of years as an architect. His enormous productivity and novel ideas have made him a star in the design world.
Figs. 18, 74

Stiletto (Frank Schreiner)
born 1959 Rüsselsheim, Germany

1979–80: worked as a locksmith for trucks and tanks; 1980–1: studied mechanical engineering in Berlin; 1981: active as a "design practitioner," involved in experimental graphics and art; 1982–6: studied visual communication in Berlin; 1987–8: studied sculpture in Düsseldorf, where he a was master-class student at the College of Art; starting in 1987: exhibitions in Vienna, Zurich, Cologne, Stuttgart, New York; 1991: opened the Studio für Gestaltungsschäden; organized *Prodomo* in Vienna; 1992: case study in collaboration with the Association of System Consultants for Product Design: "Making the Existant visible" based on the example of the Zschoppau motorcycle plant. Stiletto represents an artistically subversive current within the German design scene.
Fig. 97

Gruppo Strum
(Giorgio Ceretti, Piero Derossi,
Ricardo Rosso)

1963: Gruppo Strum established;
1972: participated in the MoMA
exhibition "Italy – the New Domestic
Landscape," where it displayed the
"Pratone" and "Tornerai" seating.
Fig. 92

Gerald Summers
born 1899 Alexandria, Egypt
died 1967

Trained in an engineering firm;
subsequently worked at Marconi
Wireless Telegraph Company, Ltd.;
furniture designs for his own
residence at the end of the twenties; 1931: established the company
Makers of Simple Furniture; 1933:
worked exclusively as a furniture
designer; collaborated with Jack
Pritchard of the Isokon furniture
company; exhibited his furniture
designs in Bristol and London;
1940: the company was closed due
to the shortage of wood during
World War II; after 1945: established Gerald Summers Ltd., which
sold ball bearings.
Fig. 42

Roger Tallon
born 1929 Paris

1944–50: trained as an engineer;
1951: directed graphic communica-
tions at Caterpillar in France; 1955:
research director for Technès, Paris;
numerous industrial designs,
including the thrifty subcompact
"Micro 3" for Peugeot; 1957: taught
industrial design at the Paris
Vocational Arts College; 1957–64:
design consultant at General
Motors; 1958: received the Compasso d'oro for the "Japy Style"
typewriter; 1962: taught at the École
National Supérieure des Arts
Décoratifs; starting in 1967: worked
for SNCF, the French Rail Company;
1971: furnished the Corail train;
1973: established his own design
studio, Design Programmes;
worked with corporate identity and
product design; 1981: established
ADSA & Partners together with
Pierre Paulin; 1986: designed the
interior for the TGV Atlantique
high-speed train; 1992: awarded
Commandeur des Arts et Lettres;
1993: solo exhibition at Centre
Georges Pompidou, Paris.
Roger Tallon is a pioneering French
industrial designer whose work
ranges from furniture design, car-
body designs, and home interiors
to corporate identity.
Fig. 80

H.V. Thaden

The only available information is
that a furniture manufacturer
named Thaden Jordan Furniture
Corporation existed in the United
States during the forties, and that
one of the proprietors was an
H.V. Thaden.
Fig. 45

Michael Thonet
born 1796 Boppard, Germany
died 1871 Vienna, Austria

Trained as a carpenter and cabinet-maker in Boppard; 1819: opened his own furniture workshop; 1830: first experiments with laminated wood; 1842: his workshop in Boppard was impounded; moved to Vienna; granted a five-year royal patent to produce bent laminated wood; employed in the workshop of the Viennese furniture producer List; 1843: created chairs for the Liechtenstein Palace; 1849: opened his own workshop in Vienna; 1850: designed chairs for the Daum café in Vienna; 1851: received a bronze medal at the London world's fair for his furniture designs; 1852: opened a sales office in Vienna; 1852: received a second patent for bending laminated wood; 1853: transferred ownership of the company to his sons under the name Gebrüder Thonet; 1855: participated in the Paris world's fair; first orders from overseas; 1856: established the first furniture plant in Korichan, Moravia; Austrian citizenship; granted the "patent for the solid bending of chairs and table legs"; 1858: closed down the Viennese workshop; opened a second sales office in Vienna; began producing chair "No. 14"; 1862: established a second factory in Bistritz, Czechoslovakia; 1866: set up a third plant in Gross-Ugrocs, Hungary.
In his role as an inventor and entrepreneur, Michael Thonet was one of the founding fathers of modern furniture production.
Fig. 2

Robert Venturi
born 1925 Philadelphia, Pennsylvania

Degree in architecture from Princeton University; 1954–6: studied at the American Academy, Rome; worked with Eero Saarinen; 1963: built the Chestnut Hill house in Philadelphia, Pennsylvania; 1964: together with John Rauch opened an architectural studio in Philadelphia; 1964: professor of architecture at Yale University; 1965: designed the Guild House in Philadelphia, Pennsylvania; 1966: published *Complexity and Contradiction in Architecture*; 1972: published *Learning from Las Vegas*; 1976: built the Allen Memorial Art Museum, Oberlin, Ohio; 1985: published *A View from the Campidoglio*; awarded Firm of the Year prize by the American Institute of Architects; 1990: built the Institute for Economics at Princeton University; until 1991: built the annex to the National Gallery, London.
Architect and theorist Robert Venturi is a leading proponent of Postmodernist architecture.
Fig. 84

Thomas E. Warren
born Troy, New York

Mentioned as a broker in *Prescott & Wilson's Troy Directory* between 1849 and 1852; 1850: patented a chair spring system; 1851: patented a railcar made out of hoop iron; presented several spring-mounted chairs at the world's fair in London; 1853: patented an "iron hull for railcars and other purposes."
Fig. 19

Hans J. Wegner
born 1914 Tonder, Denmark

Trained as a cabinetmaker; subsequently studied at Copenhagen Technical College; 1936–8: studied furniture designs at Copenhagen Vocational Art's College; 1938–40: worked in the architectural studio of Erik Moller and Flemming Lassen; 1943: employed in the architectural studio of Arne Jacobsen and Erik Moller in Arhus, where he designed furniture for the Arhus City Hall; first collaboration with cabinetmaker Johannes Hansen; 1943–6: opened his own studio in Arhus; 1946–8: worked for architect Palle Suenson in Copenhagen, then returned to his own office; 1946–53: taught at Copenhagen Vocational Art's College; 1948: participated in the MoMA competition for "Low-Cost Furniture Design"; 1950: international breakthrough with the publication of "Runde Stol" in the American magazine *Interior*; large commission in the United States; 1951: Lunning Prize; 1954: Milan Triennial Gold Medal; starting in the mid-fifties: industrial production of Wegner's designs by Fritz Hansen and Salesco.
Hans J. Wegner helped bridge the gap between craftsmanship and industrial production, and contributed with his first-class furniture to the international reputation of Danish design.
Fig. 69

Frank Lloyd Wright
born 1867 Richland, Wisconsin
died 1959 Phoenix, Arizona

1885–7: studied engineering at the Engineering School of Wisconsin; 1888–93: worked as a draftsman for architect Louis Sullivan in Chicago; 1893: opened his own architectural studio; 1897: cofounder of the Chicago Arts and Crafts Society; 1900–1: lectured; 1901: designed the Prairie House 1904: built administration buildings out of reinforced concrete for Larkin Company in Buffalo, New York; 1905: first trip to Japan; 1909: traveled to Europe, where he gave a great number of lectures; 1910–11: German-language publication entitled *Buildings and Designs of Frank Lloyd Wright* published by Ernst Wasmuth; 1911: established the Spring Green community and built his own residence in Taliesin; 1912: built his first skyscraper; 1918: published the lecture "The Art and Craft of the Machine" in the magazine *De Stijl*; 1915–22: designed and furnished the Imperial Hotel, Tokyo; 1929: built St. Mark's Tower in New York; honorary member of the Berlin Art Academy; 1936: designed the Fallingwater house in Bear Run, Pennsylvania; 1939: received a Royal Institute of British Architects gold medal; 1940: published *An Organic Architecture*; 1943: designed the Guggenheim Museum, New York; 1955: designed a furniture collection for mass production; 1959: built the Guggenheim Museum, New York.
The *œuvre* of architect and designer Frank Lloyd Wright is one of the most important and varied in the twentieth century. His visionary ideas influenced a great many architects of subsequent generations.
Fig. 77

Sori Yanagi
born 1915 Tokyo

Prior to 1940: studied painting and architecture at the State University for Art and Music, Tokyo; 1940–2: assistant to Charlotte Perriand in Japan; 1947: studied industrial design; 1951: first prize in the "First Japanese Industrial Design Competition" for a combination turntable/radio; 1952: founded the Yanagi Institute for Industrial Design in Tokyo; 1954: chair of industrial design at the Kanazawa Vocational Arts University; 1957: received a Milan Triennial Gold Medal; 1964: exhibited his works at "documenta 3," Kassel; 1977: director of the Japanese Museum of Folk Art in Tokyo.
Sori Yanagi worked predominantly as an industrial designer.
Fig. 66

Marco Zanuso
born 1916 Milan

Prior to 1939: studied architecture in Milan; 1945: opened his own office in Milan; 1947–9: chief editor of *Casabella* magazine; 1951: received Milan Triennial Gold Medal; 1958–77: joint studio with Richard Sapper; active as an architect, industrial designer, and interior designer; 1966–9: cofounder and president of the Associazione di Disegno Industriale (ADI); as of 1976: professor of industrial architecture at the Milan Polytechnic.
Marco Zanuso works as an architect, interior designer, and industrial designer.
Fig. 12

Select Bibliography

1

A. Bruchhäuser: Der Kragstuhl, Stuhlmuseum Burg Beverungen, Berlin: Alexander, 1986), p. 56.
S'asseoir 100 façons, edited by C. Fache, exhibition catalogue Grand-Hornu Images, B-Boussu (Hornu), 1993, p. 12-13.
Vitra Design Museum Collection, Poster DIN A0, Weil am Rhein: Vitra Design Museum, 1993.
M. Eisinger: Stühle des 20. Jahrhunderts, München: Klinkhardt & Biermann, 1994, p. 42-43.
T. Heider, M. Stegmann, R. Zey: Lexikon Internationales Design, Reinbek/Hamburg: Rowohlt, 1994, p. 306-307.

2

O. Bang: Thonet – Geschichte eines Stuhls, Stuttgart: Hatje, 1979, p. 58-66.
A. Bangert: Thonet-Möbel, München: Heyne, 1979, p. 12-13, 81, 134.
G. Candilis, A. Blomstedt, T. Frangoulis, M. I. Amorin: Bugholzmöbel, Stuttgart: Krämer, 1980, p. 10, 54-55, 171-172.
C. Wilk: Thonet – 150 Years of Furniture, New York: Barron's, 1980, p. 32-33.
K. Mang: Thonet Bugholzmöbel, Wien: Brandstätter, 1982, p. 42-48.
L'industrie Thonet, edited by A. v. Vegesack, exhibition catalogue Musée d'Orsay, Paris, Paris: Réunion des Musées Nationaux, 1986, p. 25-26, cat. no. 22.
Bent Wood and Metal Furniture 1850-1946, edited by D. E. Ostergard, exhibition catalogue The American Federation of Arts, New York, 1987, p. 40-44, 214-217.
A. v. Vegesack: Das Thonet Buch, München: Bangert, 1987, p. 57-61.
Sitz-Gelegenheiten, edited by C. Pese, U. Peters, exhibition catalogue Germanisches Nationalmuseum, Nürnberg, 1989, p. 21, 199-200.
A. Bangert, P. Ellenberg: Thonet-Möbel, München: Heyne, 1993, p. 18, 48-51, 167, 216.
Thonet – Pionier des Industriedesigns 1830-1900, edited by A. v. Vegesack, exhibition catalogue Vitra Design Museum, Weil am Rhein, 1994, ill. 22, 24.

3

A.G. Schneck: Der Stuhl, Stuttgart: Hoffmann (Baubücher vol. 4), 1928, p. 57, ill. 108-109.
R. Ginsburger: Gebrauchsgerät in Frankreich, in: Die Form, Berlin, 6.1931, p. 70.
G. Hassenpflug: Stahlmöbel, Düsseldorf: Stahleisen, 1960, p. 23, no. 32.
J. v. Geest, O. Mácel: Stühle aus Stahl, Köln: König, 1980, p. 146, ill. 32.
Vitra Design Museum Collection, Poster DIN A0, Weil am Rhein: Vitra Design Museum, 1991/93.
Ein Stuhl macht Geschichte, edited by W. Möller, O. Mácel, exhibition catalogue Bauhaus, Dessau, Vitra Design Museum, Weil am Rhein, Museum für Kunst und Gewerbe, Hamburg, München: Prestel, 1992, p. 40, ill. 60.

4

W. Gräff: Jetzt wird Ihre Wohnung eingerichtet, Potsdam: Müller & I. Kiepenheuer, 1933, no. 92-95.
L. Canella, R. Radici: Tavoli e piani d'appoggio, in: Quaderni di Domus, Milano, 6.1948, p. 106-107.
Marcel Breuer – Furniture and Interiors, edited by C. Wilk, exhibition catalogue The Museum of Modern Art, New York, 1981, p. 75.
A. v. Vegesack: Deutsche Stahlrohrmöbel, München: Bangert, 1986, p. 73, 130, 161, 164.
Vitra Design Museum Collection, Poster DIN A0, Weil am Rhein: Vitra Design Museum, 1991/93.
M. Droste, M. Ludewig, Bauhaus-Archiv: Marcel Breuer, Köln: Taschen, 1992, p. 92.
Ein Stuhl macht Geschichte, edited by W. Möller, O. Mácel, exhibition catalogue Bauhaus, Dessau, Vitra Design Museum, Weil am Rhein, Museum für Kunst und Gewerbe, Hamburg, München: Prestel, 1992, p. 53.
S'asseoir 100 façons, edited by C. Fache, exhibition catalogue Grand-Hornu Images, B-Boussu (Hornu), 1993, p. 55.
P. Kjellberg: Le Mobilier du XXe Siècle, Paris: Les Editions de l'Amateur, 1994, p. 98-100.

5

Neue Serienmöbel und -geräte, in: Das Werk, Winterthur, 21, 1934, p. 306-307.
F. R. Stevens Yorke, F. Gibberd: The Modern Flat, London: The Architectural Press, 1937, p. 126-127.
Wohnbedarf AG: 25 Jahre Wohnbedarf 1931-1956, Zürich, 1956, p. 21, 47-48.
J. v. Geest, O. Mácel: Stühle aus Stahl, Köln: König, 1980, p. 67, ill.14.
Marcel Breuer – Furniture and Interiors, edited by C. Wilk, exhibition catalogue The Museum of Modern Art, New York, 1981, p. 115-125.
Wohnbedarf AG: 50 Jahre Wohnbedarf 1932-1982, Basel, 1982, ill..
A. v. Vegesack: Deutsche Stahlrohrmöbel, München: Bangert, 1986, p. 122-127.
F. Mehlau-Wiebking, A. Rüegg, R. Tropeano: Schweizer Typenmöbel 1925-1935, Zürich: gta, 1989, p. 48-49, 64-65, 83-90, 140-142.
M. Droste, M. Ludewig, Bauhaus Archiv: Marcel Breuer, Köln: Taschen, 1992, p. 28-29, 118-125, 156, no. 50.
M.-L. Jousset, K. V. Posch: Portrait d'une collection – Alexander von Vegesack, Paris: Centre Georges Pompidou, 1993, p. 30.
P. Kjellberg: Le Mobilier du XXe Siècle, Paris: Les Editions de l'Amateur, 1994, p. 98-100.

6

R. Herbst: 25 années U.A.M. 1930-1955, Paris: Editions du Salon des Arts Ménagers, 1956, p. 107.
J. v. Geest, O. Mácel: Stühle aus Stahl, Köln: König, 1980, p. 146, no. 37.
Jean Prouvé-/Serge Mouille, exhibition catalogue A. Delorenzo, New York, Alan, C. Counord, Paris, 1985, p. 47.
Jean Prouvé – Mobilier 1924-1953, exhibition catalogue Galerie Down-Town, Galerie Touchaleaume, Paris, 1987, p. 11.
Jean Prouvé – Meubles 1924-1953, edited by Abaque, F. Laffanour, E. Touchaleaume, exhibition catalogue Musée des Arts Décoratifs, Bordeaux, 1989, p. 11.
Jean Prouvé 'constructeur', exhibition catalogue Centre Georges Pompidou, Paris, 1990, p. 64, 115.
Vitra Design Museum Collection, Poster DIN A0, Weil am Rhein: Vitra Design Museum, 1993.

7

Les Assises du Siège Contemporain, exhibition catalogue Musée des Arts Décoratifs, Paris, 1968, p. 49, no. 73.
Schweizer Möbeldesign 1927-1984, edited by G. Frey, exhibition catalogue Musée des Arts Décoratifs, Lausanne, Museum für Gestaltung-Kunstgewerbemuseum, Zürich, 1986, p. 71, 109, 159.
Hans Coray – Künstler und Entwerfer, exhibition catalogue Museum für Gestaltung-Kunstgewerbemuseum, Zürich, 1986, p. 14-21, 36-47.
Design Heute, edited by V. Fischer, exhibition catalogue Deutsches Architekturmuseum, Frankfurt am Main, München: Prestel, 1988, p. 25, no. 23.
Design 1935-1965 – What Modern Was, edited by M. Eidelberg, exhibition catalogue Musée des Arts Décoratifs, Montréal, and other, New York: Abrams, 1991, p. 48-49, ill. 44, 45.
K. B. Hiesinger, G. H. Marcus: Landmarks of Twentieth-Century Design, New York: Abbeville Press, 1993, p. 138-139, no. 168.
K.-J. Sembach: Möbel, die Geschichte machen, Hamburg: Gruner+Jahr, 1993, p. 36-37, no. 11.
P. Kjellberg: Le Mobilier du XXe Siècle, Paris: Les Editions de l'Amateur, 1994, p. 144.
T. Heider, M. Stegmann, R. Zey: Lexikon Internationales Design, Reinbek/Hamburg: Rowohlt, 1994, p. 78.

8

E. Noyes: Charles Eames, in: Arts & Architecture, Los Angeles, 63, 1946, p. 26-44.
An Exhibition For Modern Living, edited by A. H. Girard, W. D. Laurie, Jr., exhibition catalogue The Detroit Institute of Arts, 1949, p. 22.
Nelson/Eames/Girard/Propst – The Design Process at Herman Miller, in: Design Quarterly, Walker Art Center, Minneapolis, 98/99, 1975, p. 26.

R. Caplan: The Design of Herman Miller, New York: Whitney, 1976, p. 45,48.
Connections – The Work of Charles and Ray Eames, edited by R. Caplan, exhibition catalogue Frederick S. Wight Art Gallery, University of California, Los Angeles: UCLA Art Council, 1976, p. 48-51.
C. Greenberg: Mid-Century Modern, New York: Harmony Books, 1984, p. 31, 82.
J. Neuhart, M. Neuhart, R. Eames: Eames Design, Berlin: Ernst & Sohn, 1989, p. 54-56.
P. Kirkham: Charles and Ray Eames – Designers of the Twentieth Century, Cambridge, Mass., London: MIT Press, 1995, p. 214-219.

9
Spacious but intimate simple but subtle. In: Architectural Record, New York, Nov. 1948, p. 96-97, ill. 6.
V. Borachia, C. Pagani: Sedie, Divani e Poltrone, in: Quaderni di Domus, Milano, 8, 1950, p. 64-65.
G. Nelson: Chairs, New York: Whitney, 1953, p. 9, 26, 61.
A. Temko: Eero Saarinen, New York: Braziller, 1962, p. 42, 85, ill. 77.
E. Larrabee, M. Vignelli: Knoll Design, New York: Abrams, 1981, p. 57, 62.
C. Greenberg: Mid-Century Modern, New York: Harmony Books, 1984, p.77.
Mackintosh to Mollino, Fifty Years of Chair Design, edited by D. E. Ostergard, exhibition catalogue Gallery Barry Friedman, New York, 1984, p. 55.
Design 1935-1965 – What Modern Was, edited by M. Eidelberg, exhibition catalogue Musée des Arts Décoratifs, Montréal, and other, New York: Abrams, 1991, p. 210, ill. 307-308.
K. B. Hiesinger, G. H. Marcus: Landmarks of Twentieth-Century Design, New York: Abbeville Press, 1993, p. 163, no. 201.
R. Guidot: Design, Stuttgart: Deutsche Verlags-Anstalt, 1994, p. 42-43, 54.

10
Les Assises du Siège Contemporain, exhibition catalogue Musée des Arts Décoratifs, Paris, 1968, p. 54, ill. 91.
Charles Eames – Furniture from the Design Collection, edited by A. Drexler, exhibition catalogue The Museum of Modern Art, New York, 1973, p. 36, ill. 63.
Nelson/Eames/Girard/Propst – The Design Process at Herman Miller, in: Design Quarterly, Walker Art Center, Minneapolis, 98/99, 1975, p. 23-24.
R. Caplan: The Design of Herman Miller, New York: Whitney, 1976, p. 50.
K.-J. Sembach: Neue Möbel, Stuttgart: Hatje, 1982, p. 68, ill. 208.
C. Greenberg: Mid-Century Modern, New York: Harmony Books, 1984, p. 82-91, 141.
J. Neuhart, M. Neuhart, R. Eames: Eames Design, Berlin: Ernst & Sohn, 1989, p. 150-153.
K.-J. Sembach: Möbel, die Geschichte machen, Hamburg: Gruner & Jahr, 1993, p. 16, no. 15.
T. Heider, M. Stegmann, R. Zey: Lexikon Internationales Design, Reinbek/Hamburg: Rowohlt, 1994, p. 96-98.
P. Kjellberg: Le Mobilier du XXᵉ Siècle, Paris: Les Editions de l'Amateur, 1994, p. 211-213.

11
G. Hatje: Neue Möbel, Hatje: Stuttgart, vol.5, 1960, p. 50, ill. 113.
Charles Eames – Furniture from the Design Collection, edited by A. Drexler, exhibition catalogue The Museum of Modern Art, New York, 1973, p. 42-44.
Nelson/Eames/Girard/Propst – The Design Process at Herman Miller, in: Design Quarterly, Walker Art Center, Minneapolis, 98/99, 1975, p. 27.
Connections – The Work of Charles and Ray Eames, exhibition catalogue Frederick S. Wight Art Gallery, University of California, Los Angeles: UCLA Art Council, 1976, p. 53.
K.-J. Sembach: Neue Möbel, Stuttgart: Hatje, 1982, p. 104, ill. 347.
C. Greenberg: Mid-Century Modern, New York: Harmony Books, 1984, p. 90.
J. Neuhart, M. Neuhart, R. Eames: Eames Design, Berlin: Ernst & Sohn, 1989, p. 226-229.
K.-J. Sembach: Möbel, die Geschichte machen, Hamburg: Gruner+Jahr, 1993, p. 112, no. 23.

M.-L. Jousset, K. V. Posch: Portrait d'une Collection – Alexander von Vegesack, Paris: Centre Georges Pompidou, 1993, p. 66-67.
T. Heider, M. Stegmann, R. Zey: Lexikon Internationales Design, Reinbek/Hamburg: Rowohlt, 1994, p. 96-98.
P. Kjellberg: Le Mobilier du XXᵉ Siècle, Paris: Les Editions de l'Amateur, 1994, p. 211-213.

12
Forme Nuove in Italia, Roma: Carlo Bestetti Ed. d'Arte, 1962, p. 62-63.
G. Dorfles: Marco Zanuso – Designer, Roma: Editalia, 1971, p. 83-93.
Italy: The New Domestic Landscape, edited by E. Ambasz, exhibition catalogue The Museum of Modern Art, New York, Firenze: Centro Di, 1972, p. 42.
A. Grassi, A. Pansera: Atlante Del Design Italiano 1940/1980, Milano: Fabbri, 1980, p. 151, ill. 5/6.
G. Gramigna: Repertorio 1950-1980, Milano: Mondadori, 1985, p. 194.
A. Bangert: Italienisches Möbeldesign, München: Bangert, 1985, p. 37.
Vitra Design Museum Collection, Poster DIN A0, Weil am Rhein: Vitra Design Museum, 1991/93.
Fondazione Scientifica Querini Stampalia: Dino Gavina, Milano: Jaca Book, 1992, p. 56, no. 34.
F. Burkhardt: Design Marco Zanuso, Milano: Motta, 1994, p. 92-97.
T. Heider, M. Stegmann, R. Zey: Lexikon Internationales Design, Reinbek/Hamburg: Rowohlt, 1994, p. 301-303.

13
Les Assises du Siège Contemporain, exhibition catalogue Musée des Arts Décoratifs, Paris, 1968, p. 35, no. 32.
K.-J. Sembach: Neue Möbel, Stuttgart: Hatje, 1982, p. 116, no. 386/387.
K.-J. Sembach, G. Leuthäuser, P. Gössel: Möbeldesign des 20. Jahrhunderts, Köln: Taschen, 1982, p. 200.
W. Blaser: Element System Möbel, Stuttgart: Deutsche Verlags-Anstalt, 1984, p. 67-69, 79, 109-124.
Design Heute, edited by V. Fischer, exhibition catalogue Deutsches Architekturmuseum, Frankfurt am Main, München: Prestel, 1988, p. 29, no. 37.
Möbel aus Kunststoff, edited by A. v. Vegesack, exhibition catalogue Vitra Design Museum, Weil am Rhein, 1990, p. 16-17.
B. Mundt: Produktdesign 1900-1990, Kunstgewerbemuseum, Berlin, Berlin: Reimer, 1991, p. 184, ill. 118.
Vitra Design Museum Collection, Poster DIN A0, Weil am Rhein: Vitra Design Museum, 1991/93.
K.-J. Sembach: Möbel, die Geschichte machen, Hamburg: Gruner + Jahr, 1993, p. 22-23, no. 28.

14
E. Ritter: Design Italiano – I Mobili, Milano, Roma: Bestetti, 1968, p. 113.
Italy – The New Domestic Landscape, edited by E. Ambasz, exhibition catalogue The Museum of Modern Art, New York, Firenze: Centro Di, 1972, p. 34.
A. Grassi, A. Pansera: Atlante Del Design Italiano 1940-1980, Milano: Fabbri, 1980, p. 158, ill. 2.
Italienisches Möbeldesign, exhibition catalogue Stadtmuseum, Köln, Roma: ICE, Istituto Nazionale per il Commercio Estero, 1980, p. 54, 140-141, no. 82.
S. Casciani: Mobili come Architetture, Milano: Arcadia, 1984, p. 86-88.
A. Bangert: Italienisches Möbeldesign, München: Bangert, 1985, p. 46-47.
G. Gramigna: Repertorio 1950-1980, Milano: Mondadori, 1985, p. 248, 528, 585.
P. Sparke: Italienisches Design von 1870 bis heute, Braunschweig: Westermann, 1989, p. 194.
Ispirazione Italiana, edited by W. Schepers, P. Dunas, exhibition catalogue Kunstmuseum Düsseldorf, 1990, p. 54-55.
Möbel aus Kunststoff, edited by A. v. Vegesack, exhibition catalogue Vitra Design Museum, Weil am Rhein, 1990, p. 5, 7, 9, 30-31.
K. B. Hiesinger, G. H. Marcus: Landmarks of Twentieth-Century Design, New York: Abbeville Press, 1993, p. 238, no. 306.

15
Italy – The New Domestic Landscape, edited by E. Ambasz, exhibition cata-
logue The Museum of Modern Art, New York, Firenze: Centro Di, 1972, p. 98.
A. Bangert: Italienisches Möbeldesign, München: Bangert, 1985, p. 48,
106-107, no. 58-59.
G. Gramigna: Repertorio 1950-1980, Milano: Mondadori, 1985, p. 288.
F. Vanlaethem: Gaetano Pesce, Milano: Idea Books, 1989, p. 11, 18, 24, 52, 116.
Ispirazione Italiana, edited by W. Schepers, P. Dunas, exhibition catalogue
Kunstmuseum Düsseldorf, 1990, p. 66-67.
Möbel aus Kunststoff, edited by A. v. Vegesack, exhibition catalogue
Vitra Design Museum, Weil am Rhein, 1990, p. 5, 7, 9, 32-33.
Gaetano Pesce, exhibition catalogue Tel Aviv Museum of Art, Peter Joseph
Gallery, New York, Tel Aviv, New York, 1991, p. 40-43.
K. B. Hiesinger, G. H. Marcus: Landmarks of Twentieth-Century Design,
New York: Abbeville Press, 1993, p. 238, no. 307.
R. Guidot: Design, Stuttgart: Deutsche Verlags-Anstalt, 1994, p. 245-246.
T. Heider, M. Stegmann, R. Zey: Lexikon Internationales Design,
Reinbek/Hamburg: Rowohlt, 1994, p. 257-258.
P. Kjellberg: Le Mobilier du XXᵉ Siècle, Paris: Les Editions de l'Amateur,
1994, p. 485-487.

16
Design Since 1945, Edited by K. B. Hiesinger, G. H. Marcus, exhibition
catalogue Philadelphia Museum of Art, 1983, p. 66, 126.
M. Emery: Furniture by Architects, New York: Abrams, 1983, p. 100, 108,
no. 165.
P. Arnell, T. Bickford: Frank Gehry – Buildings and Projects, New York:
Rizzoli, 1985, p. 64-69.
Frank O. Gehry – Muebles y dibujos, edited by L. Feduchi, exhibition
catalogue b.d., Madrid, 1990, p. 15.
Frank O. Gehry, edited by K. Winter, exhibition catalogue Arkitekturmuseet,
Stockholm, 1990, p. 22.
Vitra Design Museum Collection, Poster DIN A0, Weil am Rhein:
Vitra Design Museum, 1991/93.
Frank Gehry – New Bentwood Furniture Designs, exhibition catalogue
The Montreal Museum of Decorative Arts, 1992, p. 99-101.
K. B. Hiesinger, G. H. Marcus: Landmarks of Twentieth-Century Design,
New York: Abbeville Press, 1993, p. 250, 258.
M. Eisinger: Stühle des 20. Jahrhunderts, München: Klinkhardt & Biermann,
1994, p. 94.
P. Kjellberg: Le Mobilier du XXᵉ Siècle, Paris: Les Editions de l'Amateur,
1994, p. 266-267.

17
N. Bellati: New Italian Design, New York: Rizzoli, 1990, p. 83.
R. Guidot: Design, Stuttgart: Deutsche Verlags-Anstalt, 1994, p. 292.
T. Heider, M. Stegmann, R. Zey: Lexikon Internationales Design,
Reinbek/Hamburg: Rowohlt, 1994, p. 206-207.
P. Kjellberg: Le Mobilier du XXᵉ Siècle, Paris: Les Editions de l'Amateur,
1994, p. 420-421.
Mutant Materials in Contemporary Design, edited by P. Antonelli, exhibition
catalogue The Museum of Modern Art, New York, 1995, p. 62.

18
C. & P. Fiell: Modern Chairs, Köln: Taschen, 1993, p. 133.
Grand-Hornu Images: S'asseoir 100 façons, Poster, B-Boussu (Hornu), 1993,
no. 96.
B. Sipek: Das Internationale Design Jahrbuch 1993/94, München,
Schopfheim: Bangert, 1993, p. 46-47, ill. 52.
Vitra Design Museum Collection, Poster DIN A0, Weil am Rhein:
Vitra Design Museum, 1993.
R. Guidot: Design, Stuttgart: Deutsche Verlags-Anstalt, 1994, cover, p. 262-263.
T. Heider, M. Stegmann, R. Zey: Lexikon Internationales Design,
Reinbek/Hamburg: Rowohlt, 1994, p. 318-321.
13 nach Memphis, edited by V. Albus, V. Fischer, exhibition catalogue
Museum für Kunsthandwerk, Frankfurt am Main, München: Prestel, 1995,
p. 166, ill. 6.

19
An Exhibition for Modern Living, edited by A. H. Girard, W. D. Laurie, Jr.,
exhibition catalogue The Detroit Institute of Arts, 1949, p. 10-11, 86.
Exhibition for Modern Living, in: Interieur, Zürich, 9, 1963, o.S..
Innovative Furniture in America From 1800 to the Present, edited
by D. A. Hanks, exhibition catalogue Cooper-Hewitt Museum, New York,
and other, New York: Horizon Press, 1981, p. 126-129.
S. Yates: An Encyclopedia of Chairs, London: Quintet Publishing, 1988,
p.124.

20
Moderne Bauformen, Stuttgart, 7/1908, p. 370.
A. S. Levetus: Austrian Architecture and Decoration, in: The Studio
Yearbook of Decorative Art, London, Paris, New York, 1910, p. 222-223.
D. Müller: Klassiker des modernen Möbeldesign, München: Keyser, 1980,
p. 107, ill. 81.
D. Baroni, A. D'Auria: Josef Hoffmann e la Wiener Werkstätte, Milano:
Electa, 1981, p. 63, 100-101.
K. Mang: Thonet Bugholzmöbel, Wien: Brandstätter, 1982, p. 110, 112.
Traum und Wirklichkeit Wien 1870-1930, exhibition catalogue Historisches
Museum, Wien, 1985, p. 409-410, no. 13/15/30.
Bent Wood and Metal Furniture 1850-1946, edited by D. E. Ostergard,
exhibition catalogue The American Federation of Arts, New York, 1987,
p. 257-258, no. 56.
A. v. Vegesack: Das Thonet Buch, München: Bangert, 1987, p. 134-135.
S'asseoir 100 façons, edited by C. Fache, exhibition catalogue Grand-Hornu
Images, B-Boussu (Hornu), 1993, p. 42-43.
Against the Grain, edited by G. Zelleke, E. B. Ottillinger, N. Stritzler, exhibiti-
on catalogue The Art Institute of Chicago, 1993, p. 84, no. 53.
P. Kjellberg: Le Mobilier du XXᵉ Siècle, Paris: Les Editions de l'Amateur,
1994, p. 310-313.

21
H. Eckstein: Die schöne Wohnung, München: Bruckmann, 1934, p. 110-111.
Eileen Gray, Designer, edited by J. S. Johnson, exhibition catalogue
The Museum of Modern Art, New York, London: Debrett's Peerage, 1979,
p. 42, 49.
K.-J. Sembach: Neue Möbel, Stuttgart: Hatje, 1982, p. 20, no. 35.
B. Loye: Eileen Gray 1879-1976, Architecture – Design, Analeph/J. P. Viguier,
1984, p. 30-31, 113.
P. Adam: Eileen Gray, Architect/Designer, New York: Abrams, 1987,
p. 202-203, 230, 252, 368-369, 371.
Sotheby's: Arts Décoratifs du XXᵉ Siècle, Monaco, 13.10.1991, p. 115,
Lot 323.
Grand-Hornu Images, S'asseoir 100 façons, Poster, B-Boussu (Hornu) 1993,
no. 59.
P. Garner: Eileen Gray, Köln: Taschen, 1993, p. 84-85, 144, 147, 156, no. 14, 15.
K.-J. Sembach: Möbel, die Geschichte machen, Hamburg: Gruner + Jahr,
1993, p. 159, no. 6.
T. Heider, M. Stegmann, R. Zey: Lexikon Internationales Design,
Reinbek/Hamburg: Rowohlt, 1994, p. 119-121.
P. Kjellberg: Le Mobilier du XXᵉ Siècle, Paris: Les Editions de l'Amateur,
1994, p. 274-279.

22
Mobilier et Décoration, Paris, no. 8, 1928, p. 230.
p. Chareau: Meubles, in: L'Art International d'Aujourd'hui, Paris, no. 7,
Meubles, 1929-30, plate 27.
R. Herbst: 25 Années U.A.M. 1930-1955, Paris: Editions du Salon des Arts
Ménagers, 1956, p. 95.
J. v. Geest, O. Mácel: Stühle aus Stahl, Köln: König, 1980, p. 70-71.
Bent Wood and Metal Furniture 1850-1946, edited by D. E. Ostergard,
exhibition catalogue The American Federation of Arts, New York, 1987,
p. 142, ill. 5.35.
M. Vellay, K. Frampton: Pierre Chareau, New York: Rizzoli, 1990, p. 168-169,
296.

J. M. Millon, C. Robert: Collection Jean-Claude Brugnot, Hôtel George-V, Paris, 18.06.1993, p. 110-111.
Pierre Chareau architecte, un art intérieur, exhibition catalogue Centre Georges Pompidou, Paris, 1993, p. 147-151.
Pierre Chareau, Archives Louis Moret, exhibition catalogue Fondation Louis Moret, Martigny, 1994, p. 26-30.
P. Kjellberg: Le Mobilier du XXᵉ Siècle, Paris: Les Editions de l'Amateur, 1994, p. 124-131.

23
M. Terrier: Meubles Métalliques, in: Art & Décoration, Paris, 02.1930, p. 45.
M. Casteels: L'Art Moderne Primitif, Paris: Jonquières, 1930, p. 135.
C. G. Holme, S. B. Wainwright: Decorative Art – The Studio Year-Book, London: The Studio, 1930, p. 17.
S. Papadaki: Le Corbusier, New York: Macmillan, 1948, p. 39-44.
R. De Fusco: Le Corbusier als Designer – Die Möbel des Jahres 1929, Milano: Electa, 1976, p. 23, 26, 30-41, 56-61, 90-95.
J. v. Geest, O. Mácel: Stühle aus Stahl, Köln: König, 1980, p. 72-73.
C. Wilk: Thonet – 150 Years of Furniture, New York: Barron's, 1980, p. 103-105.
A. v. Vegesack: Deutsche Stahlrohrmöbel, München: Bangert, 1986, p. 82.
Bent Wood and Metal Furniture 1850-1946, edited by D. E. Ostergard, exhibition catalogue The American Federation of Arts, New York, 1987, p. 280-281, no. 75.
A. v. Vegesack: Das Thonet Buch, München: Bangert, 1987, p. 168-169.
P. Kjellberg: Le Mobilier du XXᵉ Siècle, Paris: Les Editions de l'Amateur, 1994, p. 361-365.
G. H. Marcus: Functionalist Design, München, New York: Prestel, 1995, p. 94-114.

24
M. Terrier: Meubles Métalliques, in: Art & Décoration, Paris, 02.1930, p. 33-48.
S. Papadaki: Le Corbusier, New York: Macmillan, 1948, p. 40.
P. Blake: The Master Builders – Le Corbusier, Mies van der Rohe, Frank Lloyd Wright, New York: Knopf 1960, p. 65-70.
R. De Fusco: Le Corbusier als Designer, Milano: Electa 1976, p. 30-41, 57, 68-77.
J. v. Geest, O. Mácel: Stühle aus Stahl, Köln: König 1980, p. 72-75, ill. 5, 5A.
Charlotte Perriand – Un art de vivre, exhibition catalogue Musée des Arts Décoratifs, Paris, Paris: Flammarion 1985, p. 18-25, ill. 9, 14.
A. v. Vegesack: Deutsche Stahlrohrmöbel, München: Bangert 1986, p. 70-71, 82.
Bent Wood and Metal Furniture 1850-1946, edited by D. E. Ostergard, exhibition catalogue The American Federation of Arts, New York, 1987, p. 140-141, 282-284, no. 76.
P. Kjellberg: Le Mobilier du XXᵉ Siècle, Paris: Les Editions de l'Amateur, 1994, p. 361-365.
G. H. Marcus: Functionalist Design, München, New York: Prestel, 1995, p. 22-23, 94-114.

25
W. Lotz: Ausstellung des Deutschen Werkbundes in Paris, in: Die Form, Berlin, 5.1930, S. 281-284 (German), 284 ff (French, English).
M. Casteels: L'Art Moderne Primitif, Paris: Jonquières, 1930, p. 134.
P. Blake: Marcel Breuer: Architect and Designer, New York: The Museum of Modern Art, 1949, p. 28-35, ill. 54-58.
J. van Geest, O. Mácel: Stühle aus Stahl, Köln: König, 1980, p. 65, no. 8.
Marcel Breuer, edited by C. Wilk, exhibition catalogue The Museum of Modern Art, New York, 1981, p. 82, ill. 78.
A. v. Vegesack: Deutsche Stahlrohrmöbel, München: Bangert, 1986, p. 71, 75, 131, 161.
Bent Wood and Metal Furniture 1850-1946, edited by D. E. Ostergard, exhibition catalogue The American Federation of Arts, New York, 1987, p. 135, 286-287, no. 78.
O. Mácel: Der Freischwinger, Vom Avantgardeentwurf zur Ware, Dissertation, TU Delft, 1992, p. 65-68.
Ein Stuhl macht Geschichte, edited by W. Möller, O. Mácel, exhibition

catalogue Bauhaus, Dessau, and other, München: Prestel, 1992, p. 60-62.
M.-L. Jousset, K. V. Posch: Portrait d'une Collection – Alexander von Vegesack, Paris: Centre Georges Pompidou, 1993, p. 28-29.

26
J. van Geest, O. Mácel: Stühle aus Stahl, Köln: König, 1980, p. 145, ill. 25.
Jean Prouvé/Serge Mouille, exhibition catalogue A. Delorenzo, New York, Alan, C. Counord, Paris, 1985, p. 42-43.
Il progetto del mobile in Francia 1919-1939, in: Rassegna, Bologna, 26/2, 1986, p. 83, ill. 1.
Jean Prouvé –Mobilier 1924-1953, exhibition catalogue Galerie Down-Town, Galerie Touchaleaume, Paris, 1987, p. 9.
Jean Prouvé – Meubles 1924-1953, edited by Abaque, F. Laffanour, E. Touchaleaume, exhibition catalogue Musée des Arts Décoratifs, Bordeaux, 1989, p. 14-15.
Jean Prouvé 'constructeur', exhibition catalogue Centre Georges Pompidou, Paris, 1990, p. 63, 65, 112.
J. v. Geest: Jean Prouvé, Köln: Taschen, 1991, p. 44-47, 150, ill. 6.
Vitra Design Museum Collection, Poster DIN A0, Weil am Rhein: Vitra Design Museum, 1993.
Centre Georges Pompidou: Nouvelles Acquisitions, folder, Paris, 1993.

27
A. Bruchhäuser: Der Kragstuhl, Stuhlmuseum Burg Beverungen, Berlin: Alexander, 1986, p. 62, 65-66.
Jean Prouvé 'constructeur', exhibition catalogue Centre Georges Pompidou, Paris, 1990, p. 62, 111-112.
J. v. Geest: Jean Prouvé, Köln: Taschen, 1991, p. 19, 34-37, 150, no. 1.
K. B. Hiesinger, G. H. Marcus: Landmarks of Twentieth-Century Design, New York: Abbeville Press, 1993, p. 94, ill. 102.

28
Sitz-Gelegenheiten, edited by C. Pese, U. Peters, exhibition catalogue Germanisches Nationalmuseum, Nürnberg, 1989, p. 243-244, no. 180.
Vitra Design Museum Collection, Poster DIN A0, Weil am Rhein: Vitra Design Museum, 1991/93.

29
D. Baroni: I mobili di Gerrit Thomas Rietveld, Milano: Electa, 1977, p. 128-129.
Stoelen, Delft: Delftse Universitaire Pres, 1980, p. 186.
Rietveld. Uit de verzameling van het Stedelijk Museum Amsterdam, 1981, p. 26-27, no. 96.
P. Vöge, B. Westerveld: Stoelen, Amsterdam: Meulenhoff/Landshoff, 1986, p. 67, ill. 9.
Christie's, Amsterdam, 28.05.1987, Lot 416.
S. Yates: An Encyclopedia of Chairs, London: Quintet Publishing, 1988, p. 96-98, no. 152h.
Gerrit T. Rietveld 1888-1964, The complete works, edited by M. Küper, I. van Zijl, exhibition catalogue Centraal Museum, Utrecht, Centre Pompidou, Paris, Utrecht, 1992, p. 196-197, 209-210, no. 302, 334.
Sotheby's, Monaco, 26.04.1992, Lot 243.
S'asseoir 100 façons, edited by C. Fache, exhibition catalogue Grand-Hornu Images, B-Boussu (Hornu), 1993, p. 51.
Vitra Design Museum Collection, Poster DIN A0, Weil am Rhein: Vitra Design Museum, 1993.
P. Vöge: The Complete Rietveld Furniture, Rotterdam: 010 Publishers, 1993, p. 118-119, no. 228.

30
An Exhibition for Modern Living, edited by A. H. Girard, W. D. Laurie, Jr., exhibition catalogue The Detroit Institute of Arts, Detroit, 1949, p. 80-81.
E. Kaufmann, Jr.: What Is Modern Design? New York: The Museum of Modern Art, 1950, p. 15, ill. 22.
Nelson/Eames/Girard/Propst – The Design Process at Herman Miller, in: Design Quarterly, Walker Art Center, Minneapolis, 98/99, 1975, p. 22.

R. Caplan: The Design of Herman Miller, New York: Whitney, 1976, p. 49.
C. Greenberg: Mid-Century Modern, New York: Harmony Books, 1984, p. 89.
J. Neuhart, M. Neuhart, R. Eames: Eames Design, Berlin: Ernst & Sohn, 1989, p. 124-129, 133.
Design 1935-1965, edited by M. Eidelberg, exhibition catalogue Musée des Arts Décoratifs, Montréal, and other, New York: Abrams, 1991, p. 59-60, ill. 63.
P. Kirkham: Charles and Ray Eames – Designers of the Twentieth Century, Cambridge, Mass., London: MIT Press, 1995, p. 389.

31
P. Garner: Contemporary Decorative Arts from 1940 to the present, New York: Facts on File, 1980, p. 52-54.
E. Larrabee, M. Vignelli: Knoll Design, New York: Abrams, 1981, p. 66-75.
C. Greenberg: Mid-Century Modern, New York: Harmony Books, 1984, p. 62-63, 76.
Design 1935-1965, edited by M. Eidelberg, exhibition catalogue Musée des Arts Décoratifs, Montréal, and other, New York: Abrams, 1991, p. 214-215.
B. Mundt: Produkt-Design 1900-1990, Kunstgewerbemuseum, Berlin, Berlin: Reimer, 1991, p. 138-139, no. 82.
K. B. Hiesinger, G. H. Marcus: Landmarks of Twentieth-Century Design, New York: Abbeville Press, 1993, p. 184, no. 222.
M.-L. Jousset, K. V. Posch: Portrait d'une collection – Alexander von Vegesack, Paris: Centre Georges Pompidou, 1993, p. 56.
K.-J. Sembach: Möbel, die Geschichte machen, Hamburg: Gruner + Jahr, 1993, p. 114, no. 28.
R. Guidot: Design, Stuttgart: Deutsche Verlags-Anstalt, 1994, p. 139.
P. Kjellberg: Le Mobilier du XXᵉ Siècle, Paris: Les Editions de l'Amateur, 1994, p. 84-85.
T. Heider, M. Stegmann, R. Zey: Lexikon Internationales Design, Reinbek/Hamburg: Rowohlt, 1994, p. 47-48.

32
R. Geyer-Raack, S. Geyer: Möbel und Raum, Berlin: Ullstein, 1955, p. 11, ill. 7.
G. Hatje: Neue Möbel, Stuttgart: Hatje, vol. 4, 1958, p. 59, ill. 116.
Innovative Furniture in America From 1800 to the Present, edited by D. A. Hanks, exhibition catalogue Cooper Hewitt Museum, New York, and other, New York: Horizon Press, 1981, p. 143, ill. 120.
A. Bangert: Der Stil der 50er Jahre, München: Heyne, 1983, p. 68.
C. Greenberg: Mid-Century Modern, New York: Harmony Books, 1984, p. 59, 79, 97.
Mackintosh to Mollino, edited by D. E. Ostergard, exhibition catalogue Gallery Barry Friedman, New York, 1984, p. 58.
S. Yates: An Encyclopedia of Chairs, London: Quintet Publishing, 1988, p. 110-111, no. 172.
Vitra Design Museum Collection, Poster DIN A0, Weil am Rhein: Vitra Design Museum, 1991/93.
M.-L. Jousset, K. V. Posch: Portrait d'une collection – Alexander von Vegesack, Paris: Centre Georges Pompidou, 1993, p. 68-69.
P. Kjellberg: Le Mobilier du XXᵉ Siècle, Paris: Les Editions de l'Amateur, 1994, p. 449-451.

33
G. Hollyrod: Architecture creating relaxed intensity, in: Eames-Celebration, Sonderdruck aus: Architectural Design, 9.1966, p. 27-39.
Charles Eames – Furniture from the Design Collection, edited by A. Drexler, exhibition catalogue The Museum of Modern Art, New York, 1973, p. 30, 40-41, 55, no. 54, 68-70.
A Modern Consciousness: D. J. De Pree, Florence Knoll, exhibition catalogue National Collection of Fine Arts, Washington, Cranbrook Academy of Art Museum, Bloomfield Hills, Washington: Smithsonian Institution Press, 1975, p. 16, no. 14.
Connections – The Work of Charles and Ray Eames, edited by R. Caplan, exhibition catalogue Frederick S. Wight Art Gallery, University of California, Los Angeles: UCLA Art Council, 1976, p. 30-31.
R. Caplan: The Design of Herman Miller, New York: Whitney, 1976, p. 17, 70.
Design Since 1945, edited by K. B. Hiesinger, G. H. Marcus, exhibition

catalogue The Philadelphia Museum of Art, 1983, p. 56, 125.
J. Neuhart, M. Neuhart, R. Eames: Eames Design, Berlin: Ernst & Sohn, 1989, p. 206-208.
P. Kirkham: Charles and Ray Eames, Cambridge, Mass., London: MIT Press, 1995, p. 246, 260, 315.

34
G. Hatje, K. Kaspar: Neue Möbel, Stuttgart: Hatje, vol. 8, 1966, p. 96-98, ill. 283-284.
Nelson/Eames/Girard/Propst – The Design Process at Herman Miller, in: Design Quarterly, Walker Art Center, Minneapolis, 1975, 98/99, p. 18.
R. Caplan: The Design of Herman Miller, New York: Whitney, 1976, p. 89.
K.-J. Sembach: Neue Möbel, Stuttgart: Hatje, 1982, p. 214, ill. 745.
L'Empire du Bureau 1900-2000, exhibition catalogue Musée des Arts Décoratifs, Paris: CNAP/Berger-Levrault, 1984, p. 205, no. 149.
Treadway Gallery, Inc., Cincinnati, Ohio, John Toomey, Oak Park, Illinois: 20th Century Auction, Oak Park 02.05.1993, p. 103, Lot no. 855.
R. Guidot: Design, Stuttgart: Deutsche Verlags-Anstalt, 1994, p. 140.
T. Heider, M. Stegmann, R. Zey: Lexikon Internationales Design, Reinbek/Hamburg: Rowohlt, 1994, p. 234-235.
P. Kjellberg: Le Mobilier du XXᵉ Siècle, Paris: Les Editions de l'Amateur, 1994, p. 449-451.

35
G. Hatje, K. Kaspar: Neue Möbel, Stuttgart: Hatje, vol. 8, 1966, p. 98, ill. 284.
R. Propst: The office – A facility based on change, Elmhurst, ill.: The Business Press, 1968, p. 46-58.
Nelson/Eames/Girard/Propst, The Design Process at Herman Miller, in: Design Quarterly, Walker Art Center, Minneapolis, 98/99, 1975, p. 18.
R. Caplan: The Design of Herman Miller, New York: Whitney, 1976, p. 89, 91.
K.-J. Sembach: Neue Möbel, Stuttgart: Hatje, 1982, p. 214.
L'Empire du Bureau 1900-2000, exhibition catalogue Musée des Arts Décoratifs, Paris: CNAP/Berger-Levrault, 1984, p. 207.
Treadway Gallery, Inc., Cincinnati, Ohio, John Toomey, Oak Park, Illinois: 20th Century Auction, Oak Park 02.05.1993, p. 103, Lot. no. 856.
R. Guidot: Design, Stuttgart: Deutsche Verlags-Anstalt, 1994, p. 140.

36
G. Hatje: Neue Möbel, Stuttgart: Hatje, vol. 9, 1969, p. 38, ill. 101-102.
K.-J. Sembach: Neue Möbel, Stuttgart: Hatje, 1982, p. 150, ill. 508-509.
H. Wichmann: Industrial Design, Unikate, Serienerzeugnisse, Die Neue Sammlung (München), ein neuer Museumstyp des 20. Jahrhunderts, München: Prestel, 1985, p. 207 (cover title: Wichmann: Kunst, die sich nützlich macht).
Les Années 50, exhibition catalogue Centre Georges Pompidou, Paris, 1988, p. 569, ill. 1.
F. Sieck: Contemporary Danish Furniture Design, Nyt Nordisk Forlag Arnold Busck, 1990, p. 148.
K.-J. Sembach: Möbel, die Geschichte machen, Hamburg: Gruner + Jahr, 1993, p. 179, no. 9.
C. & P. Fiell: Modern Chairs, Köln: Taschen, 1993, p. 78.
R. Guidot: Design, Stuttgart: Deutsche Verlags-Anstalt, 1994, p. 119.
T. Heider, M. Stegmann, R. Zey: Lexikon Internationales Design, Reinbek/Hamburg: Rowohlt, 1994, p. 164.
P. Kjellberg: Le Mobilier du XXᵉ Siècle, Paris: Les Editions de l'Amateur, 1994, p. 341.

37
A. Grassi, A. Pansera: Atlante Del Design Italiano 1940/1980, Milano: Fabbri, 1980, p. 168, ill. 1/3.
Italienisches Möbeldesign, exhibition catalogue Stadtmuseum Köln, Roma: ICE, Istituto Nazionale per il Commercio Estero, 1980, p. 226-227, no. 159.
A. Bangert: Italienisches Möbeldesign, München: Bangert, 1985, p. 119, no. 74/75.
G. Gramigna: Repertorio 1950-1980, Milano: Mondadori, 1985, p. 378.
Design Heute, edited by V. Fischer, exhibition catalogue Deutsches

Architekturmuseum, Frankfurt am Main, München: Prestel, 1988, p. 30, no. 40.
Ispirazione Italiana, edited by W. Schepers, P. Dunas, exhibition catalogue Kunstmuseum Düsseldorf, 1990, p. 76-77.
B. Mundt: Produkt-Design 1900-1990, Kunstgewerbemuseum, Berlin, Berlin: Reimer, 1991, p. 202-203.
Vitra Design Museum Collection, Poster DIN A0, Weil am Rhein: Vitra Design Museum, 1991/93.
R. Guidot: Design, Stuttgart: Deutsche Verlags-Anstalt, 1994, p. 247.
T. Heider, M. Stegmann, R. Zey: Lexikon Internationales Design, Reinbek/Hamburg: Rowohlt, 1994, p. 20-21, 81-82.
P. Kjellberg: Le Mobilier du XXᵉ Siècle, Paris: Les Editions de l'Amateur, 1994, p. 153-154.

38
P. Garner: Contemporary Decorative Arts from 1940 to the Present, New York: Facts On File, 1980, p. 75.
Design Since 1945, edited by K. B. Hiesinger, G. H. Marcus, exhibition catalogue Philadelphia Museum of Art, 1983, p. 122, III-8.
A. Drexler: Architecture and Design, in: The Museum of Modern Art, New York: Abrams, 1984, p. 444-445, ill. 733.
Mario Bellini – Designer, edited by C. McCarty, exhibition catalogue The Museum of Modern Art, New York, 1987, S./p. 60-61.
P. Sparke: Italienisches Design von 1870 bis heute, Braunschweig: Westermann, 1989, p. 180.
Vitra Design Museum Collection, Poster DIN A0, Weil am Rhein: Vitra Design Museum, 1991/93.
K.-J. Sembach: Möbel, die Geschichte machen, Hamburg: Gruner+Jahr, 1993, p. 28, ill. 40.
K. B. Hiesinger, G. H. Marcus: Landmarks of Twentieth-Century Design, New York: Abbeville Press, 1993, p. 270.
P. Kjellberg: Le Mobilier du XXᵉ Siècle, Paris: Les Editions de l'Amateur, 1994, p. 78-79.
T. Heider, M. Stegmann, R. Zey: Lexikon Internationales Design, Reinbek/Hamburg: Rowohlt, 1994, p. 42-44.

39
W. Gräff: Innenräume, Stuttgart: Akademischer Verlag Wedekind, 1928, p. 27.
A.G. Schneck: Der Stuhl, Stuttgart: Hoffmann (Baubücher vol. 4), 1928, p. 56-57.
Der Stuhl, edited by A.G. Schneck, exhibition catalogue Württ. Landesgewerbeamt, Stuttgart: Hoffmann, 1928, p. 39.
H. & B. Rasch: Der Stuhl, Stuttgart: Akademischer Verlag Wedekind, 1928, p. 50-51.
Mies van der Rohe, edited by p.C. Johnson, exhibition catalogue The Museum of Modern Art, New York, 1947, p. 56, 90-91, 93, 95.
Ludwig Mies van der Rohe, edited by L. Glaeser, exhibition catalogue The Museum of Modern Art, New York, 1977, p. 20-21.
J. v. Geest, O. Mácel: Stühle aus Stahl, Köln: König, 1980, p. 95-96, ill. 2.
A. v. Vegesack: Deutsche Stahlrohrmöbel, München: Bangert, 1986, p. 62-67.
Bent Wood and Metal Furniture 1850-1946, edited by D. E. Ostergard, exhibition catalogue The American Federation of Arts, New York, 1987, p. 274-275.
M.-L. Jousset, K. V. Posch: Portrait d'une collection – Alexander von Vegesack, Paris: Centre Georges Pompidou, 1993, p. 35.

40
R. Herbst: 25 années U.A.M. 1930-1955, Paris: Editions du Salon des Arts Ménagers, 1956, p. 34.
J. v. Geest, O. Mácel: Stühle aus Stahl, Köln: König, 1980, p. 87, ill. 7.
M. Emery: Furniture by Architects, New York: Abrams, 1983, p. 131, 140, no. 243.
Il progetto del mobile in Francia 1919-1939, in: Rassegna, Bologna, 8, 1986, p. 65, ill. 1.
Design Heute, edited by V. Fischer, exhibition catalogue Deutsches Architekturmuseum Frankfurt am Main, München: Prestel, 1988, p. 24, no. 18.

S. Goguel: René Herbst, Paris: Editions du Regard, 1990, p. 64, 67, 70, 121, 197, 303.
S'asseoir 100 façons, edited by C. Fache, exhibition catalogue Grand-Hornu Images, B-Boussu (Hornu), 1993, p. 59.
Vitra Design Museum Collection, Poster DIN A0, Weil am Rhein: Vitra Design Museum, 1993.
T. Heider, M. Stegmann, R. Zey: Lexikon Internationales Design, Reinbek/Hamburg: Rowohlt, 1994, p. 136.
P. Kjellberg: Le Mobilier du XXᵉ Siècle, Paris: Les Editions de l'Amateur, 1994, p. 304-308.

41
C.G. Holme: Decorative Art, London: The Studio, 1932, p. 84.
Stahlrohr im täglichen Leben, in: Stahl überall, Düsseldorf, 6, 1933, o.S..
A. Clementi: Storia dellŌarredamento 1850-1950, Milano: Società Editrice Libraria, 1952, p. 220.
U. Kultermann: Wassili und Hans Luckhardt, Tübingen: Wasmuth, 1958, p. 142.
J. v. Geest, O. Mácel: Stühle aus Stahl, Köln: König, 1980, p. 94, ill. 3.
A. v. Vegesack: Deutsche Stahlrohrmöbel, München: Bangert, 1986, p. 47, 163, cover.
Bent Wood and Metal Furniture 1850-1946, edited by D. E. Ostergard, exhibition catalogue The American Federation of Arts, New York, 1987, p. 134-135, 294-295, no. 85.
Brüder Luckhardt und Alfons Anker, exhibition catalogue Akademie der Künste, Berlin, 1990, p. 306, ill. 1.
Ein Stuhl macht Geschichte, edited by W. Möller, O. Mácel, exhibition catalogue Bauhaus, Dessau, Vitra Design Museum, Weil am Rhein, Museum für Kunst und Gewerbe, Hamburg, München: Prestel, 1992, p. 55, ill. 81.
P. Kjellberg: Le Mobilier du XXᵉ Siècle, Paris: Les Editions de l'Amateur, 1994, p. 387.

42
N. Carrington: Design and Decoration in the Home, London: Country Life, 1938, p. 8-9.
Mackintosh to Mollino, Fifty Years of Chair Design, edited by D. E. Ostergard, exhibition catalogue Gallery Barry Friedman, New York, 1984, p. 48.
Bent Wood and Metal Furniture 1850-1946, edited by D. E. Ostergard, exhibition catalogue The American Federation of Arts, New York, 1987, p. 318-319, no. 106.
S. Yates: An Encyclopedia of Chairs, London: Quintet Publishing, 1988, p. 106.
British Design, Image and Identity, edited by F. Huygen, exhibition catalogue Museum Boymans-van Beuningen, Rotterdam, London: Thames and Hudson, 1989, p. 115.
Vitra Design Museum Collection, Poster DIN A0, Weil am Rhein: Vitra Design Museum, 1991/93.
K. B. Hiesinger, G. H. Marcus: Landmarks of Twentieth-Century Design, New York: Abbeville Press, 1993, p. 129, no. 150.
Sotheby's, Amsterdam, 31.03.1993, p. 68, Lot 990.
P. Kjellberg: Le Mobilier du XXᵉ Siècle, Paris: Les Editions de l'Amateur, 1994, p. 633-634.

43
P. Overy: De Stijl, London, New York: Studio Vista/Dutton, 1969, p. 162-163.
D. Baroni: I mobili di Gerrit Thomas Rietveld, Milano: Electa, 1977, p. 130-137.
Rietveld. Uit de verzameling van het Stedelijk Museum Amsterdam, 1981, p. 23-25, no. 70-89.
Gerrit Rietveld – A Centenary Exhibition, exhibition catalogue Gallery Barry Friedman, New York, 1988, p. 49-51.
Gerrit T. Rietveld 1888-1964, The Complete Works, edited by M. Küper, I. v. Zijl, exhibition catalogue Centraal Museum, Utrecht, Centre Pompidou, Paris, Utrecht, 1992, p. 145-147.

P. Vöge: The Complete Rietveld Furniture, Rotterdam: 010 Publishers, 1993, p. 82-83.
S'asseoir 100 façons, edited by C. Fache, exhibition catalogue Grand-Hornu Images, B-Boussu (Hornu), 1993, p. 46-47.
K. B. Hiesinger, G. H. Marcus: Landmarks of Twentieth-Century Design, New York: Abbeville, 1993, p. 135, no. 160.
K.-J. Sembach: Möbel, die Geschichte machen, Hamburg: Gruner + Jahr, 1993, p. 13-14, no. 10.

44
G. Logie: Furniture from Machines, London: George Allen and Unwin, 1947, p. 12-13.
Spacious but intimate simple but subtle, in: Architectural Record, New York, Nov. 1948, p. 92-93, 95, ill. 1, 2, 5.
E. Kaufmann, Jr.: What is modern design? New York: The Museum of Modern Art, 1950, p. 10, ill. 4.
Introduction to Twentieth Century Design, edited by A. Drexler, G. Daniel, exhibition catalogue The Museum of Modern Art, New York: Doubleday, 1959, p. 58.
K.-J. Sembach: Neue Möbel, Stuttgart: Hatje, 1982, p. 86, no. 279.
K. B. Hiesinger, G. H. Marcus: Landmarks of Twentieth-Century Design, New York: Abbeville Press, 1993, p. 142, no. 175.
M.-L. Jousset, K. V. Posch: Portrait d'une collection – Alexander von Vegesack, Paris: Centre Georges Pompidou, 1993, p. 48, 50.
K.-J. Sembach: Möbel, die Geschichte machen, Hamburg: Gruner + Jahr, 1993, p. 110-111, no. 20.
T. Heider, M. Stegmann, R. Zey: Lexikon Internationales Design, Reinbek/Hamburg: Rowohlt, 1994, p. 132.
P. Kjellberg: Le Mobilier du XXᵉ Siècle, Paris: Les Editions de l'Amateur, 1994, p. 88-89.

45
Vitra Design Museum Collection, Poster DIN A0, Weil am Rhein: Vitra Design Museum, 1991/93.
M.-L. Jousset, K. V. Posch: Portrait d'une Collection – Alexander von Vegesack, Paris: Centre Georges Pompidou, 1993, p. 52-53.
Treadway Gallery, Inc., Cincinnati, Ohio, John Toomey, Oak Park, Illinois: 20th Century Sale, Oak Park, 23.10.94, p. 114, Lot no. 716.

46
G. Nelson: Chairs, New York: Whitney, 1953, p. 55.
G. Quéant: Tradition et rupture, in: Plaisir de France, Sondernummer: L'Homme et son décor, Paris, 1953, p. 26-41.
P. Guéguen: André Bloc et la réintégration de la plastique dans la vie, Boulogne: a. a. (collection espace), 1954, p. 32-47.
C. Delloye: Le Créateur, in: L'Architecture d'Aujourd'hui, Paris, 59/60, 1967, p. 62-70.
A. Bangert: Der Stil der 50er Jahre, München: Heyne, 1983, p. 85, 88-89.
Vitra Design Museum Collection, Poster DIN A0, Weil am Rhein: Vitra Design Museum, 1993.
P. Kjellberg: Le Mobilier du XXᵉ Siècle, Paris: Les Editions de l'Amateur, 1994, p. 86.

47
R. Aloi: Mobili Tipo, Milano: Hoepli, 1952, p. 206.
G. Hatje: Neue Möbel, New York: Wittenborn, vol. 2, 1953, p. 8.
J. Pedersen: Arkitekten Arne Jacobsen, København: Arkitektens Forlag, 1954, p. 90.
F. Solaguren-Beascoa de Corral: Arne Jacobsen – Obras y proyectos, Barcelona: Gili, 1989, p. 211, ill. 15, 17.
F. Sieck: Contemporary Danish Furniture Design, Nyt Nordisk Forlag Arnold Busck, 1990, p. 122.
Design 1935-1965 – What Modern Was, edited by M. Eidelberg, exhibition catalogue Musée des Arts Décoratifs, Montréal, and other, New York: Abrams, 1991, p. 189-190, ill. 272-273.
B. Mundt: Produkt-Design 1900-1990, Kunstgewerbemuseum, Berlin, Berlin: Reimer, 1991, p. 164-165, no. 101.

F. Solaguren-Beascoa: Jacobsen, Barcelona: Santa & Cole 1991, p. 127-129.
K. B. Hiesinger, G. H. Marcus: Landmarks of Twentieth-Century Design, New York: Abbeville Press, 1993, p. 187, no. 228.
K.-J. Sembach: Möbel, die Geschichte machen, Hamburg: Gruner + Jahr, 1993, p. 17-18, no. 18.
P. Kjellberg: Le Mobilier du XXᵉ Siècle, Paris: Les Editions de l'Amateur, 1994, p. 321-323.

48
G. Hatje: Neue Möbel, Stuttgart: Hatje, vol. 4, 1958, p. 34, ill. 56.
Les Assises du Siège Contemporain, exhibition catalogue Musée des Arts Décoratifs, Paris, 1968, p. 65, ill. 122.
Willy Guhl – Gestalter und Lehrer, exhibition catalogue Museum für Gestaltung/Kunstgewerbemuseum, Zürich, 1985, p. 21, 50-51 (series Design-Pioniere 2).
Schweizer Möbeldesign 1927-1984, edited by G. Frey, exhibition catalogue Musée des Arts Décoratifs, Lausanne, Museum für Gestaltung/Kunstgewerbemuseum, Zürich, Gewerbemuseum/Museum für Gestaltung, Basel, 1986, p. 90.
Vitra Design Museum Collection, Poster DIN A0, Weil am Rhein: Vitra Design Museum, 1991/93.
Ideales Heim, Zürich, no. 6, 1994, p. 56.
Du, CH-Buchs, no. 4, 1994, p. 81.
Ideales Heim, Zürich, no. 7/8, 1995, p. 54.

49
G. Hatje: Neue Möbel, Stuttgart: Hatje, vol. 1, 1952, p. 3, ill. 5.
G. Nelson: Chairs, New York: Whitney, 1953, p. 75.
Espressione di Gio Ponti, in: Aria D'Italia, Milano, no. 8, 1954, p. 74.
R. Aloi: Esempi di Arredamento Moderno di tutto il Mondo – Sedie, Poltrone, Divani, Milano: Hoepli, 1957, p. 5-6.
A. Bangert: Italienisches Möbeldesign, München: Bangert, 1985, p. 28, 82, ill. 12.
Italien – Design 1945 bis heute, edited by H. Wichmann, exhibition catalogue Die Neue Sammlung, München, 1988, p. 81.
L. L. Ponti: Gio Ponti, Cambridge, Mass.: MIT Press, 1990, p. 174-175.
Design 1935-1965 – What Modern Was, edited by M. Eidelberg, exhibition catalogue Musée des Arts Décoratifs, Montréal, and other, New York: Abrams, 1991, p. 136-137.
K. B. Hiesinger, G. H. Marcus: Landmarks of Twentieth-Century Design, New York: Abbeville Press, 1993, p. 208, no. 265.
K.-J. Sembach: Möbel, die Geschichte machen, Hamburg: Gruner + Jahr, 1993, p. 18-19, no. 21.
R. Guidot: Design, Stuttgart, Deutsche Verlags-Anstalt, 1994, p. 91, 93.
P. Kjellberg: Le Mobilier du XXᵉ Siècle, Paris: Les Editions de l'Amateur, 1994, p. 498-499.

50
G. Hatje, E. Kaspar: New Furniture, New York, Washington: Praeger, vol. 10, 1971, p. 48.
Italy – The New Domestic Landscape, edited by E. Ambasz, exhibition catalogue The Museum of Modern Art, New York, Firenze: Centro Di, 1972, p. 112-113.
S. Casciani: Mobili Come Architetture, Milano: Arcadia, 1984, p. 89-91.
A. Bangert: Italienisches Möbeldesign, München: Bangert, 1985, p. 100, ill. 49.
Design Heute, edited by V. Fischer, exhibition catalogue Deutsches Architekturmuseum, Frankfurt am Main, München: Prestel, 1988, p. 30.
Italien – Design 1945 bis heute, edited by H. Wichmann, exhibition catalogue Die Neue Sammlung, München, 1988, p. 92-93.
P. Sparke: Italienisches Design von 1870 bis heute, Braunschweig: Westermann, 1989, p. 167.
K.-J. Sembach: Möbel, die Geschichte machen, Hamburg: Gruner + Jahr, 1993, p. 118-119.
K. B. Hiesinger, G. H. Marcus: Landmarks of Twentieth-Century Design, New York: Abbeville Press, 1993, p. 239.
P. Kjellberg: Le Mobilier du XXᵉ Siècle, Paris: Les Editions de l'Amateur, 1994, p. 260-161.

51

The New Domestic Landscape, edited by E. Ambasz, exhibition catalogue
The Museum of Modern Art, New York, Firenze: Centro Di, 1972, p. 37.
A. Grassi, A. Pansera: Atlante del Design Italiano 1940/1980, Milano: Fabbri,
1980, p. 152, ill. 1/2.
Italienisches Möbeldesign, exhibition catalogue Stadtmuseum Köln, Roma:
ICE, Istituto Nazionale per il Commercio Estero, 1980, p. 174-175, no. 114.
A. Bangert: Italienisches Möbeldesign, München: Bangert, 1985, p. 85, ill. 20.
Design Heute, edited by V. Fischer, exhibition catalogue Deutsches
Architekturmuseum, Frankfurt am Main, München: Prestel, 1988, p. 29, no. 38.
Italien – Design 1945 bis heute, edited by H. Wichmann, exhibition
catalogue Die Neue Sammlung, München, 1988, p. 89.
P. Sparke: Italienisches Design von 1870 bis heute, Braunschweig:
Westermann, 1989, p. 167.
Ispirazione Italiana, edited by W. Schepers, P. Dunas, exhibition catalogue
Kunstmuseum Düsseldorf, 1990, p. 64-65.
K.-J. Sembach: Möbel, die Geschichte machen, Hamburg: Gruner + Jahr,
1993, p. 25-26, no. 34.
P. Kjellberg: Le Mobilier du XXᵉ Siècle, Paris: Les Editions de l'Amateur,
1994, p. 491.

52

P. Starck: The International Design Yearbook 1987/88, London: Calmann and
King, 1987, p. 36, no. 13.
Design Heute, edited by V. Fischer, exhibition catalogue Deutsches
Architekturmuseum, Frankfurt am Main, München: Prestel, 1988, p. 66,
no. 141.
D. Sudjic: Ron Arad – Restless Furniture, London: Fourth
Estate/Wordsearch, 1989, p. 70-71.
K. M. Armer, A. Bangert: Design der 80er Jahre, München: Bangert, 1990,
p. 91.
Ron Arad – Sticks & Stones 1980-1990, edited by A. v. Vegesack, exhibition
catalogue Vitra Design Museum, Weil am Rhein, 1990, p. 74-75.
Vitra Design Museum Collection, Poster DIN A0, Weil am Rhein:
Vitra Design Museum, 1991/93.
S'asseoir 100 façons, edited by C. Fache, exhibition catalogue Grand-Hornu
Images, B-Boussu (Hornu), 1993, p. 80-81.
Design, miroir du siècle, edited by J. de Noblet, exhibition catalogue Grand
Palais, Paris, Paris: Flammarion/APCI, 1993, p. 252.
13 nach Memphis, edited by V. Albus, V. Fischer, exhibition catalogue
Museum für Kunsthandwerk, Frankfurt am Main, München: Prestel, 1995,
p. 26, 30, ill. 12, 13.

53

M. Bellini: Das Internationale Designjahrbuch 1990/91, München: Bangert,
1990, p. 79, ill. 134.
La Casa di Alice – Luoghi del silenzio imperfetto, edited by M. Barberis,
F. De Leonardis, E. Grazioli, exhibition catalogue Galleria Mazzocchi, Parma,
Milano: Electa, 1992, p. 33, 40-41, 47, 88-89.
S'asseoir 100 façons, edited by C. Fache, exhibition catalogue Grand-Hornu
Images, B-Boussu (Hornu), 1993, p. 82.
Vitra Design Museum Collection, Poster DIN A0, Weil am Rhein:
Vitra Design Museum, 1993.
T. Heider, M. Stegmann, R. Zey: Lexikon Internationales Design,
Reinbek/Hamburg: Rowohlt, 1994, p. 224-225.
13 nach Memphis, edited by V. Albus, V. Fischer, exhibition catalogue
Museum für Kunsthandwerk, Frankfurt am Main, München: Prestel, 1995,
p. 116, ill. 3, 4, 5.

54

H. Read: Art & Industry, London: Faber & Faber, 1934, p. 89.
Alvar Aalto – Architecture and Furniture, exhibition catalogue The Museum
of Modern Art, New York, 1938, p. 18, ill. 30.
K. Fleig: Alvar Aalto, Zürich: Girsberger, 1963, p. 42.
L. Mosso: Alvar Aalto, Helsinki: Otava, 1967, p. 34.
W. Blaser: Alvar Aalto als Designer, Stuttgart: Deutsche Verlags-Anstalt,
1982, p. 88-100, 130-132.

Museum of Finnish Architecture, Finnish Society of Crafts and Design,
Artek: Alvar Aalto Furniture, Helsinki: Museum of Finnish Architecture,
1984, p. 12, 76, 80, 86-91, 126, 132-133.
Bent Wood and Metal Furniture 1850-1946, edited by D. E. Ostergard,
exhibition catalogue The American Federation of Arts, New York, 1987,
p. 309/310.
Alvar Aalto, de l'oeuvre aux écrits, exhibition catalogue Centre Georges
Pompidou, Paris, 1988, p. 65.
En Contact Avec Alvar Aalto, exhibition catalogue Musée d'Art Moderne,
Saint-Etienne, Arc en Rêve, Bordeaux, ENSAIS, Strasbourg, Jyväskylä:
Musée Alvar-Aalto, 1992, p. 83, ill. 199.
M.-L. Jousset, K.V. Posch: Portrait d'une collection – Alexander von
Vegesack, Paris: Centre Georges Pompidou, 1993, p. 38-39.
G. Schildt: Alvar Aalto, London: Academy, 1994, p. 258.

55

L. Mosso: Alvar Aalto, Helsinki: Otava, 1967, p. 58, 166.
W. Blaser: Alvar Aalto als Designer, Stuttgart: Deutsche Verlags-Anstalt,
1982, p. 107, 131, 133.
Museum of Finnish Architecture, Finnish Society of Crafts and Design,
Artek: Alvar Aalto Furniture, Helsinki: Museum of Finnish Architecture,
1984, p. 127, 150-152, ill. 226.
Artek 1935-1985, exhibition catalogue Taideteollisuusmuseo: Helsinki, 1985,
p. 39.
Alvar Aalto, de l'oeuvre aux écrits, exhibition catalogue Centre Georges
Pompidou, Paris, 1988, p. 65.
En Contact avec Alvar Aalto, exhibition catalogue Musée d'Art Moderne,
Saint-Etienne, Arc en Rêve, Bordeaux, ENSAIS, Strasbourg, Jyväskylä:
Musée Alvar-Aalto, 1992, p. 97.
M.-L. Jousset, K. V. Posch: Portrait d'une collection – Alexander von
Vegesack, Paris: Centre Georges Pompidou, 1993, p. 42/43.
K.-J. Sembach: Möbel, die Geschichte machen, Hamburg: Gruner + Jahr,
1993, p. 178, no. 6.
T. Heider, M. Stegmann, R. Zey: Lexikon Internationales Design,
Reinbek/Hamburg: Rowohlt, 1994, p. 7-9.
G. Schildt: Alvar Aalto, London: Academy, 1994, p. 298-299, ill. 572.

56

Organic Design in Home Furnishings, edited by E.F. Noyes, exhibition
catalogue The Museum of Modern Art, New York, 1941, p. 11-15.
Eames Celebration, in: Architectural Design, London, 36, 1966, p. 2-3.
Charles Eames – Furniture from the Design Collection, edited by A. Drexler,
exhibition catalogue The Museum of Modern Art, New York, 1973, p. 4-13.
Nelson/Eames/Girard/Propst – The Design Process at Herman Miller, in:
Design Quarterly, Walker Art Center, Minneapolis, 98/99, 1975, p. 21.
Connections – The Work of Charles and Ray Eames, edited by R. Caplan,
exhibition catalogue Frederick S. Wight Art Gallery, University of California,
Los Angeles: UCLA Art Council, 1976, p. 23.
P. Garner: Contemporary Decorative Arts from 1940 to the present,
New York: Facts on File, 1980, p. 51-52.
Bent Wood and Metal Furniture 1850-1946, edited by D. E. Ostergard,
exhibition catalogue The American Federation of Arts, New York, 1987,
p. 163-165.
J. Neuhart, M. Neuhart, R. Eames: Eames Design, Berlin: Ernst & Sohn,
1989, p. 25.
R. Guidot: Design, Stuttgart: Deutsche Verlags-Anstalt, 1994, p. 53-54.
P. Kirkham: Charles and Ray Eames, Cambridge, Mass., London: MIT Press,
1995, p. 207-210, ill. 5.5.

57

What is modern industrial design?, in: The Museum of Modern Art Bulletin,
vol. XIV, no. 1, Fall 1946, p. 8.
E. Noyes: Charles Eames, in: Arts & Architecture, Los Angeles, 63, 1946,
p. 26-44.
E. Kaufman, Jr.: What is modern interior design?, New York: The Museum
of Modern Art, 1953, p. 21.
G. Nelson: Chairs, New York: Whitney, 1953, p. 52.

Eames Celebration, in: Architectural Design, London, 36, 1966, p. 5, 22-23, ill. 16, 17, 21.
Charles Eames – Furniture from the Design Collection, edited by A. Drexler, exhibition catalogue The Museum of Modern Art, New York, 1973, p. 20-21, 24.
R. Caplan: The Design of Herman Miller, New York: Whitney, 1976, p. 48, 52.
P. Garner: Contemporary Decorative Arts from 1940 to the present, New York: Facts On File, 1980, p. 24-25, 51-52.
J. Neuhart, M. Neuhart, R. Eames: Eames Design, Berlin: Ernst & Sohn, 1989, p. 53, 59, 63, 73.
Design 1935-1965 – What Modern Was, edited by M. Eidelberg, exhibition catalogue Musée des Arts Décoratifs, Montréal, and other, New York: Abrams, 1991, p. 38-39.

58
E. Noyes: Charles Eames, in: Arts & Architecture, Los Angeles, 63, 1946, p. 39.
A. Drexler, G. Daniel: Introduction to Twentieth Century Design, New York: The Museum of Modern Art, 1959, p. 60, ill. 72.
Charles Eames – Furniture from the Design Collection, edited by A. Drexler, exhibition catalogue The Museum of Modern Art, New York, 1973, p. 28-29, ill. 46, 47, 48.
R. Caplan: The Design of Herman Miller, New York: Whitney, 1976, p. 48.
Bent Wood and Metal Furniture 1850-1946, edited by D. E. Ostergard, exhibition catalogue The American Federation of Arts, New York, 1987, p. 330-331, no. 118.
J. Neuhart, M. Neuhart, R. Eames: Eames Design, Berlin: Ernst & Sohn, 1989, p. 78, 79, 82, 88.
Design 1935-1965 – What Modern Was, edited by M. Eidelberg, exhibition catalogue Musée des Arts Décoratifs, Montréal, and other, New York: Abrams, 1991, p.40.
M.-L. Jousset, K. V. Posch: Portrait d'une collection – Alexander von Vegesack, Paris: Centre Georges Pompidou, 1993, p. 56-59, cover.
P. Kirkham: Charles and Ray Eames, Cambridge, Mass., London: MIT Press, 1995, p. 153, 225.

59
G. Nelson: Chairs, New York: Whitney, 1953, p. 33.
R. Aloi: Esempi, Tavoli-Tavolini-Carrelli, Milano: Hoepli, 1957, ill. 50.
Design 1935-1965: What Modern Was, edited by M. Eidelberg, exhibition catalogue Musée des Arts Décoratifs, Montréal, and other, New York: Abrams, 1991, p. 107-108.

60
E. Kaufmann, Jr.: Prize Designs for Modern Furniture, New York: The Museum of Modern Art, 1950, p. 19-21.
Charles Eames – Furniture from the Design Collection, edited by A. Drexler, exhibition catalogue The Museum of Modern Art, New York, 1973, p. 34-35, ill. 60.
Design Heute, edited by V. Fischer, exhibition catalogue Deutsches Archi-tekturmuseum, Frankfurt am Main, München: Prestel, 1988, p. 26.
J. Neuhart, M. Neuhart, R. Eames: Eames Design, Berlin: Ernst & Sohn, 1989, p. 97-101, 138-141.
S'asseoir 100 façons, edited by C. Fache, exhibition catalogue Grand-Hornu Images, B-Boussu (Hornu), 1993, p. 63-64.
K. B. Hiesinger, G. H. Marcus: Landmarks of Twentieth-Century Design, New York: Abbeville Press, 1993, p. 168, no. 210.
K.-J. Sembach: Möbel, die Geschichte machen, Hamburg: Gruner + Jahr, 1993, p. 38, ill. 17.
P. Kirkham: Charles and Ray Eames, Cambridge, Mass., London: MIT Press, 1995, p. 231-236.

61
E. Kaufmann, Jr.: Prize Designs for Modern Furniture, New York: The Museum of Modern Art, 1950, p. 59.
Charles Eames – Furniture from the Design Collection, edited by A. Drexler, exhibition catalogue The Museum of Modern Art, New York, 1973, p. 37,

ill. 64-65.
J. Neuhart, M. Neuhart, R. Eames: Eames Design, Berlin: Ernst & Sohn, 1989, p. 96-101.
M. Bellini: Das Internationale Design Jahrbuch 1990/91, München: Bangert, 1990, p. 78-79.
Möbel aus Kunststoff, edited by A. v. Vegesack, exhibition catalogue Vitra Design Museum, Weil am Rhein, 1990, p. 10-11.
K.-J. Sembach, G. Leuthäuser, P. Gössel: Möbeldesign des 20. Jahrhunderts, Köln: Taschen, 1991, p. 164-165.
S'asseoir 100 façons, edited by C. Fache, exhibition catalogue Grand-Hornu Images, B-Boussu (Hornu), 1993, p. 63-64.
P. Dunas: Luigi Colani, München: Prestel, 1993, p. 131, ill. 200-202.
P. Kirkham: Charles and Ray Eames, Cambridge, Mass., London: MIT Press, 1995, p. 234.

62
R. Aloi: L'Arredamento Moderno, Milano: Hoepli, 1952, ill. 360.
Argomenti di Architettura, Milano, no. 3, 1961, p. 34-35.
A. Bangert: Italienisches Möbeldesign, München: Bangert, 1985, p. 122-123, 125.
G. Brino: Carlo Mollino, München: Bangert, 1985, cover, p. 44, 127, 133.
G. Berruti, C. Ratti: Il Compensato Curvato, Milano: Rima, 1988, p. 23.
L'étrange univers de l'architecte Carlo Mollino, exhibition catalogue Centre Georges Pompidou, Paris, 1989, p. 91, 93.
Design 1935-1965 – What Modern Was, edited by M. Eidelberg, exhibition catalogue Musée des Arts Décoratifs, Montréal, and other, New York: Abrams, 1991, p. 109-110.
I. de Guttry, M. P. Maino: Il mobile italiano degli anni '40 e '50, Roma-Bari: Laterza, 1992, p. 208-215, ill. 26.
K. B. Hiesinger, G. H. Marcus: Landmarks of Twentieth-Century Design, New York: Abbeville Press, 1993, p. 167.
R. Guidot: Design, Stuttgart: Deutsche Verlags-Anstalt, 1994, p. 93-96.
P. Kjellberg: Le Mobilier du XXᵉ Siècle, Paris: Les Editions de l'Amateur, 1994, p. 431.

63
R. Aloi: Esempi, Tavoli-Tavolini-Carrelli, Milano: Hoepli, no. 2, 1957, ill. 51.
C. Greenberg: Mid-Century Modern, New York: Harmony Books, 1984, p. 80-81, 104.
C. & K. Fehrman: Postwar Interior Design 1945-1960, New York: Van Nostrand Reinhold, 1987, p. 165, ill. 109.
Treadway Gallery, Cincinnati, Ohio, John Toomey, Oak Park, Illinois: 20th Century Sale, Oak Park, 15.11.1992, p. 52, Lot 322.
T. Heider, M. Stegmann, R. Zey: Lexikon Internationales Design, Reinbek/Hamburg: Rowohlt, 1994, p. 238-239.
P. Kjellberg: Le Mobilier du XXᵉ Siècle, Paris: Les Editions de l'Amateur, 1994, p. 454-455.

64
C. Greenberg: Mid-Century Modern, New York: Harmony Books, 1984, p. 80-81.
Vitra Design Museum Collection, Poster DIN A0, Weil am Rhein: Vitra Design Museum, 1991/93.
Treadway Gallery, Inc., Cincinnati, Ohio, John Toomey, Oak Park, Illinois: 20th Century Sale, Oak Park, 23.10.1994, p. 97, Lot 606.
T. Heider, M. Stegmann, R. Zey: Lexikon Internationales Design, Reinbek/Hamburg: Rowohlt, 1994, p. 238-239.
P. Kjellberg: Le Mobilier du XXᵉ Siècle, Paris: Les Editions de l'Amateur, 1994, p. 454-455.

65
A. Bangert: Italienisches Möbeldesign, München: Bangert, 1985, p. 78, ill. 3.
S. Yates: An Encyclopedia of Chairs, London: Quintet Publishing, 1988, p. 106-107, no. 166b.
L'étrange univers de l'architecte Carlo Mollino, exhibition catalogue Centre Georges Pompidou, Paris, 1989, p. 100.
Vitra Design Museum Collection, Poster DIN A0, Weil am Rhein:

Vitra Design Museum, 1991/93.
I. de Guttry, M. P. Maino: Il mobile italiano degli anni '40 e '50, Roma-Bari: Laterza, 1992, p. 214-215, ill. 25.
C. & P. Fiell: Modern Chairs, Köln: Taschen, 1993, p. 62.

66
G. Hatje: Neue Möbel, Stuttgart: Hatje, vol. 6, 1962, p. 14, ill. 3.
Les Assises du Siège Contemporain, exhibition catalogue Musée des Arts Décoratifs, Paris, 1968, p. 118, ill. 296.
Caravelles, Enjeux de l'objet, edited by F. Philip, J. Bonnot, Studio TOTEM, exhibition catalogue Grenoble, Lyon, Saint Etienne, 1986, p. 45.
F. Baudot: Les Assises du Siècle, Paris: Editions Du May, 1990, p. 87, ill. 7.
Vitra Design Museum Collection, Poster DIN A0, Weil am Rhein: Vitra Design Museum, 1991/93.
M.-L. Jousset, K. V. Posch: Portrait d'une Collection – Alexander von Vegesack, Paris: Centre Georges Pompidou, 1993, p. 48-49.
C. & P. Fiell: Modern Chairs, Köln: Taschen, 1993, p. 77.
K. B. Hiesinger, G. H. Marcus: Landmarks of Twentieth Century Design, New York: Abbeville Press, 1993, p. 202-203, ill. 255.
R. Guidot: Design, Stuttgart: Deutsche Verlags-Anstalt, 1994, p. 148-149.
P. Kjellberg: Le Mobilier du XXᵉ Siècle, Paris: Les Editions de l'Amateur, 1994, p. 676.

67
G. Hatje: Neue Möbel, Stuttgart: Hatje, vol. 4, 1958, p. 31, Abb./ill 48.
A. Temko: Eero Saarinen, New York: Braziller, 1962, ill. 79.
Les Assises du Siège Contemporain, exhibition catalogue Musée des Arts Décoratifs, Paris, 1968, p. 108, ill. 265.
E. Larrabee, M. Vignelli: Knoll Design, New York: Abrams, 1981, p. 58-59, 64-65.
M. Emery: Furniture by Architects, New York: Abrams, 1983, p. 248-249, 255, no. 469.
C. Greenberg: Mid-Century Modern, New York: Harmony Books, 1984, p. 78.
Design 1935-1965 – What Modern Was, edited by M. Eidelberg, exhibition catalogue Musée des Arts Décoratifs, Montréal, and other, New York: Abrams, 1991, p. 225-226.
B. Mundt: Produktdesign 1900-1990, Kunstgewerbemuseum, Berlin, Berlin: Reimer, 1991, p. 18-19, 140.
Vitra Design Museum Collection, Poster DIN A0, Weil am Rhein: Vitra Design Museum, 1991/93.
K.-J. Sembach: Möbel, die Geschichte machen, Hamburg: Gruner+Jahr, 1993, p. 18.
P. Kjellberg: Le Mobilier du XXᵉ Siècle, Paris: Les Editions de l'Amateur, 1994, p. 579-580.

68
Les Assises du Siège Contemporain, exhibition catalogue Musée des Arts Décoratifs, Paris, 1968, p. 93, no. 213.
G. Hatje, E. Kaspar: Neue Möbel, Stuttgart: Hatje, vol. 9, 1969, p. 14.
Design since 1945, edited by K. B. Hiesinger, G. H. Marcus, exhibition catalogue Philadelphia Museum of Art, 1983, p. 64, 132, no. III-61.
Design Heute, edited by V. Fischer, Deutsches Architekturmuseum, Frankfurt am Main, München: Prestel, 1988, p. 28, ill. 35.
Möbel aus Kunststoff, edited by A. v. Vegesack, exhibition catalogue Vitra Design Museum, Weil am Rhein, 1990, p. 2-3, 5, 7, 9.
B. Mundt: Produktdesign 1900-1990, Kunstgewerbemuseum, Berlin, Berlin: Reimer, 1991, p. 184-185.
K. B. Hiesinger, G. H. Marcus: Landmarks of Twentieth-Century Design, New York: Abbeville Press, 1993, p. 229.
K.-B. Sembach: Möbel, die Geschichte machen, Hamburg: Gruner+Jahr, 1993, p. 24-25, no. 33.
R. Guidot: Design, Stuttgart: Deutsche Verlags-Anstalt, 1994, p. 112.
T. Heider, M. Stegmann, R. Zey: Lexikon Internationales Design, Reinbek/Hamburg: Rowohlt, 1994, p. 251-252.
P. Kjellberg: Le Mobilier du XXᵉ Siècle, Paris: Les Editions de l'Amateur, 1994, p. 467-469.

69
J. Møller Nielsen: Wegner – en dansk møbelkunstner, København: Gyldendal, 1965, p. 82-83, 128.
Tema Med Variationer – Hans J. Wegner's Møbler, edited by H. S. Møller, exhibition catalogue Sønderjyllands Kunstmuseum, Tønder, 1979, p. 83.
G. Jalk: 40 Years of Danish Furniture Design, The Copenhagen cabinet-makers' Guild Exhibitions 1927-1966, København: Teknologisk Institut, 1987, p. 232, 234-235.
Hans J. Wegner – en stolemager, exhibition catalogue Kunstindustrimuseet, København, København: Dansk Design Center, 1989, p. 48-49, cover.
Vitra Design Museum Collection, Poster DIN A0, Weil am Rhein: Vitra Design Museum, 1991/93.
Grand-Hornu Images: S'asseoir 100 façons, Poster, B-Boussu (Hornu), 1993, no. 65.
Hans J Wegner, edited by J. Bernsen, exhibition catalogue Dansk Design Center, København, 1994, p. 32-33, 51, 79, 118.

70
Les Assises du Siège Contemporain, exhibition catalogue Musée des Arts Décoratifs, Paris, 1968, p. 95, ill. 226.
G. Hatje, E. Kaspar: Neue Möbel, Stuttgart: Hatje, vol. 9, 1969, p. 18, ill. 33-35.
K.-J. Sembach: Neue Möbel, Stuttgart: Hatje, 1982, p. 123, ill. 413-414.
Design Since 1945, edited by K. B. Hiesinger, G. H. Marcus, exhibition catalogue Philadelphia Museum of Art, 1983, p. 132, ill. III-63.
Vitra Design Museum Collection, Poster DIN A0, Weil am Rhein: Vitra Design Museum, 1991/93.
C. & P. Fiell: Modern Chairs, Köln: Taschen, 1993, p. 101.
R. Guidot: Design, Stuttgart: Deutsche Verlags-Anstalt, 1994, p. 186.
P. Kjellberg: Le Mobilier du XXᵉ Siècle, Paris: Les Editions de l'Amateur, 1994, p. 474-475.

71
G. Hatje, E. Kaspar: Neue Möbel, Stuttgart: Hatje, vol. 11, 1973, p. 142, ill. 427-428.
A. Fujimoto: Luigi Colani – Designing Tomorrow, Tokyo: San'ei Shobo Publishing, 1978, p. 93, ill. 8.
Möbel aus Kunststoff, edited by A. v. Vegesack, exhibition catalogue Vitra Design Museum, Weil am Rhein, 1990, p. 20-21.
Vitra Design Museum Collection, Poster DIN A0, Weil am Rhein: Vitra Design Museum, 1991/93.
P. Dunas: Luigi Colani, München: Prestel, 1993, p. 79-80, ill. 93-95.
T. Heider, M. Stegmann, R. Zey: Lexikon Internationales Design, Reinbek/Hamburg: Rowohlt, 1994, p. 75-76.

72
A. Fujimoto: Luigi Colani – Designing Tomorrow, Tokyo: San'ei Shobo Publishing, 1978, p. 93, ill. 8.
P. Dunas: Luigi Colani, München: Prestel, 1993, p. 79-80, ill. 94-95.
T. Heider, M. Stegmann, R. Zey: Lexikon Internationales Design, Reinbek/Hamburg: Rowohlt, 1994, p. 75-76.

73
Domus, Milano, no. 714, 1990, p. 67.
Decorative Arts and Design from the Powerhouse Museum, Sydney: Powerhouse Publishing, 1991, p. 155.
Vitra Design Museum Collection, Poster DIN A0, Weil am Rhein: Vitra Design Museum, 1993.
T. Heider, M. Stegmann, R. Zey: Lexikon Internationales Design, Reinbek/Hamburg: Rowohlt, 1994, p. 236.
P. Kjellberg: Le Mobilier du XXᵉ Siècle, Paris: Les Editions de l'Amateur, 1994, p. 452.
13 nach Memphis, edited by V. Albus, V. Fischer, exhibition catalogue Museum für Kunsthandwerk, Frankfurt am Main, München: Prestel, 1995, p. 130, 192, ill. 12.

74
O. Boissière: Starck, Köln: Taschen, 1991, p. 56-57, 165, cover.
P. Dunas: Luigi Colani, München: Prestel, 1993, p. 189, ill. 289.
Grand-Hornu Images: S'asseoir 100 façons, Poster, B-Boussu (Hornu), 1993,
no. 97.
B. Sipek: Das Internationale Design Jahrbuch 1993/94, München,
Schopfheim: Bangert, 1993, p. 82, ill. 113.
13 nach Memphis, edited by V. Albus, V. Fischer, exhibition catalogue
Museum für Kunsthandwerk, Frankfurt am Main, München: Prestel, 1995,
p. 160-162.

75
G. Candilis, A. Blomstedt, T. Frangoulis, M. I. Amorin: Bugholzmöbel,
Stuttgart: Krämer, 1980, p. 17, 87.
C. Wilk: Thonet: 150 years of furniture, New York: Barron's, 1980, p. 46-47.
Caravelles, Enjeux de l'objet, edited by F. Philip, J. Bonnot, Studio TOTEM,
exhibition catalogue Grenoble, Lyon, Saint Etienne, 1986, p. 24.
Bent Wood and Metal Furniture 1850-1946, edited by D. E. Ostergard,
exhibition catalogue The American Federation of Arts, New York, 1987,
p. 232-233, no. 33.
A. v. Vegesack: Das Thonet Buch, München: Bangert, 1987, p. 108-110.
Sitz-Gelegenheiten, edited by C. Pese, U. Peters, exhibition catalogue
Germanisches Nationalmuseum, Nürnberg, 1990, p. 222-223, no. 111.
A. Drexler: Architecture and Design, in: The Museum of Modern Art,
New York, 1991, p. 408-409, no. 663.
A. Bangert, P. Ellenberg: Thonet-Möbel, München: Heyne, 1993, p. 100.
Grand-Hornu Images: S'asseoir 100 façons, Poster, B-Boussu (Hornu), 1993,
no. 19.
Thonet, Pionier des Industriedesigns 1830-1900, edited by A. v. Vegesack,
exhibition catalogue Vitra Design Museum, Weil am Rhein, 1994, no. 47.

76
Deutsche Kunst und Dekoration, München, 10.1908, p. 37.
D. Müller: Klassiker des modernen Möbeldesign, München: Keyser, 1980,
p. 105, ill. 77.
D. Baroni, A. D'Auria: Josef Hoffmann e la Wiener Werkstätte, Milano:
Electa, 1981, p. 107.
Josef Hoffmann – Architect and designer 1870-1956, edited by C. Meyer,
exhibition catalogue Galerie Metropol, Wien, 1981, p. 22, 40.
Josef Hoffmann, edited by D. Gebhard, exhibition catalogue The Fort Worth
Art Museum, 1982, p. 40-41.
Mackintosh to Mollino, edited by D. E. Ostergard, exhibition catalogue
Gallery Barry Friedman, New York, 1984, p. 27.
Bent Wood and Metal Furniture 1850-1946, edited by D. E. Ostergard,
exhibition catalogue The American Federation of Arts, New York, 1987,
p. 255-256, no. 54.
Sitz-Gelegenheiten, edited by C. Pese, U. Peters, exhibition catalogue
Germanisches Nationalmuseum, Nürnberg, 1989, p. 238, no. 163.
Vitra Design Museum Collection, Poster DIN A0, Weil am Rhein:
Vitra Design Museum, 1991/93.
Against The Grain, edited by G. Zelleke, E. B. Ottillinger, N. Stritzler,
exhibition catalogue The Art Institute of Chicago, 1993, p. 86, no. 55.

77
H. T. Wijdeveld: Frank Lloyd Wright, Santpoort: C.A. Mees, 1925, p. 122,
125-126.
F. L. Wright: A Testament, New York: Bramhall House, 1957, p. 127.
The Decorative Designs of Frank Lloyd Wright, edited by D. A. Hanks,
exhibition catalogue Renwick Gallery of the National Collection of Fine Arts,
Washington, D.C., and other, New York: Dutton, 1979, p. 133.
Frank Lloyd Wright – Architectural Drawings and Decorative Art, exhibition
catalogue Fischer Fine Art Ltd, London, 1985, p. 82-83, no. 39.
S. Yates: An Encyclopedia of Chairs, London: Quintet Publishing, 1988,
p. 92-93, no. 146a.

Frank Lloyd Wright, edited by D. A. Hanks, exhibition catalogue Seattle Art
Museum, and other, New York: Dutton, 1989, p. 90-91.
Frank Lloyd Wright Retrospective, exhibition catalogue Sezon Museum of
Art, and other, Tokyo, 1991, p. 137-154, no. 88.
Vitra Design Museum Collection, Poster DIN A0, Weil am Rhein:
Vitra Design Museum, 1991/93.
Frank Lloyd Wright – Architect, edited by T. Riley, P. Reed, exhibition
catalogue The Museum of Modern Art, New York, 1994, p. 193, ill. 163.
T. A. Heinz: Frank Lloyd Wright – Interiors and Furniture, London:
The Academy Group, 1994, p. 158-159.

78
J. Sebag: Maison de la Tunisie à la Cité Universitaire de Paris, in:
L'Architecture d'Aujourd'hui, Boulogne, 47.1953, p. 66-67.
Charlotte Perriand – Un art de vivre, exhibition catalogue Musée des Arts
Décoratifs, Paris, Paris: Flammarion, 1985, p. 47.
Jean Prouvé/Serge Mouille, exhibition catalogue A. Delorenzo, New York,
Alan, C. Counord, Paris, 1985, p. 79-81.
Jean Prouvé, Mobilier 1924-1953, exhibition catalogue Galerie Down-Town,
Galerie Touchaleaume, Paris, 1987, p. 25.
Jean Prouvé 'constructeur', exhibition catalogue Centre Georges
Pompidou, Paris, 1990, p. 187.
J. v. Geest: Jean Prouvé, Köln: Taschen, 1991, p. 144-145, 153, no. 57.
Centre Georges Pompidou: Nouvelles Acquisitions, folder,
Paris, 1993.
R. Guidot: Design, Stuttgart: Deutsche Verlags-Anstalt, 1994, p. 161.

79
C. Greenberg: Mid-Century Modern, New York: Harmony Books, 1984, p. 95.
F. Baudot: Les Assises du Siècle, Paris: Editions du May, 1990, p. 53.
Design 1935-1965 – What Modern Was, edited by M. Eidelberg, exhibition
catalogue Musée des Arts Décoratifs, Montréal, and other, New York:
Abrams, 1991, p. 308-309, ill. 480, 481.
Vitra Design Museum Collection, Poster DIN A0, Weil am Rhein:
Vitra Design Museum, 1991/93.
C. & P. Fiell: Modern Chairs, Köln: Taschen, 1993, p. 79.
K. B. Hiesinger, G. H. Marcus: Landmarks of Twentieth-Century Design,
New York: Abbeville Press, 1993, p. 198, no. 247.
R. Guidot: Design, Stuttgart: Deutsche Verlags-Anstalt, 1994, p. 123.
P. Kjellberg: Le Mobilier du XXᵉ Siècle, Paris: Les Editions de l'Amateur,
1994, p. 449-451.
T. Heider, M. Stegmann, R. Zey: Lexikon Internationales Design,
Reinbek/Hamburg: Rowohlt, 1994, p. 234-235.

80
Les Assises du Siège Contemporain, exhibition catalogue Musée des Arts
Décoratifs, Paris, 1968, p. 111, no. 275.
P. Garner: Contemporary Decorative Arts from 1940 to the present,
New York: Facts on File, 1980, p. 65, 71.
Design Since 1945: Edited by K. B. Hiesinger, G. H. Marcus, exhibition
catalogue Philadelphia Museum of Art, 1983, p. 136, no. III-85.
F. Baudot: Les Assises du Siècle, Paris: Editions du May, 1990, p. 56.
Vitra Design Museum Collection, Poster DIN A0, Weil am Rhein:
Vitra Design Museum, 1991/93.
F. Mathey: Au Bonheur Des Formes, Paris: Editions du Regard, 1992, p.268.
Roger Tallon – Itinéraires d'un designer industriel, exhibition catalogue
Centre Georges Pompidou, Paris, 1993, p. 100-101.
K. B. Hiesinger, G. H. Marcus: Landmarks of Twentieth-Century Design,
New York: Abbeville Press, 1993, p. 235, no. 300.
R. Guidot: Design, Stuttgart: Deutsche Verlags-Anstalt, 1994, p. 197-198.
T. Heider, M. Stegmann, R. Zey: Lexikon Internationales Design,
Reinbek/Hamburg: Rowohlt, 1994, p. 327.
P. Kjellberg: Le Mobilier du XXᵉ Siècle, Paris: Les Editions de L'Amateur,
1994, p. 637-638.

81

A. Bangert: Italienisches Möbeldesign, München: Bangert, 1985, p. 61-66, 116, ill. 71.
G. Gramigna: Repertorio 1950-1980, Milano: Mondadori, 1985, p. 466.
Design Heute, edited by V. Fischer, exhibition catalogue Deutsches Architekturmuseum, Frankfurt am Main, München: Prestel, 1988, p. 73-76.
S. Casciani, G. Di Pietrantonio, B. Felis, D. Verzura: Alessandro Mendini, Milano: Politi, 1989, p. 86.
F. Baudot: Les Assises du Siècle, Paris: Editions Du May, 1990, p. 88.
A. Mendini: La poltrona di Proust, Milano: Tranchida, 1991.
K. B. Hiesinger, G. H. Marcus: Landmarks of Twentieth-Century Design, New York: Abbeville Press, 1993, p. 274, no. 359.
Groninger Museum: Atelier Mendini 1990-1994, Milano: Fabbri, 1994, p. 62, 170, 172-173, 197, 200-201.
R. Guidot: Design, Stuttgart: Deutsche Verlags-Anstalt, 1994, p. 250, ill. 1.
T. Heider, M. Stegmann, R. Zey: Lexikon Internationales Design, Reinbek/Hamburg: Rowohlt, 1994, p. 211-212.
P. Kjellberg: Le Mobilier du XXᵉ Siècle, Paris: Les Editions de l'Amateur, 1994, p. 422-424.

82

Design Since 1945, edited by K. B. Hiesinger, G. H. Marcus, Ausst Kat. Philadelphia Museum of Art, 1983, p. 128, no. III-39.
A. Bangert: Italienisches Möbeldesign, München: Bangert, 1985, p. 120, no. 77.
G. Gramigna: Repertorio 1950-1980, Milano: Mondadori, 1985, p. 482.
Design Heute, edited by V. Fischer, exhibition catalogue Deutsches Architekturmuseum, Frankfurt am Main, München: Prestel, 1988, p. 31, no. 43.
K.M. Armer, A. Bangert: Design der 80er Jahre, München: Bangert, 1990, p. 38-39.
B. Mundt: Produkt-Design 1900-1990, Kunstgewerbemuseum, Berlin, Berlin: Reimer, 1991, p. 236-237, no. 157.
K. B. Hiesinger, G. H. Marcus: Landmarks of Twentieth-Century Design, New York: Abbeville Press, 1993, p. 275, no. 361.
K.-J. Sembach: Möbel, die Geschichte machen, Hamburg: Gruner+Jahr, 1993, p. 122-123, no. 48.
R. Guidot: Design, Stuttgart: Deutsche Verlags-Anstalt, 1994, p. 317.
T. Heider, M. Stegmann, R. Zey: Lexikon Internationales Design, Reinbek/Hamburg: Rowohlt, 1994, p. 163-164.
P. Kjellberg: Le Mobilier du XXᵉ Siècle, Paris: Les Editions de l'Amateur, 1994, p. 339-341.

83

P. Sparke: Ettore Sottsass Jr., London: The Design Council, 1982, p. 79.
Ettore Sottsass – Mobili e qualche arredamento, exhibition catalogue Galleria Rocca, Torino, Galerie Yves Gastou, Paris, Milano: Mondadori, 1985, p. 105.
G. Gramigna: Repertorio 1950-1980, Milano: Mondadori, 1985, p. 512, 541, 570, cover.
R. Horn: Memphis – Objects, Furniture & Patterns, New York: Quarto Marketing, 1985, p. 66-67.
G. De Bure: Ettore Sottsass Jr., Paris: Rivages/Styles, 1987, p. 75.
Design Heute, edited by V. Fischer, exhibition catalogue Deutsches Architekturmuseum, Frankfurt am Main, München: Prestel, 1988, p. 73-75, 81, 310, no. 169.
B. Radice: Memphis Design, München: Bangert, 1988, p. 145.
Sottsass Associati, New York: Rizzoli, 1988, p. 38.
M. Collins, A. Papadakis: Post-Modern Design, New York: Rizzoli, 1989, p. 35, 37.
Memphis 1981-1988, exhibition catalogue Groninger Museum, 1989, p. 41, ill. 8.
H. Höger: Ettore Sottsass jun. – Designer, Artist, Architect, Tübingen, Berlin: Wasmuth, 1993, p. 99, 216.
K.-J. Sembach: Möbel, die Geschichte machen, Hamburg: Gruner+Jahr, 1993, p. 193, no. 1.

84

R. A. M. Stern: The International Design Yearbook no. 1, New York: Abbeville Press, 1985, p. 72.
J. Capella, Q. Larrea: Designed by Architects in the 1980s, New York: Rizzoli, 1988, p. 172-173.
Design Heute, edited by V. Fischer, exhibition catalogue Deutsches Architekturmuseum, Frankfurt am Main, München: Prestel, 1988, p. 87-88.
M. Collins, A. Papadakis: Post-Modern Design, New York: Rizzoli, 1989, p. 102-115.
K. M. Armer, A. Bangert: Design der 80er Jahre, München: Bangert, 1990, p. 28.
K. Takagaki, A. Sawamura, N. Maruyama: Venturi, Scott Brown and Associates – Two Naifs in Japan, Tokyo: Kajima Institute Publishing, 1991, p. 138-139.
Vitra Design Museum Collection, Poster DIN A0, Weil am Rhein: Vitra Design Museum, 1991/93.
M. Eisinger: Stühle des 20. Jahrhunderts, München: Klinkhardt & Biermann, 1994, p. 84.
P. Kjellberg: Le Mobilier du XXᵉ Siècle, Paris: Les Editions de l'Amateur, 1994, p. 655-656.
T. Heider, M. Stegmann, R. Zey: Lexikon Internationales Design, Reinbek/Hamburg: Rowohlt, 1994, p. 346-347.

85

P. Starck: The International Design Yearbook 1987/88, London: Thames & Hudson, 1987, p. 60.
Design Heute, edited by V. Fischer, exhibition catalogue Deutsches Architekturmuseum, Frankfurt am Main, München: Prestel, 1988, p. 69, ill. 145.
K. M. Armer, A. Bangert: Design der 80er Jahre, München: Bangert, 1990, p. 57.
Vitra Design Museum Collection, Poster DIN A0, Weil am Rhein: Vitra Design Museum, 1991/93.
C. & P. Fiell: Modern Chairs, Köln: Taschen, 1993, p. 122.
Grand-Hornu Images: S'asseoir 100 façons, Poster, B-Boussu (Hornu), 1993, no. 94.
K. B. Hiesinger, G. H. Marcus: Landmarks of Twentieth-Century Design, New York: Abbeville Press, 1993, p. 300.
M. Dietz, M. Mönninger: Japanese Design, Köln: Taschen, 1994, p. 68-69.
Japanese Design: A Survey Since 1950, edited by K. B. Hiesinger, F. Fischer, exhibition catalogue Philadelphia Museum of Art, 1994, p. 162-163, no. 186.
P. Kjellberg: Le Mobilier du XXᵉ Siècle, Paris: Les Editions de l'Amateur, 1994, p. 348-350.
T. Heider, M. Stegmann, R. Zey: Lexikon Internationales Design, Reinbek/Hamburg: Rowohlt, 1994, p. 175-176.

86

Barcelona Design Center: 1989 catalan designs for export, Barcelona, 1989, p. 61.
O. Tusquets Blanca: Das Internationale Design Jahrbuch 1989/90, München: Bangert, 1989, p. 40.
Neues europäisches Design, edited by A. Branzi, F. Burkhardt, exhibition catalogue Kunstmuseum Düsseldorf, Berlin: Ernst & Sohn, 1991, p. 63.
Vitra Design Museum Collection, Poster DIN A0, Weil am Rhein: Vitra Design Museum, 1991/93.
C. & P. Fiell: Modern Chairs, Köln: Taschen, 1993, p. 125.
P. Kjellberg: Le Mobilier du XXᵉ Siècle, Paris: Les Editions de l'Amateur, 1994, p. 479-480.

87

M. Bellini: Das Internationale Design Jahrbuch 1990/91, München: Bangert, 1990, p. 36, ill. 53.
Möbel aus Kunststoff, edited by A. v. Vegesack, exhibition catalogue Vitra Design Museum, Weil am Rhein, 1990, p. 5, 7, 9, 40-41.
Vitra Design Museum Collection, Poster DIN A0, Weil am Rhein: Vitra Design Museum, 1991/93.

S'asseoir 100 façons, edited by C. Fache, exhibition catalogue Grand-Hornu Images, B-Boussu (Hornu), 1993, p. 80-81.
C. & P. Fiell: Modern Chairs, Köln: Taschen, 1993, p. 128.
M. Dietz, M. Mönninger: Japanese Design, Köln: Taschen, 1994, p. 74-75, cover.
M. Eisinger: Stühle des 20. Jahrhunderts, München: Klinkhardt & Biermann, 1994, p. 95.
P. Kjellberg: Le Mobilier du XXᵉ Siècle, Paris: Les Editions de l'Amateur, 1994, p. 348-350.
T. Heider, M. Stegmann, R. Zey: Lexikon Internationales Design, Reinbek/Hamburg: Rowohlt, 1994, p. 175-176.

88
D. Baroni: I mobili di Gerrit Thomas Rietveld, Milano: Electa, 1977, p.8, 48/49.
M. Küper: Gerrit Rietveld, in: De Stijl – The Formative Years, Cambridge, Mass., London: MIT Press, 1982, p. 258-279.
Gerrit Rietveld – A Centenary Exhibition, exhibition catalogue Gallery Barry Friedman, New York, 1988, p. 4, 22-28.
Sotheby's, Amsterdam, 03.05.1988, p. 24, 26/27, 30/31, 34/35.
Rietveld and the Rietveld Academie. Christie's, Amsterdam, 07.06.1988, p. 88-91.
Gerrit T. Rietveld 1888-1964, The Complete Works, edited by M. Küper, I. van Zijl, exhibition catalogue Centraal Museum, Utrecht, Centre Pompidou, Paris, Utrecht, 1992, p. 74/75.
P. Vöge: The Complete Rietveld Furniture, Rotterdam: 010 Publishers, 1993, p. 8-41, 50-51, 58-59, 172. ill. 23, 46.
K.-J. Sembach: Möbel, die Geschichte machen, Hamburg: Gruner + Jahr, 1993, p. 105, no. 4.
K. B. Hiesinger, G. H. Marcus: Landmarks of Twentieth-Century Design, New York: Abbeville Press, 1993, p. 74-75, no. 81.
Design, miroir du siècle, edited by J. de Noblet, exhibition catalogue Grand Palais, Paris, Paris: Flammarion/APCI, 1993, p. 181.

89
Die Weissenhof-Siedlung-Stuttgart, in: Innendekoration, Darmstadt, 38, 1927, p. 441-453, ill. p. 445-449.
Neuzeitliche Innenräume in der Ausstellung: Deutsche Kunst Düsseldorf 1928, in: Innendekoration, Darmstadt, 39, 1928, p. 271-289, ill. p. 275-279.
W. Gräff: Innenräume, Stuttgart: Wedekind, 1928, p. 25, 57.
Die Form, Berlin, 4, 1929, p. 174-176.
P. Blake: Marcel Breuer – Architect and Designer, New York: The Museum of Modern Art, 1949, p. 17-18.
J. v. Geest, O. Mácel: Stühle aus Stahl, Köln: König, 1980, p. 62, 64, ill. 7.
Marcel Breuer – Furniture and Interiors, edited by C. Wilk, exhibition catalogue The Museum of Modern Art, New York, 1981, p. 37-41, ill. 24, 27, 41, 61.
A. v. Vegesack: Deutsche Stahlrohrmöbel, München: Bangert, 1986, p. 30, 33, 37.
M. Droste, M. Ludewig, Bauhaus Archiv: Marcel Breuer, Köln: Taschen, 1992, p. 4-35, 62-63, 72-73, 153, no. 12.
M.-L. Jousset, K. V. Posch: Portrait d'une collection – Alexander von Vegesack, Paris: Centre Georges Pompidou, 1993, p. 26-28.

90
J. Bier: Mies van der Rohes Reichspavillon in Barcelona, in: Die Form, Berlin, 4.1929, p. 423-431.
Mies van der Rohe, edited by P. C. Johnson, exhibition catalogue The Museum of Modern Art, New York, 1947, p. 66-75.
P. Blake: The Master Builders – Le Corbusier, Mies van der Rohe, Frank Lloyd Wright, New York: Knopf, 1960, p. 202-209.
Ludwig Mies van der Rohe, edited by L. Glaeser, exhibition catalogue The Museum of Modern Art, New York, 1977, p. 46-53.
J. v. Geest, O. Mácel: Stühle aus Stahl, Köln: König, 1980, p. 97.
W. Blaser: Mies van der Rohe – Furniture and Interiors, New York: Barron's, 1982, p. 60, 61.

A. v. Vegesack: Deutsche Stahlrohrmöbel, München: Bangert, 1986, p. 63, 66-67.
Bent Wood and Metal Furniture 1850-1946, edited by D. E. Ostergard, exhibition catalogue The American Federation of Arts, New York, 1987, p. 291-293.
K. B. Hiesinger, G. H. Marcus: Landmarks of Twentieth-Century Design, New York: Abbeville Press, 1993, p. 104, no. 120.
G. H. Marcus: Functionalist Design, München, New York: Prestel, 1995, p. 106-112, 134-139.

91
Italienisches Möbeldesign, exhibition catalogue Stadtmuseum Köln, Roma: ICE, Istituto Nazionale per il Commercio Estero, 1980, p. 182-183, no. 122.
K.-J. Sembach: Neue Möbel, Stuttgart: Hatje, 1982, p. 66, 67.
Design Since 1945, edited by K. B. Hiesinger, G. H. Marcus, exhibition catalogue The Philadelphia Museum of Art, 1983, p. 123, no. III-13.
P. Ferrari: Achille Castiglioni, Milano: Electa, 1984, p. 64-65, cover.
A. Bangert: Italienisches Möbeldesign, München: Bangert, 1985, p. 33-36, 80-81, ill. 7.
G. Gramigna: Repertorio 1950-1980, Milano: Mondadori, 1985, p. 324.
Design Heute, edited by V. Fischer, exhibition catalogue Deutsches Architekturmuseum, Frankfurt am Main, München: Prestel, 1988, p. 27, no. 31.
Italien – Design 1945 bis heute, edited by H. Wichmann, exhibition catalogue Die Neue Sammlung, München, 1988, p. 84.
K. B. Hiesinger, G. H. Marcus: Landmarks of Twentieth-Century Design, New York: Abbeville Press, 1993, p. 208-209, no. 266.
K.-J. Sembach: Möbel, die Geschichte machen, Hamburg: Gruner + Jahr, 1993, p. 199-200, no. 14.
R. Guidot: Design, Stuttgart: Deutsche Verlags-Anstalt, 1994, p. 170-171.

92
Italy – The New Domestic Landscape, edited by E. Ambasz, exhibition catalogue The Museum of Modern Art, New York, Firenze: Centro Di, 1972, p. 100, 101.
Galerie Wolfgang Ketterer: 79. Auktion, Italienisches Design 1951-1973, München, 24.03.1984, p. 120, ill. 182.
P. Sparke: Italienisches Design von 1870 bis heute, Braunschweig: Westermann, 1989, p. 193.
Möbel aus Kunststoff, edited by A. v. Vegesack, exhibition catalogue Vitra Design Museum, Weil am Rhein, 1991, p. 28, 29.
Vitra Design Museum Collection, Poster DIN A0, Weil am Rhein: Vitra Design Museum, 1993.
R. Guidot: Design, Stuttgart: Deutsche Verlags-Anstalt, 1994, p. 244.

93
N.-J. Kaiser: Verner Panton, København: Bording Grafik A/S, 1986.
C. & P. Fiell: Modern Chairs, Köln: Taschen, 1993, p. 89.

94
G. Hatje, E. Kaspar: Neue Möbel, Stuttgart: Hatje, vol. 10, 1971, p. 36.
Italy – The New Domestic Landscape, edited by E. Ambasz, exhibition catalogue The Museum of Modern Art, New York, Firenze: Centro Di, 1972, p. 103.
A. Grassi, A. Pansera: Atlante del design italiano 1940/1980, Milano: Fabbri, 1980, p. 161, no. 4.
Galerie Wolfgang Ketterer: 79. Auktion, Italienisches Design 1951-1973, München, 24.03.1984, p. 88, ill. 136.
A. Bangert: Italienisches Möbeldesign, München: Bangert, 1985, p. 109, ill. 61.
G. Gramigna: Repertorio 1950-1980, Milano: Mondadori, 1985, p. 287.
Vitra Design Museum Collection, Poster DIN A0, Weil am Rhein: Vitra Design Museum, 1991/93.
M. Eisinger: Stühle des 20. Jahrhunderts, München: Klinkhardt & Biermann, 1994, p. 85.
T. Heider, M. Stegmann, R. Zey: Lexikon Internationales Design, Reinbek/Hamburg: Rowohlt, 1994, p. 20-21.

95

S. Casciani, G. Di Pietrantonio, B. Felis, D. Verzura: Alessandro Mendini, Milano: Politi, 1989, p. 39, 59.
Groninger Museum: Atelier Mendini 1990-1994, Milano: Fabbri, 1994, p. 197-198, 205-206.
La Sindrome di Leonardo – Art e Design in Italia 1940/1975, edited by E. Biffi Gentili, exhibition catalogue Palazzina di Caccia di Stupinigi, Torino, Torino: Allemandi, 1995.

96

R. Horn: Memphis, New York: Quarto Marketing, 1986, p. 40.
G. Berruti, C. Ratti: Il Compensato Curvato, Milano: Rima, 1988, p. 83.
Design Heute, edited by V. Fischer, exhibition catalogue Deutsches Architekturmuseum, Frankfurt am Main, München: Prestel, 1988, p. 83, 310.
B. Radice: Memphis Design, München: Bangert, 1988, p. 175.
G. Albera, N. Monti: Italian Modern – A design heritage, New York: Rizzoli, 1989, p. 85.
Memphis 1981-1988, exhibition catalogue Groninger Museum, 1989, no. 143.
K. M. Armer, A. Bangert: Design der 80er Jahre, München: Bangert, 1990, p. 23.
F. Baudot: Les Assises du Siècle, Paris: Editions Du May, 1990, p. 95.
Vitra Design Museum Collection, Poster DIN A0, Weil am Rhein: Vitra Design Museum, 1991/93.
S. Kicherer: Michele De Lucchi, Milano: L'Archivolto, 1992, p. 63.
A. Buck, M. Vogt: Michele De Lucchi, Berlin: Ernst & Sohn, 1993, p. 35.
S'asseoir 100 façons, edited by C. Fache, exhibition catalogue Grand-Hornu Images, B-Boussu (Hornu), 1993, p. 83.
C. & P. Fiell: Modern Chairs, Köln: Taschen, 1993, p. 119, 140.
N. Börnsen-Holtmann: Italian Design, Köln: Taschen, 1994, p. 2, 112, 161.

97

Gefühlscollagen – Wohnen von Sinnen, exhibition catalogue Kunstmuseum Düsseldorf, Köln: DuMont, 1986, cover.
P. Teichgräber: Stiletto – Kraft durch Design, Wien: Prodomo, 1987, p. 4-5.
K. M. Armer, A. Bangert: Design der 80er Jahre, München: Bangert, 1990, p. 70.
Vitra Design Museum Collection, Poster DIN A0, Weil am Rhein: Vitra Design Museum, 1991/93.
V. Albus, C. Borngräber: Design Bilanz, Köln: Dumont, 1992, p. 44-45, 155, 262.
C. & P. Fiell: Modern Chairs, Köln: Taschen, 1993, p. 120, 153.

98

Gefühlscollagen – Wohnen von Sinnen, exhibition catalogue Kunstmuseum Düsseldorf, Köln: DuMont, 1986, p. 233.
Design Heute, edited by V. Fischer, exhibition catalogue Deutsches Architekturmuseum, Frankfurt am Main, München: Prestel, 1988, p. 69, 309.
W. Schepers, S. Voggenreiter, M. Erlhoff: Pentagon – Informal Design, Köln: Taschen, 1990, p. 84, 85, 154.
V. Albus, C. Borngräber: Design Bilanz, Köln: DuMont, 1992, p. 190, 191.
La Casa di Alice, edited by M. Barberis, F. De Leonardis, E. Grazioli, exhibition catalogue Galleria Mazzocchi, Parma, Milano: Electa, 1992, p. 84-85.

99

Caravelles, Enjeux de l'objet, edited by F. Philip, J. Bonnot, Studio TOTEM, exhibition catalogue Grenoble, Lyon, Saint Etienne, 1986, p. 62/63, 81-87.
Gefühlscollagen – Wohnen von Sinnen, exhibition catalogue Kunstmuseum Düsseldorf, Köln: DuMont, 1986, p. 143.
A. Branzi: Domestic Animals – The Neoprimitive Style, Cambridge, Mass.: MIT Press, 1987, ill..
J. Capella, Q. Larrea: Designed by Architects in the 1980s, New York: Rizzoli, 1988, p. 34-37.
P. Sparke: Italienisches Design von 1870 bis heute, Braunschweig: Westermann, 1989, p. 217.
F. Baudot: Les Assises du Siècle, Paris: Editions du May, 1990, p. 97.
Vitra Design Museum Collection, Poster DIN A0, Weil am Rhein: Vitra Design Museum, 1991/93.
R. Guidot: Design, Stuttgart: Deutsche Verlags-Anstalt, 1994, p. 265, 302.
P. Kjellberg: Le Mobilier du XXᵉ Siècle, Paris: Les Editions de l'Amateur, 1994, p. 97.

100

K. M. Armer, A. Bangert: Design der 80er Jahre, München: Bangert, 1990, p. 89.
G. H. Marcus: Functionalist Design, München, New York: Prestel, 1995, p. 31, no. 20.

Photograph Credits

P. 22: *Brockhaus Enzyklopädie*, (Mannheim, 1993) Vol. 19, p. 371; Tecta, Lauenförde. P. 24: Archive A. v. Vegesack; Basel Mission Archive, Basel. P. 26: F. Baudot, *Les Assises du Siècle*, (Paris, 1990), p. 38; from the catalogue of a German mail order company, 1976. P. 28: E. Dieckmann, *Möbelbau*, (Stuttgart 1931, reprint VDM, Weil am Rhein, 1990), p. 69; L. Canella, R. Radici, *Tavoli e Piani d'Appoggio*, (Milan, 1948), p. 22. P. 30: *Wohnbedarf AG, Zurich advertisement brochure*, (Thirties, VDM Archive). P. 32: Archives Modernes de L'Architecture Lorraine, Nancy. P. 34: Museum für Gestaltung Zurich, Kunstgewerbemuseum, *Hans Coray – Künstler und Entwerfer*, (Zurich, 1986). P. 36: VDM Archive. P. 38: VDM Archive; *Saturday Evening Post*, May 16, 1959. P. 40: VDM Archive; sales catalogue: *The Herman Miller Collection*, 1952, pp. 97-8. P. 42: *Interieur*, No. 2, 1963, p. 26; Alcoa Aluminum flyer, 1958; Flyer: The Eames Aluminum Group by Herman Miller, 1958; Information pamphlet by Herman Miller Inc., Assembly Operations for Eames Aluminum Group Chairs, undated (c. 1960). P. 44: François Burkhardt, *Design Marco Zanuso*, (Milan, 1994), pp. 93-4. P. 46: Archive Helmut Bätzner; Menzolit company flyer; Kraichtal-Menzingen. P. 48: Archive Zanotta, Nova Milanese, Milan. P. 50: B&B Italia company flyer, Novredate, Como; Archive Gaetano Pesce; Archive B&B Italia, Novredate, Como; VDM collection. P. 52: VDM Archive. P. 54: Archive Alberto Meda, Alias Company, Grumello del Monte. P. 56: VDM Archive. P. 62: David A. Hanks, *Innovative Furniture in America from 1800 to the Present*, (New York, 1981), Ill. 105. P. 64: A. S. Levetus: "Austrian Architecture and Decoration," in: *The Studio Yearbook of Decorative Art*, (London, Paris, New York, 1910), p. 222; Jacob & Josef Kohn catalogue, Vienna, 1916, p. 68. P. 66: P. Adam, E. Gray: *Architect/Designer*, (New York, 1987), p. 202; VDM collection. P. 68: B. B. Taylor, P. Chareau: *Designer and Architect*, (Cologne, 1992), p. 139; *L'Art International d'Aujourd'hui*, No. 6, (Paris, 1929–30); VDM collection. P. 70: *The Studio Year Book of Decorative Art*, (London, Paris, New York, 1930), p. 17. P. 72: R. De Fusco, *Le Corbusier as Designer*, (Milan, 1976), p. 73; *Art & Décoration*, Feb. 1930, p. 41; *Charlotte Perriand – Un art de vivre*, exhibition catalogue (Musée des Arts Décoratifs, Paris, 1985); catalogue of Thonet Frères Paris, *Meubles en tubes d'acier*, undated (1933) p. 44. P. 74: *Die Form*, Vol. 5, 1930, p. 285; VDM collection. P. 76: Jean Prouvé Archive Prof. Peter Sulzer, University of Stuttgart; *Jean Prouvé/Serge Mouille*, exhibition catalogue, (A. De Lorenzo, New York, A. & C. Councord, Paris, 1985), p. 42. P. 78: *J. Prouvé – Architecture/Industry*, (Paris, undated), p. 91. P. 147. P. 143. P. 80: VDM Archive; catalogue of Gebrüder Thonet AG, Siesta Medizinal, undated (c. 1940), p. 1. P. 82: *Gerrit T. Rietveld 1888–1964, The Complete Works*, ed. M. Küper, I. v. Zijl, *exhibition catalogue Centraal Museum Utrecht*, (Centre G. Pompidou, Paris, Utrecht, 1992), p. 115; p. 197; p. 209; VDM collection. P. 84: *Arts & Architecture*, Sept.1946, p. 40; Pat Kirkham, *Charles and Ray Eames – Designers of the Twentieth Century*, (Cambridge, Mass., London, 1995), p. 321; *The Herman Miller Collection*, sales catalogue 1952, p. 105; *Organic Design in Home Furnishings*, exhibition catalogue Museum of Modern Art, New York, ed. Eliot F. Noyes, (New York, 1941), p. 29. P. 86: VDM Archive; VDM collection. P. 88: collection catalogue *The Museum of Modern Art*, New York, ed. S. Hunter, (New York, 1984), p. 207; VDM Archive. P. 90: Herman Miller pamphlet, undated; VDM Archive; Herman Miller pamphlet, Fifties. P. 92: VDM Archive. P. 94: E. Kold Christensen, Copenhagen advertising brochure, undated; *Bent Wood and Metal Furniture 1850–1946*, ed. D. E. Ostergard, exhibition catalogue (The American Federation of Arts, New York, 1987), p. 324. P. 96: A. Bangert, *Italienisches Möbeldesign – Klassiker von 1945 bis 1985*, (Munich, 1985), p. 119. P. 98: P. Garner, *Contemporary Decorative Arts from 1940 to the Present*, (New York, 1980), p. 75. P. 104: *Ein Stuhl macht Geschichte*, ed. W. Möller, O. Mácel, (exhibition catalogue Bauhaus, Dessau, Vitra Design Museum, Weil am Rhein, Museum für Kunst und Gewerbe, Hamburg, Munich, 1992), p. 57; VDM Archive; *S'asseoir 100 façons*, ed. C. Fache, exhibition catalogue (Grand-Hornu Images, B-Boussu, 1993), p. 60; sales catalogue of Berliner Metallgewerbe J. Müller, (Berlin, undated). P. 106: sales catalogue of Formes Nouvelles, *R. Herbst – Aciers et Sandows*, (undated), p. 19; S. Goguel, *René Herbst*, (Paris, 1990), p. 70; p.197. P. 108: VDM Archive; U. Kultermann, *Wassili und Hans Luckhardt*, (Tübingen, 1958), p. 149; sales catalogue of Desta Stahlmöbel, (undated). P. 110: VDM Archive; *Bent Wood and Metal Furniture 1850–1946*, ed. D. E. Ostergard, exhibition catalogue (The American Federation of Arts, New York, 1987), p. 319. P. 112: *Bent Wood and Metal Furniture 1850–1946*, ed. D. E. Ostergard, exhibition catalogue (The American Federation of Arts, New York, 1987), p. 147; D. Baroni, *Il mobili di Gerrit Thomas Rietveld*, (Milan, 1977), p. 137; VDM collection. P. 114: D. A. Hanks, *Innovative Furniture in America from 1800 to the Present*, (New York, 1981), Ill. 139; sales catalogue (Knoll, 1950). P. 116: *Bent Wood and Metal Furniture 1850–1946*, ed. D. E. Ostergard, exhibition catalogue (The American Federation of Arts, New York, 1987), p. 309; Archive A. v. Vegesack. P. 118: A. Bangert, *Der Stil der 50er Jahre*, (Munich, 1983), p. 88; *L'Homme et son décor*, June 1953, (Paris, 1953), p. 29. P. 120: sales catalogue Fritz Hansen-Furniture No. 6802, (undated), p. 6; VDM collection; J. Pedersen, *Arkitekten Arne Jacobsen*, (Copenhagen, 1954), p. 63. P. 122: Archive Willy Guhl; P. Dunas, *Luigi Colani*, (Munich, 1993), p. 135; P. Vöge, *The Complete Rietveld Furniture*, (Rotterdam, 1993), p. 157; VDM collection. P. 124: L. Litrica Ponti, *Gio Ponti*, (Cambridge, Mass., 1990), p. 174; Archive L. Litrica Ponti, Milan; *Domus* 351, (Milan, 1959), p. 44. P. 126: *Mobili Come Architetture*, (Milan, 1984), pp. 90-1. P. 128: Archive Anomima Castelli p.p.A., Ozzano (Bologna). P. 130: VDM Archive; D. Sudjic, *Ron Arad – Restless Furniture*, (London, 1989), p. 85; *Ron Arad – Sticks and Stones 1981–1990*, ed. A. v. Vegesack, exhibition catalogue (Vitra Design Museum, Weil am Rhein, 1990), p. 74. P. 132: J. Morrison, *Designs, Projects and Drawings 1981–89*, (London, 1990), p. 61, cover. P. 138: VDM Archive; K. Fleig, Alvar Aalto, (Zurich, 1963), p. 127; Alvar Aalto Foundation, Helsinki; *Alvar Aalto: Furniture and Glass*, exhibition catalogue (The Museum of Modern Art, New York, ed. J. S. Johnson, New York, 1984); p. 140: *Artek 1935–1985*, exhibition catalogue. Taideteollisuusmuseo, Helsinki, 1985, p. 39; K. Fleig, Alvar Aalto, Zurich, 1963, p. 61. P. 142: VDM Archive; VDM Archive; VDM collection; *Organic Design in Home Furnishings*, exhibition catalogue (Museum of Modern Art, New York, ed. Eliot F. Noyes, New York, 1941), p. 12. P. 144: VDM collection; VDM Archive; VDM collection; *Arts & Architecture*, Sept. 1946, Cover. P. 146: VDM Archive; J. &. M. Neuhart, *R. Eames, Eames Design*, (Berlin, 1989), p. 78; VDM collection. P. 148: VDM collection; I. Noguchi, *A Sculptor's World*, (New York, Evanston, 1968), Ill. 190, 240. P. 150: sales catalogue *The Herman Miller Collection*, 1952. P. 152: *An Exhibition For Modern Living*, exhibition catalogue (The Detroit Institute of Arts, Detroit, 1949), p. 80. P. Dunas, *Luigi Colani*, (Munich, 1993), p. 131; exhibition catalogue The Museum of Modern Art, (New York, ed. S. Hunter, New York, 1984), p. 156; VDM Archive. P. 154: P. Sparke, *Italienisches Design*, (Braunschweig, 1989), p. 93; G. Brino, *Carlo Mollino*, (Munich, 1985), p. 50; F. Ferrari, *Carlo Mollino*, (Turin, 1985), p. 105; G. Brino, *Carlo Mollino*, (Munich, 1985), p. 44. P. 156: VDM collection; Herman Miller flyer, 1945. P. 158: *L'étrange univers de l'architecte Carlo Mollino*, exhibition catalogue (Centre G. Pompidou, Paris, 1989); p. 100, p. 109. P. 160: *Kalligraphie v. Yoshinobu Hagita*, Düsseldorf; *Der große Polyglott – Japan*, (Munich, 1972), p. 237. P. 162: VDM Archive; A. Wilkie, *Biedermeier*, (Paris, 1992), p. 90; sales catalogue Knoll, 1962; A. Temko, *Eero Saarinen*, (New York, 1962), Abb. 102. P. 164: Archive V. Panton, Basel; VDM Archive; VDM collection. P. 166: *Hans J. Wegner*, ed. J. Bernsen, exhibition catalogue (Dansk Design Center, Copenhagen, 1994), p. 31, p. 51; *Hans J. Wegner – en stølemager*, exhibition catalogue (Kunstindustriemuseet, Dansk Design Center, Copenhagen, 1989), p. 45, p. 48. P. 168: G. Hatje, E. Kaspar, *Neue Möbel*, (Stuttgart, 1969), p. 18; VDM collection. P. 170: Archive P. Dunas; *Top System* (Burkhard Lübke, Gütersloh). P. 172: Archive P. Dunas; *Domus* 714, (Milan, March 1990); *13 nach Memphis*, ed. V. Albus, (S. Fischer, exhibition catalogue Museum für Kunsthandwerk, Frankfurt/M., Munich, 1995), p. 127. P. 174: A. Bangert, S. Ellenberg, *Thonet-Möbel*, (Munich, 1993), p. 118; *13 nach Memphis*, ed. V. Albus, (S. Fischer, exhibition catalogue Museum für Kunsthandwerk, Frankfurt/M., Munich, 1995), p. 170; F. Bertoni, *Philippe Starck – Architektur*, (Munich, 1994), p. 111; *Afrikanische Sitze*, ed. S. Bocola, exhibition catalogue (Vitra Design Museum, Weil am Rhein, Africa Museum, Tervuren, Munich, 1994), p. 129. P. 180: Archive A. v. Vegesack. P. 182: sales catalogue Jacob und Josef Kohn, (Vienna, 1909); *Bent Wood and Metal Furniture 1850–1946*, ed. D. E. Ostergard, exhibition catalogue (The American Federation of Arts, New York, 1987), p. 109; p. 184: *Frank Lloyd Wright – Architect*, ed. T. Riley, P. Reed, exhibition catalogue (The Museum of Modern Art, New York, 1994). P. 192: Y. Futagawa, B. B. Pfeiffer, *Frank Lloyd Wright - Monograph 1914–1923*, (Tokyo, 1991), p. 28. P. 186: *L'Architecture d'Aujourd'hui*, No. 47 (April/May 1953), p. 67;

Les anneés 50, exhibition catalogue Centre G. Pompidou, (Paris, 1988), p. 164/165. P. 188: J. Russell, S. Gablik, Pop Art – Redefined, (New York, 1969), Ill. 98; *Design 1935–1965: What Modern Was*, ed. M. Eidelberg, exhibition catalogue (Musée des Arts Décoratifs, Montréal, New York, 1991), p. 309. P. 190: Sentou Galerie, Paris. P. 192: *Brockhaus Enzyklopädie*, (Mannheim, 1993), Vol. 20, p. 265; Groninger Museum, *Atelier Mendini 1990–1994*, (Milan, 1994), p. 117; *Ispirazione Italiana*, ed. P. Scarzella, W. Schepers, P. Dunas, exhibition catalogue (Kunstmuseum Düsseldorf, Düsseldorf, 1990), p. 85; Groninger Museum, *Atelier Mendini 1990–1994*, (Milan, 1994), p. 199. P. 194: Cassina flyer, (Milan). P. 196: *Design 1935–1965: What Modern Was,* ed. M. Eidelberg, exhibition catalogue (Musée des Arts Décoratifs, Montréal, New York, 1991), p. 327; *Ettore Sottsass – Mobili e qualche arredamento*, exhibition catalogue (Galleria Rocca, Turin, Galerie Yves Gastou, Paris, Milan), 1985, p. 56; H. Höger, *Ettore Sottsass jr. – Designer, Artist, Architect*, (Tübingen, Berlin, 1993), p. 216. P. 198: *Post-Modern Design*, (New York, 1989), p. 110; p. 113; p. 109. P. 200: Shiro Kuramata, *Shiro Kuramata 1967–1987*, (Tokyo, 1988), p. 107; VDM collection; *Star Piece: Sketch of Image by S. Kuramata*, (Tokyo, 1991), p. 68. P. 202 Amat 3 flyer, (Martorell, Barcelona, undated); J*orge Pensi, Barcelona; Gaudí*, ed. H.-R. Hitchcock, exhibition catalogue (The Museum of Modern Art, New York, 1957), p. 31. P. 240: M. Diez, M. Mönninger, *Japanese Design*, (Cologne, 1994). P. 210: S. Overy, L. Büller, F. den Oudsten, B. Mulder, *The Rietveld Schröder House*, (Cambridge, Mass., 1988), p. 73; *Sotheby's*, (Amsterdam, May 3,1988), p. 24; S. Overy, L. Böller, F. den Oudsten, B. Mulder, *The Rietveld Schröder House*, (Cambridge, Mass., 1988), p. 74; p. 48. P. 212: *Innendekoration*, 29 (Darmstadt, 1928), p. 275; *Marcel Breuer – Furniture and Interiors*, ed. C. Wilk, exhibition catalogue (The Museum of Modern Art, New York, 1981), p. 38; *Thonet Frères Paris: Meubles en métal*, (Paris, 1929). P. 214: *Ludwig Mies van der Rohe,* ed. L. Glaeser, exhibition catalogue (The Museum of Modern Art, New York, 1977), p. 11; p. 46; VDM collection; *Bent Wood and Metal Furniture 1850–1946*, ed. D. E. Ostergard, exhibition catalogue (The American Federation of Arts, New York, 1987), p. 293; VDM collection; VDM collection. P. 216: collection catalogue, The Museum of Modern Art, New York, ed. S. Hunter, (New York, 1984), p. 129; Archive A. Castiglioni, Milan. P. 218: Gufram flyer, (Balangero, undated); catalogue pamphlet Gufram Multipli, (Balangero, 1986). P. 220: Bayer flyer: *Visionen und Bayer-Chemiewerkstoffe für die Möbelzukunft!*, (Leverkusen, 1970); VDM Archive. P. 222: G. Gramigna, Repertorio 1950–1980, (Milan, 1985), p. 287; S. Blake, *The Master Builders – Le Corbusier, Mies van der Rohe, Frank Lloyd Wright*, (New York, 1960), p. 167; e.g. *Stühle – Ein Streifzug durch die Kulturgeschichte des Sitzens*, exhibition catalogue. Deutscher Werkbund e.V., (Giessen, 1985), p. 193. P. 224: *Italienische Metamor-phose 1943–1968*, exhibition catalogue Wolfsburg Art Museum, (Wolfsburg, 1994-5), Ill. 180; Archive A. Mendini. P. 226: Memphis as Poster, (Milan, 1983); Archive M. De Lucchi. P. 228: S. Teichgräber, *Stiletto – Kraft durch Design*, (Vienna, 1987), pp. 4-5; K. Varnedoe, *Duane Hanson*, (New York, 1985), p. 44. P. 230: W. Schepers, S. Voggenreiter, M. Erlhoff, *Pentagon – Informal Design*, (Cologne, 1990), pp. 120-1; Archive W. Laubersheimer. P. 232: Andrea Branzi, *Domestic Animals – The Neoprimitive Style*, (Cambridge, Mass., 1987). P. 234: A. Tzonis, L. Lefaivre, *Architektur in Europa seit 1968*, (Frankfurt, New York, 1992), p. 221; Cassina flyer, (Meda, Milan, undated)